Praise for **The Working Brain**

Finally, a user's manual for your brain. *The Working Brain* is a must-read to improve your cognitive performance and mental wellness at work. Dr. Winegard masterfully distills the wisdom of mind-body and lifestyle medicine into a succinct framework. As a proponent of exercise medicine and culinary medicine, I believe the focus on movement and nutrition as levers for professional optimization makes this book essential reading. "Health care" starts with "self care," and this comprehensive guide is indeed the missing professional manual for your own better wellness, happiness, and performance.

EDWARD PHILLIPS, MD, author and podcast host of *Food, We Need to Talk*, founder and director of the Institute of Lifestyle Medicine, and associate professor of Physical Medicine and Rehabilitation at Harvard Medical School

My friend and colleague Dr. Brynn has crafted a brilliant book on how to perform to your potential while optimizing your brain. She presents a powerful framework and clear path to better mental health and performance for her readers. Her recommendations are based in research and science, as well as her extensive expertise in the business world. I am thrilled that this book has made its way into the world!

GREG WELLS, PHD, senior scientist at the Hospital for Sick Children and author of *The Ripple Effect*

A fantastic "brain blueprint" filled with practical tips, tricks, and evidence-based strategies designed to enhance cognition and improve performance at work and in life. Dr. Winegard's MERIT framework (how you move, eat, rest, interact, and think) beautifully encapsulates the pillars and practices of lifestyle medicine as they pertain to cognitive health. A must-read for any professional looking to optimize their health, performance, and longevity.

    DR. JONATHAN BONNET, physician and author of the *Lifestyle Medicine Handbook*

Dr. Winegard's explanation of brain function in *The Working Brain* provides compelling motivation to optimize our cognitive potential using the MERIT framework. As a university professor, I am excited to apply these actionable insights in my courses to help students achieve peak mental performance. This book is a must-read for anyone looking to elevate their productivity and unlock the full power of their mind.

    DR. KATHLEEN RODENBURG, associate dean academic, University of Guelph

Even as a physician, I learned so many new things from this book about how my brain works that I never learned in medical school. Dr. Winegard eloquently breaks down the brain's function in a way that is accessible to all readers. *The Working Brain* is for everyone who wants to improve their mind's function at work, regardless of profession.

    DR. ANDREA MERRILL, surgeon and medical writer

DR. BRYNN L. WINEGARD

THE WORKING BRAIN

Optimize Your Workday Performance

Copyright © 2024 by Dr. Brynn L. Winegard

All rights reserved. No part of this book may be reproduced, stored in a retrieval system or transmitted, in any form or by any means, without the prior written consent of the publisher or a licence from The Canadian Copyright Licensing Agency (Access Copyright). For a copyright licence, visit accesscopyright.ca or call toll free to 1-800-893-5777.

The information provided in this book is for educational or informational purposes only and should not be considered a substitute for professional psychological, neurological, psychiatric, or medical advice, diagnosis, treatment, and consultation with licensed providers. Consult a medical professional, PCP, or healthcare provider for health, fitness, psychological, medical advice, diagnoses, or treatment. The author assumes no responsibility or liability for any errors or omissions in this book's content nor any resulting actions taken by readers. The information is provided on an "as is" basis without guarantees of completeness, accuracy, usefulness, or timeliness.

Cataloguing in publication information
is available from Library and Archives Canada.
ISBN 978-1-77458-490-3 (paperback)
ISBN 978-1-77458-388-3 (ebook)

Page Two
pagetwo.com

Edited by James Harbeck, Sandra E. Leppan
Copyedited by Melissa Kawaguchi, Sandra E. Leppan
Cover and interior design by Fiona Lee
Cover illustration by Allan Chu
Interior illustrations by Fiona Lee

DrBrynn.com

For Adam, Mum, and Dad

Contents

Preface *1*

PART I   INSIDE YOUR WORKING BRAIN

  1 **Marvel, Masterpiece, Misfit** *7*

PART II YOUR BRAIN'S PRODUCTIVITY CYCLE

  2 **The Rhythm of Your Brain** *27*
  3 **The Climb** *57*
  4 **The Peak** *73*
  5 **The Fall** *85*
  6 **The Valley** *99*

PART III YOUR WORKDAY BRAIN AT ITS BEST: THE MERIT FRAMEWORK

7 **Move** *115*

8 **Eat** *147*

9 **Rest** *189*

10 **Interact** *215*

11 **Think** *239*

Conclusion:
Putting It All Together *263*

Nutritional Reference Lists *271*

Acknowledgements *287*

Notes *291*

Further Reading *338*

For Adam, Mum, and Dad

Contents

Preface *1*

PART I INSIDE YOUR WORKING BRAIN

1 **Marvel, Masterpiece, Misfit** *7*

PART II YOUR BRAIN'S PRODUCTIVITY CYCLE

2 **The Rhythm of Your Brain** *27*
3 **The Climb** *57*
4 **The Peak** *73*
5 **The Fall** *85*
6 **The Valley** *99*

PART III **YOUR WORKDAY BRAIN AT ITS BEST: THE MERIT FRAMEWORK**

7 **Move** *115*

8 **Eat** *147*

9 **Rest** *189*

10 **Interact** *215*

11 **Think** *239*

Conclusion:
Putting It All Together *263*

Nutritional Reference Lists *271*

Acknowledgements *287*

Notes *291*

Further Reading *338*

Preface

*If the brain were so simple we could understand it,
we would be so simple we couldn't.*

LYALL WATSON

YOUR BRAIN is still the most impressive, complex technology ever to have existed. You may have noticed, however, that it didn't come with anything like a user's manual. Worse, our culture, popular lore, corporate narratives, and mainstream understanding of the brain are replete with myths, mysticism, and misinformation. Even for those of us who study the brain scientifically, our understanding of all the inner workings of the human brain is still in its infancy, with discoveries being made every day.

The good news is that technology has accelerated more in the last decade than in all the history of the world, and along with it, so have the neuroimaging techniques required to understand and investigate how the human brain works. This has increased our collective understanding as brain research has advanced and entered popular culture and mass media. Gone are the days of the "black box" concept of the brain, where we assumed that what happened inside your skull was effectively unknowable. This has been replaced by new and exciting discoveries that give us a better idea of how the brain operates throughout the many phases of our existence, including while we sleep and dream, during our lived days, under stress, while we shop, and even—as we will see in this book—during our workday.

It's time for you to benefit from this knowledge so you can appreciate how impressive you are, how much potential you have, and how you might unleash this potential each day at work and throughout your career. *The Working Brain* is intended to help empower you to reach your highest professional and career potential in a sustainable manner. My hope is that a better understanding of your brain at work—unmarred by myths, narratives of work culture, or beliefs of yesteryear—will help you perform at your peak each workday and throughout your career.

This book is specifically designed to help non-academic, non-neuroscientist working professionals understand and work with your own brain's natural cycles, requirements, and tendencies throughout your workday. It is intended to help you organize yourself, your thinking, and your scheduling so that you feel more motivated, get more done, and unlock your latent brain abilities, productivity, and potential.

The Working Brain is intended to be:

- A practical survey or overview guide of some recent relevant brain science for your workday productivity, with a focus on topic breadth, so you have a map for further investigation into areas of particular professional interest to you

- A collection of brain-based, science-backed how-to tips for optimizing your brain's workday performance

- Informative for healthy, highly functioning professionals looking to move the professional developmental needle from "good" to "best yet"
- A distilled compilation of insights from my 25 years of research, teaching, consulting, coaching, and corporate career

The Working Brain is not:

- An exhaustive manual for career or lifetime brain functioning
- A self-help alternative for medical advice for those struggling with psychopathology, psychiatric disorders, neurological problems, or medical challenges (please consult your primary care physician)
- An attempt to cover all the latest brain-science research and discoveries, because there simply is too much advancement happening at breakneck speed

Everything you will read in this book is backed by research and based in "hard science," but it only includes as much brain science and references as I think will be useful for you to understand suggested tips and techniques and investigate areas of interest further on your own. This material is intended to help you:

- Have a more accurate, "fiction-free" understanding of your working brain during your workday
- Use your brain more effectively each day by gaining some insights from the disciplines of applied neuroscience and positive psychology

- Be more sustainably productive, composed, and motivated in your professional life
- Perform better, succeed more often, and flourish at work

Your brain is the primary tool for your work. *The Working Brain* is here as your guide, map, or "missing manual" to help you make sure your workday brain is performing as optimally as possible—so *you* are performing as optimally as possible.

PART I

INSIDE YOUR WORKING BRAIN

The brain immediately confronts us with its incredible complexity. The human brain weighs only three to four pounds but contains about 100 billion neurons. Although that extraordinary number is of the same order of magnitude as the number of stars in the Milky Way, it cannot account for the complexity of the human brain.

GERALD FISCHBACH

1

Marvel, Masterpiece, Misfit

*The human brain is the highest bloom of
the whole organic metamorphosis of the earth.*
FRIEDRICH WILHELM JOSEPH SCHELLING

YOU ARE likely familiar with—or at least have heard—some commonly held beliefs about how the brain works:

- You are using only 10 percent of your brain.
- Most of the decisions you make are conscious.
- The brain is separate from and acts independently of the body, and vice versa.
- The brain works on the same 24-hour circadian cycle as the body.
- You are born with mostly preprogrammed neural structures and operating systems that can't really be altered.

- Your neuroanatomy and thinking processes work basically like everyone else's.
- IQ, EQ, personality, and mindset are effectively set for life once they are developed in childhood.
- Neural and cognitive decline are inevitable throughout life.
- The brain operates like a computer.
- Introspection gives an accurate picture of your brain's inner functioning.
- Thoughts are from the head, but emotions are from the heart.
- Your brain doesn't need breaks like the body does.
- Your body works like a machine, and your brain is its computer.
- The less you sleep, the more usable hours you reclaim, the more productive you will be.
- Food and exercise affect your body much more than your brain.
- Other people's inner thoughts, emotions, and beliefs are confined to their minds and don't affect yours.
- The spontaneous thoughts you think and your inner monologue are not editable or changeable.

These are all mistruths. Before you can learn how to make your brain perform better, you need a myth-free understanding of how your brain works.

We start with three undergirding assertions: your brain is (1) a marvelously complex, super-efficient, mostly serial "processor" (Marvel); (2) a personalized and specific tool susceptible to your own making (Masterpiece); and (3) potentially an ill fit to the standard modern 9:00 to 5:00 workday (Misfit).

A Marvelous Supertechnology

Popular urban lore, Silicon Valley narratives, and shared understandings about the human brain have left most of us with the impression that our brains are messy, complex organs that (1) work much like computers but (2) basically not as well. In reality, neither is accurate.

Let's address the second point first. You have ready access right now—and all the time—to the most impressive, intelligent technology yet known to humankind, and it's right there in your skull. Your brain performs one exaflop of calculations (a billion billion) every second using approximately 20 watts of power. At the time of this writing, the most advanced supercomputer on earth—an HP monstrosity named Frontier that looks into deep space, among other things—is capable at peak capacity of performing approximately two exaflops, just twice as many as your brain, but using a whopping 21 million watts of power, and only for relatively short bursts of uptime. Your brain is half a million times as energy efficient as HP's Frontier, it can do more operations faster than almost every other computer on earth, and it does this for your whole life without breaks, let alone long periods of nonoperation.

While OpenAI, Google, Meta, and other software companies come up with new eye-catching products almost daily, at this time those systems are still limited to mostly technological domains and have nowhere near your intellectual abilities to predict personal cause and effect, forecast your future, or often even distinguish fact from fiction. Further, there is no current evidence that any computer could approximate your various other, arguably more important, types of intelligence (e.g., spatial, emotional, bodily, kinesthetic, linguistic, naturalistic, musical, interpersonal), nor is there current evidence of a computer problem-solving as effectively and efficiently as your brain can (and *does*) every second of your day.

Now to address the first point: Silicon Valley hasn't yet approximated all of your brain's phenomenal capacity, intelligences, and functioning because your amazing brain isn't built like their computational machines. People are often surprised that the brain doesn't work like a computer—likely due to pop culture metaphors for describing the brain and its functioning. Although you possess untapped cognitive "computing power," and both human and computer have what might be described as "neural networks," most of your neural processing is (1) not knowable to you because it is non-conscious and developed over time (whereas the computer's was knowable and was once purposefully built by people); (2) operated consciously in a serial fashion (X then Y), not simultaneously (X and Y) like the average computer; and (3) more "plastic" as your neural networks renegotiate themselves constantly (while AI is predicated on the idea that the computing models can learn and are intelligent themselves, they learn less efficiently because they require much more information and power than your brain does, and the result is often less accurate or precise because of an inability to think critically, even if autonomously).

Most of your neural processing is non-conscious. While at one time conscious processing was thought to constitute approximately 10 percent of all neural activity (one of the many origins of the famous 10 percent myth), we now believe it is much less than this. Experts estimate that as much as one percent of brain operation is conscious, and some indicate it may be as little as 0.01 percent. Most of what is happening in our brains is too quick and too quiet to enter our conscious awareness, which, it turns out, has relatively limited bandwidth compared with our non-conscious capacity because of the mostly serial nature of conscious processing. Despite what proponents of multitasking might assert, your conscious brain does only one thing at a time, while both your subconscious and the average computer are considered "simultaneous processors," which can calculate or work on multiple things at once. It's an inaccurate metaphor therefore to refer to your brain as a "super-computer," though it is indeed what you might consider to be a remarkable marvel of complexity, ingenuity, and ability—a marvelous "supertechnology."

Understanding how much more efficient and impressive your brain is than any human-made computer to date should empower you. Computers are valuable tools when used properly by a human operator, but they aren't smarter than you and won't soon take your job. As has been the case all along, your job may evolve to incorporate new technologies, and therefore so must you. In chapter 11 we will discuss ways to stay more mentally and cognitively agile, as well as the advantages of leaning in to change and trying new things. Fortunately, it is your brain's natural imperative to update and improve daily so it is the most specific, efficient, and useful tool it possibly can be for you.

Your Working Masterpiece

Your brain (and spinal cord, together the central nervous system) is mostly made of special cells called neurons (communicators) and companion cells like neuroglia (physical and chemical supporters, connectors, protectors). Each neuron has tentacles called dendrites that connect to other neurons.

These connected neurons form neural networks, which are the basis of conscious and non-conscious thought when activated in a specific order, pattern, or combination. Neural networks are part of the central nervous system, which is connected through the brainstem and spinal cord to the peripheral nervous system in your body. We begin life with about 100 billion neurons or so, each with approximately 2,500 connections to other neurons—called synapses. As we grow, we develop many more of each, especially synapses. By the time you are three years old, each neuron has as many as 15,000 synapses. While brains vary, by approximately age 25 your brain is thought to be fully formed into its adult version, with approximately 128 billion neurons (including cerebellum) and as many as 100 trillion connections.

Think of your brain and nervous system as a series of cellular (neural) networks communicating through electrochemical pulses. Sometimes these neural networks form discrete regions or areas where certain types of reasoning or activities are consistently managed (e.g., the hypothalamus in the ventral brain, directly above the pituitary gland, helps in managing your bodily functions like hunger, thirst, mood, sex drive, blood pressure, and sleep). However, sometimes these networks are highly diversified and spread out (e.g., the "autopilot" default mode network, which talks to you about the memories, associations, and recent events it recruits so you will be able to contemplate and plan while your mind wanders). The idea that your brain's functionality is localized to specific areas (e.g., amygdala, hippocampus, limbic system) may be helpful conceptually but isn't necessarily strictly true for every region, function, or person. As it turns out, you likely have a lot more variability than this because of the magic of neuroplasticity and the networked way your brain wires, stores, and relays information.

The brain's functionality is a series of networked patterns of neural firing and interconnected activity. As your brain changes, wires, rewires, and fires connections and networks in response to events in your life, so does the function of each network. At varying rates, depending on life stage, events, or circumstances, your brain is continually changing both physically and functionally. Learning, memory, knowledge, and resulting intelligence are held in networks through neural connections, not in the neurons themselves. All neural networks are active at least sometimes, but only some are active at any one moment—you use all of your brain, just not all at once. Some sources indicate that at any given millisecond, depending on the activity, about 10 percent of the entire brain is active—another source of the 10 percent usage myth. We gain and preserve neural connections and networks through our experiences, learning, focus, efforts, attention, and deliberate practice. So by working age you are one brilliant masterpiece of ever-evolving supertechnology.

You are one brilliant, personal masterpiece of continuously evolving supertechnology.

All this exciting neural network construction and change is energetically expensive and psychologically taxing—it feels draining and will tire you quickly. Neuroplasticity makes all your neural individuality and uniqueness possible; the brain can cultivate neurons, make connections between them, and scaffold up whole networks because it is plastic—capable of being shaped and reshaped. The brain is most flexible, plastic, or "spongy" during childhood, and we used to believe that it tapered off after puberty. Now we know that much neuroplasticity can be maintained throughout your life with conscious and deliberate effort.

Because of how draining neuroplastic change can feel and how taxing learning is, the brain will wire everything possible into networks so that novel stimuli, people, interactions, actions, behaviors, and circumstances don't require a laborious learning curve every time you witness or experience them repetitively. The more you witness, think, do, or experience something, the more solidified those connections and resulting networks become. This "hardwiring" imperative ultimately saves your whole system energy, oxygen, calories, and time, and it lets you get through your day without having to consciously decide how to do a whole bunch of small acts.

Neuroplasticity starts at the microscopic level in your brain: it is survival of the fittest for individual neurons, like everything else in life. We know that networks that have not been active for a while get disbanded in favor of other networks or more popular neural activities as neurons migrate their connectivity and activity to more relevant networks. A neuron can be eliminated if it doesn't work to be as involved in as many neural networks as possible. After all, no neuron has any way of predicting which neural networks you will continue or cease to use. Inside your skull, not even something as small as a neuron can take up resources and space without being useful—you are indeed using 100 percent of your brain.

For a neuron to survive, the signals that affect it must occur approximately every six hours. To the neuron, being included in a network is like a wild party with college friends. There's a supply of food (serum glucose), drink (fresh water), drugs (dopamine, serotonin, norepinephrine), fresh air (oxygen), excitement (action potential), energy (protein, fat, glucose), fireworks (electrical activity), matchmaking (new synaptic connections), and even a cleaning crew (phagocytes, glymphatic system) and repair technicians (glial cells) that take over when the event is done. Being excluded from neural networks is isolating and impoverishing enough that without relevance and the resulting metabolic activity, the neuron may perish. Networks you stop using as a result of different circumstances can plastically reorganize themselves or cease to exist. This results in brain wiring that is highly unique to you, based on your experiences, what you attend to, the things you think, and the choices you make in life.

Neurons are electrochemically drawn to other affiliated neurons in a network so that the connections are deeper, broader, and easier to activate—to keep the party going, so to speak. All day long, your brain is collecting information from within your systems (thoughts, conclusions, hunger levels, hydration levels, energy levels, etc.) and outside your systems (environment, context, circumstance, situation, timing, friends, foes), watching for patterns, predicting your future, and drawing up potential actions that might benefit you now. (To some extent, the brain considers future actions, but it much prefers making decisions for the here and now, since the future is unknown and uncertain.) In response to this mass of information, your plastic brain is constantly learning, adapting, and honing itself to be the best possible tool it can be for you in your current life circumstance. This is especially true at work, where so many resources are gleaned, your social connections are material, and the stakes are high.

From a biological perspective, your brain is a survival tool. It is designed to help you survive anything life throws at you as best it can. It does this by (mostly subconsciously) assessing your circumstances—environment, resources, abilities, allies, enemies, and probabilities—and helping you make the best decisions based on those variables. Your brain (with help from bodily systems) directs your thoughts, feelings, attitudes, emotions, and beliefs so that you continually act in your own self-interest. This means it has to be perpetually highly adaptive, changing in response to what it understands about the outside world as well as its internal one. At any given moment, your mostly subconscious brain is combining thoughts, emotions, information, feelings, resources, and internal and external factors to come to conclusions, form connections, make predictions, formulate reactions, and help make all your decisions.

You can use the propensity of neurons to "fire and wire together" to your advantage to create functional habits that will help you do more, feel better, be more productive, and master your own mindset for productivity and success. Finding out that you can regulate and be directive about how your brain functions and changes allows you to be more deliberate about the brain you build and use every day at work. Still no computer on earth is as intelligent, plastic, or multipurposed as your brain and every neuron in it, and there is no other brain like yours on earth. Your brain's potentially infinite neural connections are ever-changing and may be considered your very own ongoing masterpiece. Whether you are aware of it or not—and you probably are not, because most of this networking was put together in non-conscious brain areas while you were sleeping—your neural networks are based on your life experiences, choices, circumstances, and thoughts (both conscious and non-conscious). Because your experiences, perceptions, emotions, cognitions, and development are unique to you, to a large extent so are your brain's networking, wiring, programming, and functioning.

Here's a hypothetical example you've likely experienced something similar to. Two colleagues may be in the same place at the same time, immersed in the same happenings at work, but come away with very different impressions and recollections depending on their subjective thoughts, cognitive systems, and past experiences. The first person may not even notice negative elements in their environment, situations, or interactions—or if they do, may externalize and ignore them effectively—allowing them to reflect on the positive occurrences, feel happy about their time and circumstances, and move on with their day in a productive, prosocial manner. The second person, meanwhile, may attend almost exclusively to the negative occurrences in the circumstance and ignore the positive aspects, internalizing their perceptions and allowing all of it to irritate, distract, or slow them down for the remainder of their day. Both people were in the same place at the same time, but because their neural networks are constructed and primed differently, what they attend to, perceive, think, feel, and respond to may be entirely different. These brain-based differences may compound outcomes over time: the first person may become a top performer given they can effectively ignore the negative and focus on the people, processes, and tools that can help them perform. They may win the president's award for sales performance that quarter and get a promotion after a couple of months, for example. The second person, meanwhile, may fall behind—inundated with performance review requests, asked to partake in extra training sessions, losing valuable sleep at night, and demotivated—disappointing their employer, their colleagues, and themselves. The respective upward and downward career spirals in this hypothetical but understandable example aren't explained by the circumstances but by differently constructed, wired, and primed brains.

The differing neural infrastructure responsible for people's unique perceptions and responses to life experiences are built of well-practiced network pathways that are easier and more efficient to use—like mental shortcuts. We call these "cognitive schemata." The more you think a thought (e.g., "The world is a dangerous place"), experience the same thing over and over (e.g., the drive to work every morning), repeat an action (switching lanes in traffic), or are subjected to similar or repetitive stimuli (lineups of slowing taillights in rush-hour freeway traffic), the more solidified the connections between neurons (learning) and networks (knowledge) become. Solidified networks (e.g., the network for scanning rush-hour traffic) can often link to others (e.g., the network for reacting swiftly to other drivers' actions) in a consistent and practiced pattern. After years of witnessing and practicing a behavior, we unconsciously link the relevant networks and automate their sequence, such as when you witness a car move into your lane (network for monitoring your vehicular environment) and automatically slow down to give both vehicles a safe amount of space (network for reacting appropriately). Meanwhile, networks for other experiences and behaviors (e.g., commuting to work every morning on the train and knowing all the routes and connections) attenuate and even disintegrate over time if you don't practice them—if you don't use it, you lose it. Every experience, thought, and behavior is contributing to "tuning" some connections and networks while typically also "pruning" others.

These shortcuts can accumulate to whole cognitive systems that allow us to operate largely on autopilot for many repetitive or familiar tasks in our everyday lives. Take the example of driving home after a long day at work. You are likely conscious of your decisions and actions at the beginning of the drive as you enter the freeway and merge into traffic. But somewhere along the familiar route you traverse every day, you aren't consciously aware any more—your mind is wandering, thinking about what you can make quickly for dinner, your unfinished task list from the day and spillover into tomorrow's schedule, what Suzy from finance said to you about your weak P&L this quarter relative to other portfolios, and that comment your boss made about needing to be "immediately quicker with the numbers off the top of your head." Through your ruminations, you may be "awakened" or brought back to the present, where you realize you were driving all the while. You are still in rush-hour traffic, same route, same scenery, different cars surrounding you, a few miles ahead of when you last checked in. *Who was driving the car?* you may ask yourself, as you reflect on the last few minutes of daydreams. The short answer is your basal ganglia (nuclei embedded deep in the center of your brain) and default mode network, though in fact it was many more cognitive systems, specific to you, that have been built with time, experience, and repetition in your life. These personalized systems allowed you to zone out (or zone in to your own mind), imagine, remember, contemplate, and plan while they all worked together automatically to do the driving. In this common example, it all acted quite literally as your autopilot. Practiced neural pathways become well-oiled systems and shortcuts that are more time efficient, allow your mind to wander, give your brain a break from learning, and conserve valuable system resources like oxygen and glucose.

Even your neural functionality common to all humans can vary significantly based on your unique experiences, development, and thought patterns. As we will discuss further in chapter 11, much of what you attend to, ignore, perceive, feel, believe, and act on is based on how your inner world is wired and the mindset you developed (and vice versa)—which can have major implications for your motivation, productivity, and performance at work and in life.

A Misfit for the Modern Workday

For all its complexity, intelligence, and uniqueness, in many ways, your brain may be the right thing in the wrong place—at least during the modern workday.

The human brain's fundamental components, physical systems, and ways of organizing evolved in remote, technologically rudimentary, pre-agrarian, pre-industrial, slow-paced, often nomadic hunter-gatherer tribes that typically had no more than about 80 members. Aside from the odd in-group disagreement, a prowling predator, or a sudden storm, the days were likely relatively quiet and consistent. Work and waking hours were physically active, psychologically challenging, seasonally predictable, and limited to the sun's light. Much of this is quite different from the environment and circumstances most of us find ourselves in today.

Now, many of us are in environments that are primarily urban, technologically advanced, post-agrarian, fast-paced, unpredictable, highly populated, relatively stationary, highly industrialized, commercially driven, and lit 24/7 by electricity. We no longer need to hunt or gather our own food; we are typically surrounded by more than 80 people; and our days often feel too long and over-scheduled. Unsurprisingly, some biologists argue that modern society is mismatched to the human brain's original environment. Of course, evolution and adaptation are possible, but they take much longer than a couple of hundred years and a few generations for their effects to be known.

Modern schedules and workdays are not necessarily set up to be conducive to our brains' preferred circumstances for learning, development, motivation, performance, or productivity. In humanity's early days, there were no offices, stationary desks, or 9:00-to-5:00, Monday-to-Friday jobs.

It could be argued that the normalized daily or weekly Western work schedule is ineffective and potentially harmful, given how far from the original circumstance it seems to be for the human brain.

If the modern workday isn't conducive to our brain's functioning, how did this schedule come to be? During the exciting upswing of the Industrial Revolution in nineteenth-century England, it wasn't uncommon for laborers to have 18- or 20-hour workdays in factories. Workers were keen for wages, while manufacturers were keen to turn profits. After years of grueling work schedules, labor unions started to form, demanding more reasonable working conditions and treatment for workers. The 8-8-8 concept was born, with workers demanding eight hours for rest, eight hours for leisure, and (only) eight hours for labor. In response to union demands, as well as reports of burnout, injury, and high turnover, one factory owner named Sir John Lubbock (also a bank owner) studied the circumstances under which workers could work safely and sustainably in his facilities. Based on his findings, Lubbock fought for reforms in the British Parliament: laws to ensure shorter laborer hours and a maximum number of weekly shifts. His most lauded win was the Bank Holidays Act, which proposed statutory holidays for all workforce members many times a year.

The efforts of Lubbock, unions, and others during this era resulted in workers' hours being limited to eight hours per shift, more typically during the middle of the day. Similar efforts spurred the two-day weekend and the typical office work week: 9:00 a.m. to 5:00 p.m., Monday through Friday, with three breaks a day (typically a longer one for lunch plus two shorter breaks), two weeks of vacation a year, and statutory holidays most months. Each evening, after the 5:00 p.m. clock-out, a typical person would go home, have dinner with their family, do some domestic chores, perhaps attend to children, climb into bed, set an alarm for 7:00 a.m., and be asleep by 11:00 p.m. or so—to do it all over again the next day until the weekend. This cadence is the backdrop of most Western life, schooling, employment contracts, films, and books. It is the usual schedule for most professionals to this day.

Our idea of what a standard workday should entail is likely ineffective and uncomfortable from your brain's perspective.

The challenge remains that twenty-first-century knowledge work is not nineteenth-century factory work. While the reforms during the industrial era were adequate for a specific purpose for a limited time in nineteenth-century England, Lubbock-era workers were mainly employed doing physical, repetitive, or rote activities. They weren't expected to be consistently creative or cognitively active throughout their entire workday as you probably are. They could set their minds on autopilot, thanks to increasingly practiced and solidified neural networks, shortcuts, and cognitive systems they had likely developed through their work. While they may have had eight productive working hours each day (though without issues, injuries, or errors seems unlikely), there's no reason to expect that to translate to knowledge workers in the modern professional context, surrounded by technology and mostly using their brains to produce their outputs. Many professional workers today have few or no physical aspects to their jobs, and much of their labor comes from their cognitive abilities. (This is true even in modern factories, where an increasing amount of work is accomplished by robots operated by highly trained computer programmers, engineers, and technicians.)

Much of our normalized idea of what a workday should be—how long and in what intervals—is likely misplaced, inefficient, and uncomfortable from your brain's perspective. Your brain doesn't work exactly like your body does (even though they are highly interconnected), and it shouldn't be expected to. As we will continue to uncover in the coming chapters, while the human brain is one of the great marvels of all time, it is remarkably short in its active working span, quick to need rest, energetically expensive (more so than any other single organ or system), and not possible to fully understand through introspection, and it operates on a unique, variable rhythm all its own.

Our brains likely don't have eight hours of productivity each day, all at once, in an extended block of time in the middle of the day. As wonderfully powerful and complex as our brains are, their arousal, energy, and performance ebb and flow all day long. In the coming chapters, we will discuss the various cycles your brain and body operate on, with special attention to the brain's specific rhythm. If your brain is a misfit in the modern work world, in a world of standardized schedules and expectations, it's persistently specific and unique. Because your brain is exceptional, its schedule for work should be, too. It's unreasonable to assume that one size fits all in terms of workdays, work schedules, and work methods. In the coming section you will learn about the rhythm your brain works on, as well as how you might be able to optimize your tasks, thinking, schedule, and workday for higher productivity and performance.

To add to the complexity of all this, it is much more likely—given what we know about human physiology, psychology, functioning, perception, reaction to circumstances, and the varying resources each day (quality sleep, hydration, nutrition, etc.)—that your rhythms vary depending on the hour, day, week, or month. While you can't know exactly where you are in your own chronobiological cycling at any given moment of the day, you are almost certainly further ahead if you understand that your brain is constantly in flux and cycling, and that it is perpetually attempting to account for incoming inputs while simultaneously adapting decision-making to variable resources, rhythms, and expectations.

We'll start in the next section with a look at your brain's specific rhythm, an ultradian rhythm—a four-phase cycle (Climb, Peak, Fall, Valley) that your brain goes through many times each day. You can benefit from learning how each of the four phases might feel or be identified, so you can modify and optimize your activities during each one and schedule your workday accordingly.

In the final section we will look at my MERIT framework, composed of all the levers you can control for optimizing your brain's overall workday functioning and performance: the physical activity (Move), nutrition (Eat), sleep (Rest), social connections (Interact), and thought patterns (Think) that can help you function in top form every day. From here, each chapter will include a lengthy how-to section with tangible suggestions for how to optimize the phase of (e.g., Peak) or domain for (e.g., nutrition) brain functioning and workday performance.

PART II

YOUR BRAIN'S PRODUCTIVITY CYCLE

The question of how the ebb and flow of a highly developed mind can be catered to by a physical brain, and the related question of how the one impacts the other, are the hardest-ever challenges to human ingenuity and imagination.

SUSAN GREENFIELD

2

The Rhythm of Your Brain

*In the past thirty years, we have
learned more about the workings of the human
brain than in previous history.*

DANIEL H. PINK

YOU HAVE probably heard of the circadian rhythm, your sleep-wake physiological pattern that repeats every 24 hours. It helps control your body's mental and physical functioning and is affected by light. Scientists used to believe that our brains operated only on this cycle as well; it seemed logical that your brain and body would be on the same wavelength, so to speak, since they work in tandem.

It wasn't until the 1950s that sleep researcher Nathaniel Kleitman discovered that the brain had another, different rhythm from the body. Kleitman's sleep research revealed that sleep patterns followed a shorter cycling in the brain throughout the night. More recently, researchers determined that these shorter cycles continue through waking hours, accounting for variable levels of attention, energy, and alertness throughout the wakeful day and therefore inconsistent motivation, performance, and productivity. For example, Jim Loehr and Tony Schwartz, authors of *The Power of Full Engagement*, measured heart rate, hormone levels, muscle tension, and brain waves to determine that as all of these increase during the first part of the ultradian cycle, so do alertness, energy, attention, productivity, and performance. As alertness and energy begin to wane somewhere around 60 to 90 minutes, the back end of the ultradian cycle marks the brain and body's increasing need for rest and recovery. This basic rest-activity cycle (BRAC) operates continuously throughout the day, is characterized by approximately 90 minutes of activity followed by 20 minutes of required rest, and is typically referred to as the brain's ultradian rhythm.

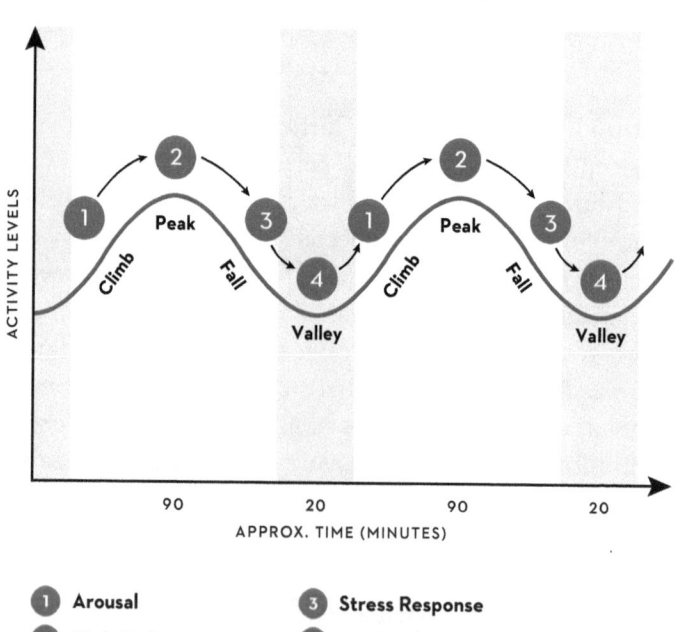

Figure 2.1: Your Brain's Ultradian Cycle

This cycle has four phases:

- **Arousal** (The Climb) is when the brain has to rally resources, overcome fatigue, and tune out distractions to focus on a task. During this stage, your brain and body use oxygen, glucose, and other fuel.

- **High Performance** (The Peak) is when the brain is at its cognitive and energetic maximum, engaged in its deepest thinking, production, and cognitive outputs, and using many resources to accomplish this. During this stage, metabolic waste, cellular debris, and other by-products of your mental and physical exertion build up.

- **Stress Response** (The Fall) is when the brain experiences diminishing productivity, a decrease in energy, and a stress response from exertion. This phase is characterized by declines in focus or concentration: fatigue, wandering attention, fogginess, irritability, distractedness, hunger, thirst, and potential cravings (especially for processed foods, snacks, salt, fat, sugar, caffeine, and—if you smoke—nicotine).

- **Healing Response** (The Valley) is a healing period during which the brain rests, clears some debris, recuperates, restores, and resets its synapses and neurochemistry as it prepares for the next cycle's Climb.

It often frustrates high-achieving professionals that, despite their best efforts and intentions, their attention spans and productivity ebb and flow significantly throughout the day and often fall off altogether midafternoon. Their brains' natural Valleys come more frequently than they would like and feel almost impossible to power through as the workday nears its end. Their ability to get things done or remain in high-performance mode often feels too limited. But there's no point in fighting it; the ultradian rhythm is a universal human phenomenon. This is also why thinking of your workday as one long marathon is a mistake from your brain's perspective. Your brain is not consistently capable of sustained periods of uninterrupted focus, attention, or productivity. Instead, your day should be thought of as a series of sprints, varying in length and intensity over the course of the day and from day to day. You need more, short breaks throughout your workday to be sustainably and optimally productive.

Because of your brain's unique, physiological ebb and flow, your workday should be thought of as a series of shorter work sprints, not one long marathon.

It's worth noting that your own ultradian rhythm is a physiological cycle that proceeds independent of your cognitive, mental, or psychological state and activities—what you do or think won't stop it, even if they can alter it slightly. While the physiology proceeds, your perceived ability to fully reap the benefits at each ultradian phase can be thwarted by your actions, behaviors, or thoughts. The ideal circumstance is one where you've matched your activities and psychology to your ultradian rhythm, so you feel cognitively and productively in line with it. While the language herein melds the concepts of physiology, psychology, and cognitions of each phase, it's important to know they are indeed separate. For example, you can be in an ultradian Peak physiologically and be completely unproductive cognitively; you can be in an ultradian Climb and be gathering none of your own requisite attentional resources or focus, and so on. The goal here is to try to understand how you might align your intentions, thoughts, and actions to your physiological phases so you can be your own most productive self.

A Rhythm All Your Own

Circadian is from Latin, meaning "around the day." *Ultradian* means "outside of the day" and is intended to mean "longer than an hour but shorter than a day," which is likely intentionally vague because we know this cycle is somewhat variable. Your brain isn't the only bodily system that cycles through an ultradian rhythm. Other ultradian cycles of various lengths in your body include blood circulation, blinking, pulse, hormone secretions, urinary activity, bowel activity, and appetite, among others. All of these, as you well know from personal experience, can vary significantly from hour to hour, day to day, or depending on the circumstances.

Your brain and body are inextricably linked through electrical, nervous, hormonal, and chemical messenger systems that cycle continually, with feedback loops and interference. Your ultradian cycle is constantly being adjusted according to variable system resources (e.g., sleep, stress, fatigue, hydration, salt, energy, and glucose levels). In parallel, your brain continuously attempts to collect data and renegotiate its connections and networks in response to the stimuli you experience and subject yourself to all day. This means that the 90/20 cycle concept (as depicted in Figure 2.1) is likely oversimplified or even hypothetical. Because your brain is in constant flux and resource management, to some extent your rest-activity performance cycles almost certainly vary by hour, day, week, situation, work type, life stage, or even season.

During each ultradian cycle, your body and brain go through the four phases, each characterized by different physiological, neurochemical, and hormonal levels and changes. Levels of neurotransmitters and hormones—such as dopamine, cortisol, serotonin, acetylcholine, glutamate, and adrenaline—vary from phase to phase, moderating your mood, energy, alertness, and performance.

Your brain is an electrochemical system that creates rhythmic patterns of electrical activity we call brainwaves, which can be measured using neuroimaging technology like electroencephalogram (EEG) or magnetic resonance imaging (MRI), among others (e.g., fMRIs, MEGs, PTs, CTs). Just as your system circulates varying neurohormones during each phase of the ultradian cycle, so are there varying brainwaves associated with each phase. There are five main types of brainwaves to consider. You can't feel brainwaves, and without imaging technology it would be near impossible to know exactly which are active, but it's nice to know some basics about your own neural activity. Figure 2.2 depicts your various brainwaves as they might be seen on a neuroimaging machine.

1 **Beta waves** are associated with heightened mental activity, alertness, attention, focus, concentration, and problem-solving. You will experience them alone or in combination with other waves. Beta waves and high beta waves are most notably associated with the Peak, though they are also present during the later Climb and early Fall. Beta waves can block your more relaxing alpha waves. Prolonged beta activity is associated with perceived anxiety, inability to relax, and sometimes stress.

2 **Alpha waves** are associated with more relaxed wakefulness, daydreaming, deep work, creativity, and information absorption, as well as wakeful rest, rejuvenation, and

Figure 2.2: What Your Brainwaves Look Like

Gamma 32-100 Hz
Heightened perception, learning, problem-solving tasks, cognitive processing

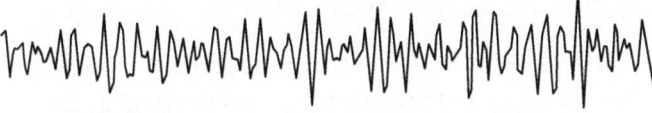

Beta 13-32 Hz
Awake, alert consciousness, thinking, excitement

Alpha 8-13 Hz
Physically and mentally relaxed

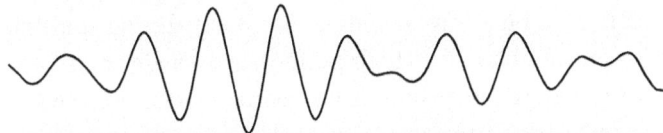

Theta 4-8 Hz
Creativity, insight, deep states, dreams, deep meditation, reduced consciousness

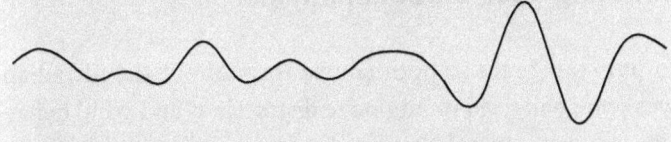

Delta 0.5-4 Hz
Deep (dreamless) sleep, loss of bodily awareness, repair

healing. When alpha waves are blocked or underactive, you may feel restless, anxious, irritable, stressed, or unable to concentrate. You may experience alpha waves alone or in combination with others during any of the phases, though they are most synonymous with the Valley.

3. **Theta waves** are slower waves associated with relaxation, meditation, mind wandering, creativity, healing, and the initial phases of falling asleep. During your waking hours, a combination of theta and alpha waves are most likely to occur during the Valley, as an example.

4. **Delta waves** are the slowest brainwaves and are associated with deep sleep.

5. **Gamma waves** are associated with learning, memory, executive functioning, information processing, and alert consciousness. You will experience these typically in concert with beta waves, and most notably during the Peak, when your brain is in high-performance mode or attempts to integrate everything it has learned, accomplished, or wants to remember or make decisions about.

Honoring Your Ultradian Rhythm

To put your brain to optimal use throughout the ultradian cycle, you will need to minimize distractions and avoid behaviors you can control that hinder your progress and proper functioning—which often takes a bit more preplanning, organizing, and discipline than you might realize. Reaching peak performance can be physically, psychologically, and cognitively demanding, especially later in the day or if you haven't had enough breaks or restful sleep. In today's world, we are constantly bombarded with distractions that can reduce our attention span and focus (e.g., phones ringing, people talking, people walking by your desk), which can increase irritation and frustration, hindering concentration or productivity.

For instance, you might be happily focusing on something essential during a Peak when an email arrives. You think, *This will need just a quick response. I'll answer it now.* However, the ultradian wave may have passed by the time you finish the email and attempt to refocus on your priorities. You may feel slightly disorganized and out of sorts at this point, making it tempting to answer more emails, take a break, or do other unimportant (if urgent) tasks. It's surprising how a whole day can go by without accomplishing much, even tasks that you thought were high priority at the start of the morning. This is often at least partially because we don't honor our own functioning and ultradian phases, allowing other things to distract, thwart, or redirect our attention and activities. Wherever a distraction or task avoidance comes from (externally or internally initiated), it hinders productivity.

Behaviors such as task avoidance, self-distraction, procrastination, or multitasking can hurt our progress or productivity, but they can also provide valuable information about our motivations and which ultradian phase we are in. For example, if you feel too tired, unprepared, or overwhelmed, you may be in a Fall or a Valley. In this case, sometimes the best thing to do is put the task off and come back to it when you feel fresher or better equipped (such as when you're in the Climb or Peak phases). It's better to acknowledge this early on in the phase than to try to tackle a task you are not in the right mental space for, lest you prolong your stress response, fail, spin your wheels, and increase the opportunity for further distractions or productivity sinkholes to take hold of your day. Failing to honor your ultradian phase in the here and now may hurt your productivity in the moment, but it can also pay negative dividends through successive cycles if you've deepened or prolonged the ultradian stress response or skimped on adequate rest. This is why it's important to choose tasks and activities deliberately based on your current abilities and ultradian phase: so you can optimize where you're currently at, as well as honor successive phases throughout your workday.

Technology: Both Friend and Foe

Among top distractors, technology ranks right up there. Tech can have positive and negative effects on the ultradian rhythm of the brain and resulting productivity, depending on what it is and how it's used.

On the positive side, technology can be an excellent tool to help you stay organized and to manage your time and energy more efficiently. It can help you strike better work-life balance and ensure more opportunities for rest during the appropriate phases of your ultradian rhythm or workday. For example, a calendar app can help someone schedule their workday more effectively, make adequate time for breaks intermittently throughout the day, work concertedly during the productive ultradian phases, have purposeful activities during the lull of the afternoon, and include the scheduling of highest-priority tasks first thing in the day.

However, technology can also disrupt the natural rhythm of the brain as well as disturb your ability to concentrate or be productive. Exposure to blue light from electronic device screens such as phones and computers can interfere with the brain's melatonin production, disrupt overall circadian cycling, make it more difficult to fall asleep, and compromise the ultradian healing response phase, as examples.

In addition, the constant notifications and distractions from technology can overwhelm and disrupt the natural flow of thought, focus, work efforts, and your attempts to concentrate, leading to increased frustration or a stress response. This can be especially problematic for professionals who may feel pressure to always be connected and available through digital means, yet continually creative, efficient, and cognitively productive.

Technology can help or hinder the brain's physiology, functioning, and resulting productivity, depending on what it is and how it's used.

Neuroscientist Susan Greenfield asserts that people's attention spans decrease when they use technology and that sustained, chronic use of technology can permanently shorten a person's working attention span. Greenfield's work suggests that most of us who use technology for hours every day at work will likely have shortened periods of peak mental performance because focus, attention, and concentration are more challenging to sustain in the context of technology use. This can have many consequences, the most obvious of which is that the uptime of the ultradian cycles may be—or at least feel—shorter than the BRAC graphs depict. Depending on how often and how early in life you use technology, your brain's productive ultradian uptime could be 45 to 60 minutes long, for example, instead of the hypothetical

90 minutes, while your required refractory period of ultradian healing and downtime would likely remain consistent—15 to 20 minutes or so. Based on the evidence so far, using more technology more persistently and earlier in life can decrease your ability to gather your attentional resources and cognitive focus for extended periods throughout your waking day, while simultaneously increasing how quickly distractions and the stress response (the Fall) may take over. While your Peak duration may be compromised, your ultradian healing periods are not thought to be simultaneously shortened. They are likely to be just as long—if perhaps less effective—and even more required.

Technology isn't all bad; it's in how you use it. It is a wonderful tool for productive work when used correctly and, like all things, in moderation. It's essential to be mindful of how and how much you use technology and to find ways to incorporate deliberate screen-free periods into your day to allow for natural fluctuations in the ultradian rhythm and decrease how much exposure to blue light you are getting each day. This can help promote better productivity, focus, creativity, and overall brain functionality.

Excessive Stress: A Real Downer

The stress response phase, an ordinary and necessary part of the ultradian cycle, is designed to help us respond to the everyday needs of the brain in its natural ebb and flow. During this phase, the brain facilitates the release of small amounts of stress hormones, which cause physiological, mental, and psychological changes, such as increased heart rate, blood pressure, slight irritability, and mental alertness. This adaptive process is designed to ensure you take a break and allow your systems to clear, replenish, and reset, so you can come back to your tasks fresher and stronger. However, when the stress response becomes more severe, pervasive, or chronic, these active hormones can be released continuously, disrupting the natural flow of the ultradian rhythm and negatively affecting both Peak cognitive performance and the healing response, which can be detrimental to overall physical, physiological, and psychological functioning. Deeper or chronic stress can significantly impact every system in the brain and body—no surprise that it also affects the BRAC and resulting functioning of the brain, especially in regard to your ability to think, focus, work, and perform.

Significant stress may make it feel as though you can never fully focus and concentrate nor fully heal, replenish, and reset. It both stands to reason and has likely been your subjective experience that if you perceive many external threats and/or feel much internal stress, your brain's ability to perform at the Peak and heal or replenish properly in the Valley is—and feels—compromised. Instead, a chronically stressed person is likely to feel as if they are stuck in some type of productivity purgatory or limbo: unable to fully focus and be deeply productive, and unable to fully replenish or recuperate.

Chronic, prolonged, or severe stress can also lead to brain chemistry and structure changes, affecting cognitive function, emotional regulation, and overall health. Stress is a known preceding factor in just about every health issue. It has been linked to the development of anxiety, depression, and other mental health disorders; suppresses the immune system and your ability to fend off infection; and can contribute significantly to physical ailments, disorders, and diseases. It's important to manage stress through stress-reducing techniques like meditation, exercise, breaks, positive self-talk, boundary-setting, and deep breathing, to allow for the natural flow of all rhythms and systems, and to promote overall health and well-being.

Optimizing Stress: Striking Hormesis

People often ask how they can eliminate stress altogether, as if it is all bad and undesirable. Actually, some stress is highly functional and instrumental for your performance. The trick is to know the difference between the functional and the dysfunctional kinds or amounts for you. To maximize your brain's (and body's) rhythms and performance, start paying attention to your own stress levels throughout your days and various activities.

The Yerkes-Dodson law asserts that there is an optimal level of perceived stress, resulting in optimal productivity or performance. On one end of the curve, when stress levels are too low, cognitive performance quality also suffers—you are just not engaged, aware, attentive, or interested enough to perform at your peak. On the other end of the curve, cognitive performance and productivity deteriorate under the burden of anxiety and a significant uptick in stress response. Moderate levels of stress, meanwhile, are thought to help the alignment of mental systems, invigorate you psychologically and cognitively, and allow for the right neurochemical activation to help you be attentive and interested enough to excel at the task at hand. People often wonder why they do their best work when a deadline is looming, for example. The answer is simple: the deadline provided the right amount of external pressure—stress—to shift them into their highest cognitive gear. This is what scientists call "hormesis," when some amount of a substance, stressor, or "insult" to the system is stimulating and beneficial. However, these beneficial effects are seen to reverse at both lower and higher amounts or levels. Many systems in the brain and body follow the phenomenon of hormesis, as depicted by the Yerkes-Dodson curve (Figure 2.3).

Figure 2.3: The Yerkes-Dodson Curve

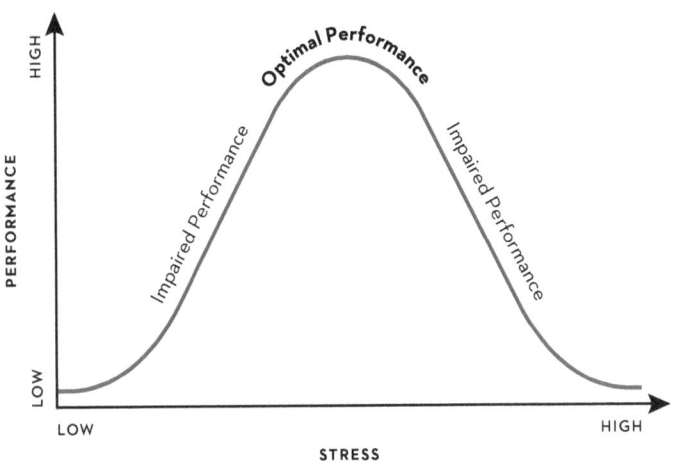

You know the subjective experience of feeling too-high levels of stress. You panic and suddenly adrenaline is coursing through your veins, your heart rate spikes, you may blank out for a bit, and your hands get sweaty. This overstimulated or panic state is biologically designed to help you be as effective as possible at confronting or getting away from something the brain perceives to be critically stressful for you ("fight or flight"). This state is not functional for sustained optimal performance and output and is not going to help you do your best—or even think consciously, rationally, and productively.

While likely less bothersome, you also know the subjective experience of feeling too-low stress levels for performance. You are ambling along, not particularly interested in the tasks at hand, feeling fairly relaxed, maybe bored, definitely willing to procrastinate or even zone out. You aren't likely to perform particularly well at tasks that elicit these feelings in you.

Often, learning that some stress is useful is enough to bring people back to the optimal zone of performance, because they were stressed about being stressed. Further, with a little conscious thought many types of non-functional or abundant stress can be converted into functional stress. Feeling anxious about your presentation to the board next week? Redefine anxiety as excitement and your perspective about your presentation changes completely. You have likely heard the adage, "When you change the way you look at things, the things you look at change." This is the crux of how to transform stress. You can reframe your own stress perceptions to view them as helpful, catalyzing, and even functional in the circumstance, rather than overwhelming or hindering.

How can you continually ensure optimal stress levels? It's likely to be an ongoing and active (not passive) practice you hone over time and through experience. Only you can really know when you are feeling either too much or too little stress to be maximally functional, motivated, and feeling optimally stimulated. What motivates you and gets you into the right cognitive gear will differ from what motivates others. What tips the scales and causes undue, over-the-top, or unmanageable stress that hinders performance will also be different for you than others. When you start to acknowledge, understand, and anticipate your stress levels, you can modify your circumstances, perceptions, and behaviors accordingly.

Stress is an inevitable—and potentially highly functional—part of work and life. In order to consistently perform, especially at work, you must deal with stress consciously and appropriately. Because of its pervasiveness in modern life and its essential relationship to performance, stress management will come up again in Part III's MERIT Framework, where we look at five levers for managing stress and your allostatic load (cumulative burden of ongoing stress in your life) to function and feel your best.

The upcoming chapters will look at the four ultradian stages individually and specifically to understand how to optimize each phase. But first, let's consider the following tactics intended to help you directly or indirectly honor your own overall ultradian cycling through the BRAC, during each workday.

Stress is inevitable but you can learn to manage it more deliberately, so it's working for you, not against you.

Optimizing Your Ultradian Rhythm: How-Tos

Think Workday Sprints—Not a Marathon

Your brain has four distinct phases of the ultradian rhythm, but only one of them is considered high performance. While it isn't necessarily possible to determine precisely what stage of each phase you may currently be in, you can typically tell based on how you feel. That's why it's helpful to structure your day into multiple sprints, with breaks between them, that align with the BRAC and your own physiology. Treating your day like a marathon without breaks can backfire and decrease productivity as stress hormones rise. Instead, plan your day in 45- to 90-minute intervals, depending on how you feel or what works best for you, with 15- to 20-minute breaks in between (and perhaps a longer one for lunch). This may feel like a lot of breaks, but the science is clear: downtime will ultimately *increase* your output during your uptime, not detract from it. It's a double-win: you will have *both* more productivity and more downtime. Take *more short* breaks during your day to increase your overall motivation and productivity while also staving off a deeper or longer stress response.

Use the Pomodoro Technique—Or Devise Your Own

In the 1980s, Francesco Cirillo developed what he called the Pomodoro Technique: a method of time management using a kitchen timer. This is still an often-touted productivity method in which you set a timer for 25 minutes and focus on a specific task until the timer goes off. Then you take a five-minute break before starting another 25-minute work session. After four cycles, you take a longer break of 15 to 30 minutes. This can work well for some people, but it isn't for everyone. Not all tasks are suited to this technique. While the Pomodoro Technique is closer than the "marathon approach" for how your brain works during the day, it doesn't necessarily follow the natural ultradian cycling of your brain, either.

High performers often find a hybrid approach works best. You can develop your own method based on your preferences, tasks or projects of the day, or how you are feeling. Whatever duration you choose for work versus breaks, the point is that you work for short periods with short, frequent breaks in between—which is more in line with the "sprints approach" advocated above. You will likely find this increases your overall motivation, productivity, and performance because your day feels more energetically and psychologically manageable for you.

Don't shy away from rest or taking breaks. Your current workday schedule may include sessions that are too long for your brain to operate optimally, so it may be helpful to experiment with different work-break intervals to find what works best for you. Many workday breaks do not a slacker make; they are a best practice of the highest performers.

Enable Your Focus by Deleting Your Distractions
As Susan Greenfield highlights in her work, things like the changing nature of culture (people talk faster, type faster, expect everything faster these days), society (people even walk more quickly), and especially technology (the pace of innovation is mind-blowing) all put downward pressure on our attention span and ability to focus. Forewarned is forearmed here: each day, you must equip yourself with the circumstances (e.g., a quiet room), conditions (e.g., well fed and hydrated), tools (e.g., noise-canceling headphones), and practices (e.g., setting an out-of-office notification on your inbox) that will help you to extend your focus (directing your mental effort), concentration (intensity of mental effort), and attention (selectively concentrating on one thing to the exclusion of others) at work. What you need and what works for you to delete your distractions and enable your focus will be different from what is required or works for others—it's up to you to figure this out. Your focusing requirements may vary by day, project, or work environment, also. The more you practice concentrating and focusing, forcing yourself to pay attention to only one thing at a time, weeding out and actively inhibiting distractions, the easier it will become to know which circumstances and practices are right for you to deeply engage with your work.

Focusing on the here and now is essential for being immediately productive: you can't expect to get much done on something you are not attending to. You also need cognitive focus for your brain to make sense of new information (learning), assimilate it into neural networks (knowledge), and ultimately be able to retrieve it (memory). Think of your efforts to focus not just as an excellent way to quicken a taxing ultradian Climb to get to the rewarding Peak faster, but also as helpful in making you more knowledgeable, skilled, and productive. Avoiding distractions and facilitating focus should be a cognitive state you aim for throughout your workday to avoid negative emotions and extra stress, but especially during your mornings, when your well-rested, fresher brain is most likely to be productive.

Put Your Working Brain in Its Preferred Environment
In order to be able to work most productively, you need to make sure you are physically and mentally comfortable. Being too relaxed can interfere with focus, but being in an uncomfortable work environment (e.g., noisy, poorly lit, too hot) will also interfere with your attention and productivity. Having the appropriate lighting, temperature, ambient noise, and environment can help your brain function optimally. Before you start tackling tasks, take a moment to organize and optimize your space for your own comfort, preferences, and productivity. Wear appropriate attire, sit straight in a chair, and adjust the temperature. When you feel your environment has been tailored to you, you will find it easier to become mentally engaged in your work, which will result in much better output and productivity. Some people find that ambient noise helps them focus, while others find they need silence. Some require a relaxed work environment, while others feel more capable of producing when there's ambient noise or peer influence around them to spur their own work efforts. And so on. This may take some concerted self-observation as well as preplanning.

Ensure Your Technology Works for You, Not Against You
Technology is a wonderful tool for workday productivity when used properly and not routinely overused. Our brains were developed when electronic technology didn't exist. As a result, the technology we use can sometimes have the opposite effect of what is intended, decreasing effectiveness, attention span, or performance. Avoiding technology altogether is impossible, but it helps to use it mindfully or limit yourself to one device at a time, for example, or for limited intervals throughout the day. You may aim to have tech-free, screen-free moments during leisure time and daily breaks, since it isn't likely you can get away from technology during your working hours. The break from blue light is helpful to many systems in your brain, but especially your pineal gland and its daily gradual melatonin production—the hormone that facilitates falling and staying asleep at night.

Another way to minimize negative consequences of tech use is to turn off notifications to help reduce unwanted disruptions or the temptation to multitask. Studies have found that even if your mobile device is silent, turned off, and not sending or receiving data, it can still distract you if it is in the same room. I liken these findings to the idea that your subconscious thinks of your phone like a sleeping baby that it knows will eventually wake and need your attention, so it's always (semiconsciously) listening for any signs of need, notifications, or activity. Try this: don't just turn off your phone when you want to focus. If you can put it out of sight, perhaps even in another room, you have a better shot at putting it completely out of your mind so you can attend fully to the tasks at hand. I have found it effective to hide my phone in a drawer in another room when I'm really in need of concerted attention to focus on a task. This may seem extreme at first, but it is a healthy brain practice and can be liberating to feel free of the constant demands of technology, even for just a little while.

Schedule Your Task List into Your Calendar
To work within the likely BRAC time posts throughout your workday, you can organize your to-do list in your calendar on a schedule that breaks things up into ultradian blocks of time (e.g., 45 minutes on, 15 minutes off). This forces you to prioritize and organize your tasks more succinctly. It also gives each task a time allowance, with a planned start and end time, which is especially helpful for difficult, daunting, new, or potentially time-consuming tasks. Parkinson's Law states that work expands (or contracts) to fill the time available for its completion, so giving yourself a specific length of time can be helpful for ensuring tasks or projects don't go on endlessly and get done in a timely manner. Task lists that are scheduled are also typically easier to tackle because they are better prioritized, sequenced, and conceptualized. Tasks without a set timeslot can feel disorganized, unstructured, or endless.

Bonus tip: Put the task list into your calendar the night before (perhaps at the end of your workday or after dinner) so that while you sleep your brain can work on it, visualize it, or even prioritize things further. When you wake up, you will feel that much more ready to take on the tasks and highest priorities of the day.

Be Mindful and Deliberate in Your Work—Don't Multitask
Being your most productive self and doing your best work happens when you are cognitively deliberate, focusing on the task at hand, and being fully immersed in the work of the present moment. Similar to the concept of deliberate practice—when you practice something for the purpose of improvement and full engagement rather than for enjoyment

or reward per se—practicing cognitive deliberateness allows you to be fully present and consciously engaged in your current work for the sake of ensuring its quality and expediency.

Being more deliberate and present allows you to consciously select your thoughts, emotions, and resulting behaviors as they pertain to your work. This, in turn, can help you prioritize, focus, rally resources, and align cognitive systems by engaging your conscious attention. Although being more deliberate requires mental and psychological effort—and can feel quite challenging—it ultimately pays dividends because your engagement increases your effectiveness and efficiency (read: progress) on the tasks at hand. Short periods spent being more deliberate about a task or activity can help you focus genuinely, learn maximally, be more purposeful in your behaviors and actions, and develop skills more quickly. You will also notice your tendencies sooner and more specifically—things like self-distraction efforts, avoidance behaviors, self-sabotage, resistance, or frustrations, to name a few.

Multitasking backfires. Focusing on one task at a time deliberately is the fastest, most effective way to get more things done.

Some people will engage in attempts to multitask to cope with a stressful environment or an overwhelming workload. Unlike computers, which can accomplish simultaneous processing and aren't disturbed by other people or distractions, the human brain can consciously focus on only one thing at a time. Even attempting to multitask requires so much extra mental effort, energy, and code switching between tasks that it increases the rate of errors, stress, blood pressure, fatigue, anxiety, and frustration, while simultaneously decreasing deliberate attention, executive functioning, precision, performance, efficiency, and overall output. Focusing on one task at a time deliberately is the fastest, most effective way for humans to get more things done.

To ensure more engagement, cognitive deliberateness, and maximum productivity in your work, try the following:

1. Get rid of as many distractions in your work environment as possible (e.g., hide your silenced phone in a drawer, close the email inbox tab, ensure you are alone).

2. Give yourself a relatively short period for the current work stint, aligned to your ultradian timeposts (e.g., 60 minutes).

3. Give yourself something to look forward to on the ensuing break (e.g., have some tea, take your dog for a short walk).

4. Set a relatively challenging goal for what you want to achieve in that length of time (e.g., follow up with five clients).

5. Focus on each task at a time successively for that duration and don't attempt to multitask.

These tactics help rally all your cognitive resources to focus singularly on the task at hand for a concerted (but not endless) period of time, which will ensure higher performance and deeper cognitive engagement.

Clarity Through Chaos—
Prioritize Your Tasks with This Matrix

Failing to prioritize your tasks can be as detrimental for your productivity as attempting to multitask. Not prioritizing tasks prevents you from focusing, being deliberate, or completing anything specific, which can ultimately be anxiety-producing, frustrating, or stressful.

Especially when time and resources are scarce (and when isn't that the case?) or demands are coming at you quickly, it's essential to minimize your reliance on immediate cognitive efforts, energy, and willpower. You can prioritize your tasks by eliminating anything that isn't important to your work, which simplifies your to-do list, making it easier to navigate, with less friction or frustration.

Figure 2.4: The Eisenhower Matrix
(Urgent vs. Important Task Prioritization)

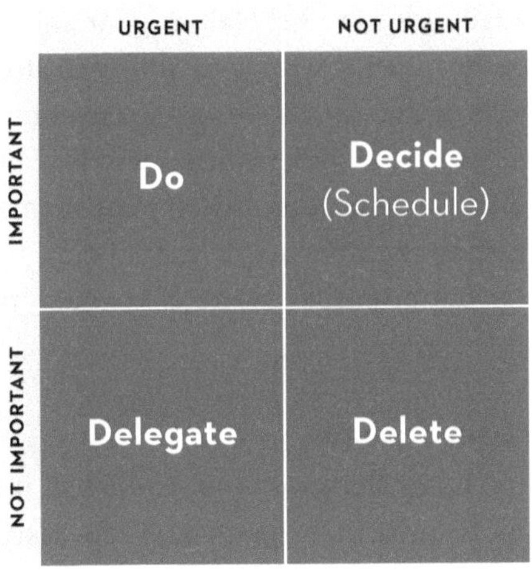

	URGENT	NOT URGENT
IMPORTANT	Do	Decide (Schedule)
NOT IMPORTANT	Delegate	Delete

Prioritization can be tricky, though, because perceived urgent tasks often elicit stronger uncomfortable emotions (e.g., anxiety), allowing them to precede important tasks. The following simple 2×2 matrix (Figure 2.4; popularized by Stephen Covey and named after President Eisenhower) is often recommended for how you can think about your time and tasks more strategically. You can categorize tasks based on their relative importance and urgency to you and your work. Once you determine where a task fits in the "important/not important" and "urgent/not urgent" categories, the prescribed action is labeled in the corresponding quadrant. Incoming emails, as an example, typically fall into the category of urgent for others but not necessarily for you, and as either important (Do now or Decide when to do) or unimportant for you (Delegate or Delete). Because emails often represent menial tasks that get in the way of your highest priorities or deepest cognitive work, many professionals have started scheduling specific times in their day to answer emails instead of answering them continuously as they arrive. Incoming emails are not likely (all) urgent and attending to them continuously can thwart your ability to attend to more important tasks of the day. As we will see in coming chapters, the best time for email inbox management is likely not in the morning but in the afternoon, when your mental resources for deep, creative, cognitive work might be flagging, but you are still adequately attentive, aware, and energetic to engage in such administration.

Target One Daily Triumph

If you have too many things on your to-do list, it can be hard to know how to prioritize them, and it's easy to become overwhelmed, procrastinate, or lose focus. To combat this, try my "Rule of One" method, which is backed by cognitive science. What is *one* thing you care about most, know you can focus on fully, and can realistically accomplish today? It should be a goal, task, or to-do item that is big enough and satisfying enough that, if you get nothing but this done today, you would still consider the day productive and satisfying. It may depend on the day, varying energy levels, motivation, resources, circumstances, and to-do items. Targeting *one* daily triumph will help you stick to only that priority and increase your momentum, self-efficacy, task satisfaction, and intrinsic rewards (e.g., jolts of dopamine and serotonin) from at least one good "job well done" for the day.

Try this: At the end of your day, list everything you want to accomplish for the following day, then choose one major priority you think is realistic and impactful enough from that list, and cross everything else off. Then rewrite that single task on a new piece of paper and list the subtasks required to complete it. These subtasks should be small, specific, and sequenced. Each subtask is an item on its own and gets checked off as it is accomplished. By the end of the workday, ideally, the major item (and all pertaining subtasks) has been accomplished, often in addition to items that were unavoidable throughout the day or were completed afterward (e.g., spoke with accountant, paid bills). You may add unavoidable, unexpected tasks to your working to-do list as you go through the day. Completing any task, even if it wasn't originally on your to-do list, can boost dopamine, serotonin, and norepinephrine, which in this case act as the "get it done," "contented," and "pay attention" neurohormones, respectively, and are helpful for your overall workday productivity, output, momentum, feelings of satisfaction, and performance. By doing this, your to-do list may look longer at the end of the day than it did at the beginning, but all items will be marked as complete, so you will feel adequately satisfied with your efforts and accomplished for the day. At the end of your workday, you'll likely feel more motivated to repeat this process for tomorrow: listing all your desired tasks, choosing the highest priority, and crossing the rest off, etc.

Bonus tip: Write this list the old-school way—on paper. Physically checking things off your to-do list once completed can feel very satisfying and comes with the same positive neurochemistry mentioned above.

Leverage Reward and Anticipation Psychology

Happiness scholars attest that having something to look forward to can be highly uplifting and motivational. It can be a daily thing, like what you are excited about this evening (e.g., a fancy dinner, a yoga class) or something happening during the workday (e.g., lunch with a work friend). It can also be much more significant, like the weekend, a wedding, a vacation, or an important holiday. It doesn't have to be big or expensive—anything will do, as long as you genuinely look forward to it and find it motivating. Figure out what it is that tickles you and hold it in your mind's eye, actively reminding yourself of it throughout the workday, especially during mentally challenging moments. The psychology of positive anticipation is such that imagined future happiness increases your present happiness and can also motivate and energize you through each task of your day, toward improving your overall productivity and performance.

Set (SMART) Goals

There is a vast body of research on the merits and methods of goal setting for achievement. Deliberate goal setting typically provides outcomes and an action plan that helps you achieve what hopes, dreams, ideas, or intentions on their own cannot. Setting goals and deadlines for yourself can help you avoid procrastination, fully engage, and stay on track in your work. It helps your brain prepare, visualize, problem-solve, make decisions, organize your thinking, and set expectations. Objectively measuring your progress and accomplishments can enhance your sense of intrinsic motivation, confidence, and self-efficacy (your belief in your capacity to act to reach specific goals), as well as increase your neurochemistry for feelings of satisfaction and motivation. Small, meaningful, manageable goals can motivate you throughout your entire workday. SMART goals have been shown to aid in goal attainment. SMART stands for specific (or simple), measurable, attainable (or achievable), relevant (or realistic), and time-bound (or time-based).

Say someone has a dream to be more physically fit. They could turn this vague intention into a SMART goal by registering for a 5 km race event that happens eight weeks from today. In this case, their goal is specific (to be physically fit enough to run the race continuously), measurable (five kilometers), attainable (they walk this distance daily), relevant (cardiovascular endurance is one part of physical fitness), and time-bound (they have to be able to accomplish this in eight weeks from now).

Start a Daily Self-Monitoring Diary

Instead of relying on the memory of how your typical day or week goes, pay special attention to your own performance by keeping a log of some kind. You can record your thoughts, feelings, activities, energy levels, and output throughout each workday to understand how your brain works throughout working hours and how you can optimize your work efforts. While the ultradian, circadian, and other cycles predict some of your likely high and low productivity points during the workday, every person's chronobiology is different. Only you can really know when you are in the zone, focused, productive, and feeling good, or the opposite. If you keep track of your experiences for a week, you can gain insight into how to structure your days and tasks for better overall balance, satisfaction, output, and performance.

While there may be some worksheet templates available online for recording your workday activities and productivity proclivities, you can easily make a table or spreadsheet yourself with variables (e.g., energy, positive emotions, motivation, productivity, ability to focus) listed down the first column, and the remaining columns representing hours in your workday. You might give each variable a score (say, from one to five) every hour and then total them for the hour (bottom of the column). These totals will help you quickly determine which parts of your day are typically lower in energy, motivation, or productivity, and in which parts you typically experience higher performance. You might add some notes as well for each hour—so you have both a quantitative and a qualitative account of how your time was spent and felt. A more accurate sense of your own typical energy, emotions, stress, and performance throughout the workday can help guide how you schedule your day better or differently to align your typical peak periods with your top priorities or toughest tasks. Being aware of yourself physically and mentally makes it easier to determine which phase of the ultradian cycle you are in, how much actual progress you are making at any given moment, and what improvements you could incorporate into the current work session or your typical workday scheduling for better overall productivity and performance.

3

The Climb

*I could never have done what I have done without the
habits of punctuality, order, and diligence, and
the determination to concentrate on one subject at a time.*

CHARLES DICKENS

THE CLIMB phase may be perceived as the most challenging part of the ultradian cycle, physiologically, psychologically, and cognitively, because, exactly as it sounds, some heavy lifting is often necessary to get yourself in gear and gain momentum in your tasks, concentration, or work. This phase is also often slower than we hope it to be. During this phase, the brain activates and aligns the various required systems, decides what to focus on, tries to ignore other things, and uses many resources to work on the tasks at hand.

The Climb features increased heart rate, blood pressure, respiration, energy, and oxygen consumption. This phase is crucial for developing your concentration toward peak awareness, attention, cognition, and functioning. The first Climb of the day will likely be the easiest and might be why many of us feel the most productive and motivated first thing in the morning, when our brains feel the freshest after a good night's sleep.

Functionally, the Climb typically lasts 5 to 25 minutes. However, moments of hesitation, procrastination, or distractions can hinder your perceived progress here. How successfully you rally your own attentional and cognitive resources depends on your effort and discipline to overcome the obstacles and distractors and reach a state of cognitive clarity, engagement, and focus.

The perceived time needed for the Climb can also vary depending on the day, task, time of day, and factors such as age, health, and lifestyle habits. For instance, older adults, people with chronic health conditions (e.g., sleep apnea), or those in chaotic circumstances may have a more challenging time ignoring distractions to muster the cognitive, psychological, and physical resources necessary to overcome the initial difficulties to fully focus, concentrate, or engage during this phase.

During the Climb, you may find yourself semi-consciously negotiating the size or duration of a task and reassessing what's most important or realistic for the present moment. Success in this phase of building toward deeper work often requires prioritizing what you will concentrate or work on and simplifying the task to make it more psychologically manageable and easier to tackle.

The Climb is crucial preparation mentally for reaching your Peak. Without adequately engaging in the Climb, attaining optimal cognitive performance levels in your workday becomes less likely. In general, a successful Climb requires that you are rested, reasonably fueled, focused, and relatively calm.

A Peek Inside: What's Happening in There

During the ultradian arousal phase, a network of brain regions work together to regulate bodily functions and resources for the brain. The hypothalamus is active and partly controls BRAC cycles, the thalamus relays sensory information, and the neocortex processes information and generates voluntary movements. Hormones (e.g., adrenaline and cortisol) in these regions trigger the release of neurotransmitters (e.g., dopamine and norepinephrine), which results in a neurochemical cocktail that helps us build alertness and concentration to function most effectively.

Here are some neurotransmitters that are typically active during this phase and some of their effects:

- **Epinephrine** (adrenaline) in small amounts helps increase heart and breathing rates, blood pressure, and the oxygen supply to the brain. It also stimulates the release of neurotransmitters that enhance alertness, attention, and focus.

- **Norepinephrine** increases alertness, attention, and focus, and affects blood vessels and other vascular tissue. Its release is triggered by a small brain area that regulates mental arousal and attention.

- **Cortisol** in small amounts is released by our adrenal glands, resulting in heightened alertness and focus during the arousal phase. In small doses, cortisol is beneficial for optimum motivation and productivity.

- **Dopamine** is a neurotransmitter crucial in motivation, reward, pleasure, satisfaction, and getting things done. It also contributes significantly to learning, memory, and action.

- **Acetylcholine** is a neurotransmitter that significantly affects attention, learning, and memory by exciting and activating the relevant neural areas. Increased levels may boost cognitive function, attention, and awareness through this phase.

- **Glutamate** is not a neurotransmitter per se, but rises through this phase to help transmit signals between brain nerve cells, particularly during heightened alertness. It is important for attention, cognition, learning, and mood regulation.

- **Glutamine** is an essential amino acid and an important energy source for the brain, so its levels increase to meet the sudden demand of energy during this phase.

During the Climb, the brain starts using more oxygen, glucose, water, micronutrients, neurotransmitters, and system resources to activate neural areas and concentrate. The Climb presents a slight challenge because the brain and body must allocate limited resources while dealing with external stimuli, making it a potentially physically and mentally challenging experience.

It is in this phase that your brain transitions from more relaxed alpha and theta waves characteristic of the Valley to more alert and excited beta waves. The beta waves become more synchronized and organized as the brain becomes more engaged, facilitating efficient communication between different brain regions. This beta activity is associated with thinking, problem-solving, and focusing. During the Climb phase, you should feel alert and mostly consciously aware of your thinking, attention, efforts, and engagement. Failure to properly rally mental resources during the Climb phase (e.g., not eliminating distractions, not prioritizing tasks, getting flustered) may result in stress, frustration, and even prolonged beta wave activity (associated with feelings of overwhelm, anxiety, or overstimulation). At the latter end of this phase, toward the Peak, gamma waves make their appearance. Gamma waves are associated with higher brain functions, cognition, focus, working memory, and long-term memory functions, including learning, knowledge, and memory processes.

How It Feels: Common Climb Challenges

The increases in arousing neurotransmitters, hormones, and brainwaves during the Climb can lead to some common challenges.

- **Impatience:** The heightened state of arousal, various neurohormones, and increasing beta and gamma waves can lead to feelings of impatience and restlessness, which can be challenging when dealing with tasks that require patience or attention to detail.

- **Difficulty concentrating:** Paradoxically, the increased arousal levels during this phase can make it difficult to focus on any one task at a time and make it easier to get distracted. Because the brain seeks stimulation, staying on track here may be more difficult. Decreasing distractions is especially important through this phase.

- **Impulsivity and increased self-distraction:** The increased energy and confidence levels during this phase can also lead to a higher tendency to self-distract or avoid the current tasks at hand, which can have negative consequences. Because this stage is a period of flux (like the Fall), the brain is even more likely than usual to make decisions based on emotion rather than logic, making it perhaps more challenging to think critically, stick to the current work, and make rational decisions about work efforts, among other things.

- **Difficulty managing energy levels:** Because this phase is associated with increased energy expenditures, it becomes apparent in this phase if you haven't had enough sleep, haven't taken enough breaks, aren't fueled properly, or are otherwise stressed. You may more readily notice feelings of tiredness or sluggishness, which may be a sign that you need to take more or longer breaks during the Valley phases to recharge, or get more sleep at night.

- **Negative emotions:** The Climb can also cause some negative emotions, especially if it is prolonged or ineffective toward your work efforts. If you have been procrastinating, have many distractions, are in a hectic environment, have been spinning your wheels, are feeling extra stress, or are sick or tired, you may find it harder to rally mental and cognitive resources through this phase. This can feel tiring, frustrating, irritating, or hopeless. You know something isn't quite right if you have to try really hard to concentrate or attend to something in this phase, because your natural physiology should be helping you along.

- **Perceived stress:** This phase can highlight how stressed you are or by itself can feel almost stressful as the brain waves alter and neurochemistry changes. The increased alertness and slight uptick in cortisol can lead to feeling slightly more anxious, agitated, or overwhelmed if you are already dealing with other things. Increased perceived stress may make it challenging to stay calm or relaxed enough through this phase to focus and get things done.

Gearing Up Cognitively Through the Climb: How-Tos

Identify Your Own Task-Avoidance Behaviors to Quell Procrastination

Everyone has their own ways of procrastinating. You are particularly susceptible to these during the Climb, when you are ramping up your productivity and having to align all your cognitive systems. The first step in overcoming task-avoidance behaviors is identifying what they are or look like for you and honestly acknowledging when you are engaging in them so you can stop them in their tracks. Consciously or subconsciously redirecting your energy and attention away from completing a task happens because of anxiety, perceived difficulty, distraction, disengagement, fear of failure, or a lack of current motivation. Recognizing these task-avoidance behaviors is the first step in stopping them, which is important for accomplishing your highest-value tasks and progressing toward your goals each day.

One way to recognize task-avoidance behaviors is to monitor yourself when you are procrastinating. While task-avoidance behaviors might start subconsciously, you will likely have flickers of realization throughout your other activities, including escalating stress or anxiety about the original as-yet-unaccomplished task(s). Some common task-avoidance behaviors are procrastinating, multitasking, self-distracting, scrolling on social media, over-planning, engaging in low-priority or mindless tasks, socializing, doing other chores or errands, daydreaming, zoning out, or asking too many questions, among many others. If you find yourself engaging in any of these, stop what you're doing, move around a little bit to get the blood flowing, give yourself a pep talk, and re-center your energy on your highest-priority tasks. Self-awareness and preplanning will also help you overcome procrastination or other task-avoidance behaviors so you don't have to rely too heavily on your mental resources, energy, or willpower in the moment.

Break Up Big Tasks into Chewable Chunks

One of the best ways to overcome procrastination or tackle a daunting project is to break it up into many smaller, more manageable pieces—something I often refer to as "chewable chunks." Once you have identified the smaller pieces, you can more clearly see what needs to be done and in what order. The smaller the subtasks, the more psychologically manageable you will likely perceive the overall project to be.

Just because they are smaller doesn't mean you should necessarily start with the *easiest* subtasks. You might tackle the project's most challenging or complex parts at the beginning of your day when your energy and motivation are likely to be highest and you're most likely to feel the freshest. This is the logic behind the old "eat your frogs for breakfast" adage, stemming from the famous Mark Twain quotation, "If it's your job to eat a frog, it's best to do it first thing in the morning and the rest of your day shall surely improve. And if it's your job to eat two frogs, it's best to eat the bigger one first." The idea is that by starting with the most challenging subtask in your day and conquering it, you increase your confidence, momentum, sense of progress, satisfaction, self-efficacy, and all the upcycle of neurochemistry that comes with these positive states.

Conversely, if you aren't feeling particularly confident or motivated, starting with the easiest or preferred subtasks can bolster your sense of confidence and satisfaction by providing quick wins right away. It can help you get warmed up and psyched up, and jump-start your momentum.

The order you put subtasks in will depend on the day, the overall project, how you are feeling, and the circumstances surrounding you. Being strategic here can be very helpful for getting started and making progress. Just breaking things into bite-sized subtasks makes any project more mentally manageable and can increase both the motivation to start and the stamina required to finish.

Just Start—The Zeigarnik Effect

Speaking of starting and finishing, psychologist Bluma Zeigarnik investigated why people typically finish what they start. She discovered that interrupted tasks are easier to remember than uninterrupted ones. This is because people tend to feel dissatisfied with unfinished tasks and continue thinking about them. This can lead to slight anxiety or mental discomfort, especially when we want or need to finish the task but we haven't yet for some reason. We can use this "Zeigarnik effect" to our advantage in tasks or projects that we don't like or have been avoiding, for example. The trick here is to just start on the project—anywhere. Don't wait for the right timing, resources, sequence, or permission—just begin somewhere. According to Zeigarnik, you are significantly more likely to finish a project you have already started, and if you get interrupted or take a break, you will be more likely to return to it because leaving something unfinished will effectively bother you too much. Zeigarnik's principle is analogous to Nike's "Just Do It" slogan. If you overthink when, where, and how to start something, you likely just won't, whereas according to the science, if you jump right in, you are more likely to try, continue, and finish, at least eventually.

Jump-Start with the 15-Minute Challenge

If you are struggling with a task or subtask that feels too challenging at the moment, there's a trick you can use to temporarily motivate yourself and jump-start your efforts. The 15-minute challenge is used by psychologists and fitness trainers alike and is very simple: Select the task, set the timer for 15 minutes, and attempt to complete as much as possible in just those 15 minutes. Once the timer goes off, you can take a break, stop, or continue working on the task for as long as you can tolerate. As Zeigarnik might assert, even if you decide to take a break after 15 minutes, you will be more likely to return to the task eventually because you will want to finish what you started. Also, your task-related self-efficacy and confidence will be boosted from the first 15-minute stint, so you are also more likely to carry on. The concept is a bit like jump-starting a car—you need that first jolt of energy to get the wheels turning. Committing to just 15 minutes can build up momentum, stamina, progress, confidence, and willpower for more extended sessions. You can choose any time for this challenge (5, 10, 20 minutes), but 15 minutes is often touted because it's perceptually short enough to tolerate and yet long enough to give you time to make some progress.

This trick is often used by people who lack any or all of the three confidences (task, situational, or personal). For example, it can get disorganized people started in clearing things out at long last or people new to physical exercise moving their bodies. A person may not feel confident about decluttering or running to start with, but if they know they must engage in it for only 15 minutes, they are usually willing to at least *try*, which increases their overall confidence, efficacy, and progress.

Here's an example: I know a fitness trainer who uses this trick to get people started with exercise routines after long periods of sedentary living and who lack confidence to work out again. He asks that his clients commit to only 15 minutes of time on the treadmill to start. If after 15 minutes they want to keep going, great, but if not, they have accomplished the intended objective for the day's session. That same trainer uses another trick, which is similar psychologically but doesn't have a time component to it: They don't have to commit to any specific duration exercising, but they do have to put on all their workout clothes, lace up their runners, get out their water bottle, and stand on the road with him. Then, if they feel like running, jogging, or walking, great. If not, they have accomplished his requirements for the session. (No surprise that most people do some physical activity after they have gone to all the trouble of getting ready.) In both cases his clients "jump-start" a task that might have originally seemed too psychologically daunting to even begin.

Switch Up Overwhelming Tasks Spontaneously

If you find that you can't concentrate, are overwhelmed by a given task, or cannot even commit to it for 15 minutes to start, try switching immediately to a different task from your to-do list that you feel more capable of handling at the specific moment. This is different from trying to multitask, which is counterproductive. Instead, it's about switching your immediate (singular) activity based on what you feel capable of right now, what your environment will allow, or what you think might help increase your momentum, satisfaction, or confidence. Switching tasks spontaneously can help you feel better and increase overall motivation, whereas trying to work on a task you aren't up to can lead to diminishing marginal returns, decreased overall performance, and increased stress response—the longer you spend spinning your wheels, the worse you will feel. If you struggle significantly at some point during your day, strategic, spontaneous task-switching can jolt your confidence, motivation, momentum, willpower, stamina, and progress in the immediate term to help get you back on track in your workday.

That said, there's a limit here. You don't want to switch tasks too frequently, as this can be a sign that something else is amiss, like you have more pressing issues to attend to or you haven't organized your day properly. The outcome of immediate task-switching should be to decrease anxiety or frustration while increasing your current sense of progress and motivation, allowing you to more readily get back on track with your previously planned tasks and activities.

All Work and No Play Wrecks a Workday
Play can be both a physical activity and a state of mind. A sense of play can enhance attention, concentration, focus, and brain function, ultimately leading to increased enjoyment and productivity. Humans naturally prefer to do things they find enjoyable, so engaging in tasks you find entertaining, fun, or even playful can increase your sense of engagement and "Flow." Entering a cognitive state of play through gamification can help you concentrate on tasks for longer periods without frustration, which can lead to more progress, higher productivity, more creativity, and better outputs.

Turning your tasks into games can help also you rally your cognitive resources more effortlessly, so you feel as though you are reaching peak performance faster and with greater ease. You can create games with the clock (e.g., finish five small tasks in the next 30 minutes), with yourself (e.g., outdo your previous performance), or with colleagues (e.g., compete with them to do something). Competition is an excellent way to gamify anything, stimulate your social brain regions, engage different neural and psychological areas, and help buoy your progress and productivity. Gamification can also be a great way to motivate a group of people to focus on a task simultaneously and productively. It can decrease task-related frustration and friction, too, because you and your colleagues focus on each other (using subconscious, social parts of your brain) instead of the specific task, challenge, or project (which often uses conscious, logical, laborious parts of your brain). As we will discuss in greater detail in chapter 10 (Interact), there are plenty of social regions in your brain, and positive social interactions stimulate your overall creativity, motivation, productivity, happiness, performance, and well-being. Generally, doing what you can to make your work as enjoyable as possible is best practice for reaching your own peak performance.

Do what you can to make all of your tasks each day as enjoyable as possible for you.

Reframe Immense Challenges

Perception is everything. A common challenge for rallying cognitive resources is being unable to focus because you feel overwhelmed with your tasks and how much you have to get done—especially at the beginning of a major or daunting project. You might need to consider paring down the project, breaking it into smaller tasks as discussed above, or reconceptualizing the whole thing. This is often referred to as reframing, relabeling, or reinterpreting the nature or magnitude of the challenge at hand. In this method, you are challenging your own thoughts, changing your focus, questioning the objectives, and altering your perceptions.

Even more specifically, there are three components of a challenging task you can reframe or reconsider: your ability relative to the overall task ("Yes, I can do it"), the magnitude or duration of the task itself ("It is doable, in 15-minute intervals"), or the emotion associated with the challenge of the task ("This doesn't have to feel overwhelming; feeling challenged is an opportunity for growth and improvement. This is exciting!"). It might feel emotionally or psychologically uncomfortable at first, but deliberately looking at the challenge differently will help you perceive it newly, and will often help make it feel more possible or manageable for you. Find a way to reframe challenging tasks or projects for yourself so you can view them as doable, if not interesting, stimulating, and even enjoyable.

Say No Sometimes
When all else fails, don't let others, or even yourself, overwhelm you to the point of undue, chronic, or non-optimal stress. Sometimes saying no to tasks or projects is the healthiest, best way to proceed. Only you can know and communicate your boundaries—you are the only one who knows when too much is too much for you. Honor that. Listen to your mind, intuition, and body. If you have tried other reasonable courses of action—such as reframing the task, questioning your own thoughts and emotions, attempting to reclaim your sense of control, trying the 15-minute challenge, switching tasks at strategic times, starting anywhere, or giving yourself confidence-boosting pep talks—and none of it is working to decrease task-specific stress, there's likely a reason.

Saying no isn't a sign of weakness; it's a sign of healthy self-awareness and self-respect. When you respect yourself, your energy, and your time this way, you signal for others to respect these as well. Of course, it is also important not to give up too soon—give yourself time to work through the challenge and attempt to meet it. Whenever possible, it's important to set boundaries and expectations up front with others, so that you are not disappointing colleagues unexpectedly. It is essential, especially for high achievers (who tend to score higher on perfectionism and people-pleasing scales), to remember that saying no is a viable option and is sometimes the best course of action.

4

The Peak

*Peak performance begins with
your taking complete responsibility for your life
and everything that happens to you.*

BRIAN TRACY

DURING YOUR brain's ultradian journey, the Peak might be considered "the main event." Reaching the Peak of your ultradian rhythm is a pinnacle state and serves as a reward for the work of the Climb. At this stage, all your neural and physiological systems should be working optimally, resulting in heightened alertness, awareness, activity, and energy expenditure. During this phase, your brain may function at its highest level of productivity, and your body typically feels ready for action.

Many people report feeling their most clear-headed and perceptive at the Peak, and their mood tends to be the most positive and upbeat. Cognitively, this is the time to capitalize on a heightened ability to pay attention, concentrate, or focus. This heightened alertness and concentration may also give rise to a state of Flow—an optimal psychological and cognitive experience where you feel completely absorbed in an activity and derive great satisfaction and fulfillment from it, even in the face of some challenges. Some people refer to this as being "in the zone" or "on a roll." Flow, originally described by Mihaly Csikszentmihalyi, is considered an ideal state in positive psychology, characterized by a feeling of effortless action and full engagement, where everything seems to fall into place while time and your surroundings may feel irrelevant. You may feel so immersed you become one with the activity and lose track of time. Ultradian Peak phases are not the same as the Flow state. While heightened productivity and Flow *can* occur during the Peak, they don't always.

The challenge with the Peak, especially for high performers, is that it never feels long enough—you almost always wish you had more of that optimal state to feel fabulous and get more done. Enough time at the Peak is essential to maximize your productivity and progress. Unfortunately, we all sometimes do things that keep us from experiencing peak performance for as long as we might like. Failing to fuel ourselves properly, allowing distractions to take over, pushing ourselves too hard for too long, or failing to recognize signs of fatigue are examples of errors that may decrease the duration and perceived height of this phase—how great you feel and how much you are able to get done.

A Peek Inside: What's Happening in There

During the Peak, there is a surge of activity in several brain regions. Here are some:

- **The prefrontal cortex** is responsible for executive functions such as planning, decision-making, and attention to tasks. It activates the anterior cingulate cortex.

- **The anterior cingulate cortex** manages error detection (so that useful, accurate work gets done) and response inhibition (like getting distracted by incoming emails).
- **The hippocampus** is critical in memory formation and retrieval, helping you remember what you discovered or accomplished and retrieve pieces of information you already know that might help with the task at hand.
- **The amygdala** is involved in emotional processing and regulation, may spur feelings of task interest or excitement, and can aid motivation to keep working.

Brain areas work together to promote peak performance by increasing alertness, focus, information processing, reasoning, decision-making, creativity, enhanced learning, and memory. This phase typically lasts for about 30 minutes, after which there is a decline in activity (the beginning of the Fall), followed by the rest and recovery (the Valley) phase before the cycle begins again.

At the Peak, some expected neurochemical and hormonal processes also occur:

- **Dopamine** levels can rise, resulting in increased focus, motivation, an orientation toward your goals, and feeling able to accomplish tasks.
- **Acetylcholine** levels rise, resulting in enhanced cognitive function, information processing, attention, learning, and memory.
- **Serotonin** levels may rise, resulting in improved mood, overall sense of well-being, cognitive flexibility, contentedness, and focused mental state.

- **Endorphins**, which regulate pain and pleasure, may rise, resulting in balanced mood and a sense of pleasure or well-being.

- **Cortisol**, released by the adrenal glands, may rise slightly to facilitate heightened energy, focus, or performance.

- **Glutamate**, involved in the transmission of signals between nerve cells in the brain, may rise and results in increased neural activity, network activation, and cognitive functioning.

- **Norepinephrine**, involved in arousal, alertness, and attention, may rise to facilitate cognitive performance, readiness for action, and response to incoming information.

The Peak phase most commonly involves beta (including high beta), gamma, and sometimes alpha waves. Beta waves are thought to help with active thinking, concentration, engagement, cognitive processing, and focused attention. Gamma waves are thought to allow for heightened perception, better learning, more effective problem-solving, efficient information processing, superior decision-making, new insights, and stronger connections among multiple brain areas. Alpha waves may also be present during this phase and are linked to a relaxed and focused mental state, aiding sustained attention and innovative thinking, balanced with relative calmness or decreased psychological tension. The combination of beta and gamma waves (and sometimes alpha waves) can facilitate cognitive processing (e.g., deep or challenging work), information integration (e.g., pattern recognition, network formation, learning), and the ability to work with information more effectively (e.g., problem-solving, reasoning, decision-making). All this variable activity and synchronization allows the brain to balance focused attention and effort with relative calmness (as opposed to stress), ideally resulting in a psychological Flow state or a sense of optimal cognitive performance. These desirable states are more assured when someone engages routinely in activities that promote these states of mind (such as mindfulness, meditation, or physical exercise), manages their own workday time and energy deliberately, and actively avoids distractions so as to stay focused.

How It Feels: Common Peak Challenges

Although the Peak phase of the ultradian cycle feels fulfilling when properly supported, several typical challenges or mistakes can compromise, shorten, or hinder your experience and output during this phase. Here are some common issues:

- **Pressure to perform:** The heightened mental state during the Peak can lead to perceived pressure (usually from yourself) to maintain high levels of performance indefinitely, which can be stressful and even backfire. It may also lead to a tendency to take on too much work, which can result in more prolonged stress, anxiety, or feeling overwhelmed.

- **Distraction:** During the Peak phase, attention, focus, and concentration aren't guaranteed, and it's possible to become overstimulated, avoid tasks, or allow external distractions to creep in. You might start to feel overwhelmed, be quickly drawn to new stimuli, or be tempted to multitask, which can make it even more challenging to stay on task and complete your work. This is especially a problem when there are multiple demands on your attention, your environment is hectic, or technology interrupts your work.

- **Mental fatigue and errors:** You may feel pressure to sustain high performance, or you may be so mentally stimulated that you fail to recognize overall fatigue and start making more mistakes than usual—especially nearing the end of this phase. The energy and positive feeling of the Peak can also lead to increased errors due to overconfidence, impulsivity, or because you start rushing through tasks to "strike while the iron is hot."

- **Physical fatigue:** You may feel so mentally active that you don't notice (or might not heed) your body's physical warning signs. Fatigue can make some tasks more difficult, especially those requiring physical exertion, a high level of precision, attention to detail, or maximum accuracy. It can also contribute to prolonged fatigue over the rest of the day if you fail to take regular breaks and replenish properly.

- **Agitation:** Because of heightened awareness, excitation, energy, and attention in this phase, it can sometimes be challenging to feel cool, calm, collected, or composed. While excitement can be helpful for performance and productivity, it can sometimes tip you over the edge, decrease your output, or lead to more negative feelings.

More Powerful Peaks: How-Tos

Foster Habits That Facilitate Your Cognitive Performance

In chapter 1 we discussed how our brains store information we have seen or experienced more than once into networks and shortcuts, allowing us to conserve future energy by creating efficient neural pathways. You can use this "hard-wiring" to your advantage by purposefully practicing functional behaviors throughout your workday to facilitate habits for productivity and cognitive performance. Routinizing various activities or parts of your day can help reduce your reliance on mental resources in the moment, and help push you through moments of difficulty or distraction. The more routinized or habitual a behavior is, the less you need to consciously think about engaging in it and the easier it feels to accomplish.

Here's an example. Mary is a content creator who works in a busy office that she finds distracting and overwhelming, and that has contributed to many unproductive, frustrating workdays for her. To combat this, every morning she sits at her desk and does the exact same things to start her day. With her favorite tea in hand, she has a quick look at her inboxes and messages to ensure nothing is detrimentally urgent, and then sets an out-of-office message until after lunch—she wants to use her freshest, best brain for her own work, not others' requests or correspondences. She also verifies her calendar she organized the night before, and she schedules any meeting requests for the afternoons wherever possible. Next, she takes out her handwritten to-do list she put together yesterday, crosses off all but her highest-priority item, and starts in on the task anywhere (hoping to conjure the Zeigarnik effect), promising herself only 15 minutes of effort, at first. This usually propels her into a full 60 minutes with the help and momentum of her freshest physiology, at which point she takes a 15-minute break to refresh, reset, and tackle the next part of her project. Mary is very consistent in this morning routine and has modeled these behaviors to others, who now understand her patterns and boundaries to the point where they very rarely ask her for morning meetings and often won't even send her emails until the afternoon. All this allows Mary to ensure her best brain is deployed on her own work first thing in the morning with fewer distractions, conscious decisions, or discussions to be had at the outset of her day. Mary doesn't need to rely on her willpower, stamina, energy, or variable motivation to kick-start her day—she need only follow her routine habits to reach peak cognitive performance and focus with greater ease. Now her morning routine is second nature to her and those around her, and her once-conscious actions are now habitual.

It is best practice to be mindful of what you practice consistently, because these practices become habits that easily perpetuate themselves. Whatever you repeat becomes increasingly wired into your neural networks. Undesirable habits like watching TV all evening, scrolling on Instagram for hours, or drinking three cups of coffee each day are as easily habituated as more desirable ones like working out every day, eating a salad at lunch, taking more frequent breaks, and going for an evening walk. The more often you repeat anything, the more you will naturally be drawn to doing it because of something called habit inertia. Well-practiced behaviors become habits that can eventually feel like second nature for you, as they become increasingly automated, and can even feel uncomfortable *not* to engage in. Establishing deliberate and consistent behaviors requires more conscious organization and effort at first, but with practice, these preferred behaviors can become as automatic as the less-functional ones. Facilitating your own cognitive performance during the Peak is critical for your productivity. Fostering habits specifically to help you pay attention, concentrate, and focus gets easier over time, helping you progress toward your goals each day with less mental anguish and resources.

Seek Challenge to Stimulate a Flow State

Back in 1975, psychologist Mihaly Csikszentmihalyi coined the term "Flow" to describe a mental state wherein a person is intrinsically motivated and fully absorbed in what they are doing. According to Csikszentmihalyi, it is essential to balance the task's challenge with the performer's skill level to achieve a Flow state (Figure 4.1). Similar to Yerkes and Dodson's assertions, it was conceived that a state of Flow couldn't be reached if the task was either too easy (e.g., apathy, boredom) or too difficult (e.g., anxiety, worry).

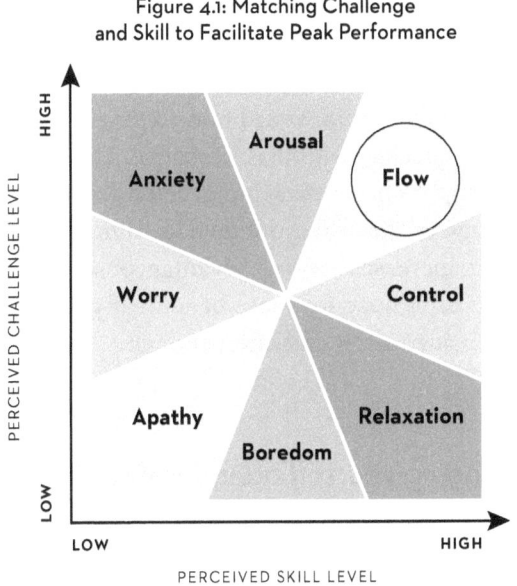

Figure 4.1: Matching Challenge and Skill to Facilitate Peak Performance

Therefore, to optimize productivity and usher in Flow, motivation scholars suggest engaging in activities that you find rewarding in and of themselves (known as autotelic experiences or autotelic activities) and that you feel naturally and intrinsically motivated to engage with, but that are also relatively challenging for you. Engaging in autotelic work and achieving a Flow state can help prolong your peak performance and help you be more productive. When you enjoy what you are doing, you will probably do more of it, though

Csikszentmihalyi believed that autotelic enjoyment isn't enough in itself to kick you into high gear—a certain level of perceived challenge is also necessary to hold your attention and motivate your exertion. Striking the right balance of your own *perceived* skill (high) and challenge (high) on a project or task is the key here. Perception, framing, and self-talk shape how you *perceive* both your abilities and the challenges in front of you and therefore determine your performance at anything, including your ability to get into Flow. Challenging yourself adequately should help you reach your maximum performance range, excite your brain to develop and learn, and even spur valuable neuroplastic change. The saying "use it or lose it" applies here: engaging in activities that are challenging enough to stimulate your own learning, growth, and development increases lasting advantageous neuroplastic change—you can't hope for these benefits if you don't challenge yourself adequately and often enough.

Challenging yourself adequately and often is optimal. Comfort zones can impede learning, growth, and our own peak performance.

If you find that your task list, projects, or work don't command your attention, aren't absorbing, or don't spur you into action, it could be because you just aren't challenged enough. Comfort zones can be great for healing and recuperating, but there can be too much of a good thing: staying too much or too often within your comfort zones can inhibit psychological, cognitive, mental, professional, and even physical amelioration and growth.

Reclaim Your Sense of Task Autonomy, Control, Choice

A significant factor in helping you feel like you are deeply engaged with your work and can achieve optimally is feeling as if you have autonomy, control, or choice in your work. If you feel as if a task is beyond your perceived ability and frustrating or difficult *and* you can't control how it proceeds, then your focus, concentration, positive emotions, and confidence may dip, while your stress response increases.

Whenever possible, try to choose the tasks you work on, as well as how, when, where, and with whom you work on them. When you can remind yourself that you chose the current task (or at least how it proceeds), you decrease perceived anxiety and stress while increasing your sense of autonomy, control, choice, and agency. Whether you chose the task or it was assigned, do what you can to personalize or make it feel like your own, such as by breaking it up your way, infusing your personality into it, or following a process that you know works for you. Whenever possible, delegate parts you don't like or don't feel up to, or ask for help. Feeling like you have some control, choice, or autonomy in your work will quiet the natural "alarm bells" in your brain and help you feel like you have better circumstances or competencies to get the job done. Working on tasks or projects for which you have intrinsic motivation (the stuff you really want to do, that no one told you to do) also leads to a better sense of personal agency, self-efficacy, and confidence. If you feel you have autonomy and freedom of choice for what you work on, you are more likely to perform at your best for longer periods of time.

Turn on Some Tunes

Many people find that listening to music helps them focus. When selecting music for concentration, it is best to keep music at a low enough volume that it does not interfere with your information processing or thought processes—and to protect your eardrums. Depending on the task, studies have shown that classical and rhythmic music without lyrics can help you study by helping you zone in and tune out distractions, especially if you're in a busy environment such as a library or an open office space. The "Mozart effect" suggests that classical music has unique patterned, mathematical, and rhythmic properties that aid in assimilating new information into neural networks (learning). Research shows that music without lyrics can help attention, whereas music with lyrics can be more distracting, whether the listener is aware of it or not. Musical preferences vary, though the crucial aspect of music that aids in attention, concentration, focus, and productivity is that it helps (a) block out environmental distractions and (b) direct your attention so you can engage more deeply, work more efficiently, focus for longer, and make more progress.

There's an App for That
Various tools and technologies claim to help enhance your focus, concentration, or Flow experience. At the time of this writing, websites like Brain.fm, Focus@Will, StudyStream, and Study Together, as well as tech options like noise-canceling headphones and productivity apps, are intended to help you stick to the task longer and more meaningfully, although new innovations come out all the time. I don't endorse or use these myself because I find they require too much distracting interaction or affiliation with technology. However, everyone is different in terms of what will or won't work for them, and getting aid is better than struggling through and getting frustrated. If you're so inclined, experimenting with the available apps or tech may help you get in the zone and stay there longer—and if so, more power to you.

5

The Fall

*Stress response is simply the adaptation
of our bodies and minds to change.*

PETER G. HANSON

THE FALL phase is the ultradian stress response. Coming after the high of the Peak, it can feel frustrating, anticlimactic, or lackluster. This is the phase of the ultradian cycle when your brain and body start to signal that they need to rest and reset. Unfortunately, this can happen even when you are feeling otherwise productive or on a roll.

If you continue to work on tasks despite this stress response gaining momentum, you may experience decreasing benefits, outputs, performance, or productivity. During the Fall is when HALT sensations—hungry, angry, lonely, tired (or thirsty)—may start to creep in. HALT sensations are common in the ultradian stress response, and the acronym isn't an accident—they can all signal a good time to rest, recuperate, or take a break. When you enter the Fall, you experience heightened stress, and your body produces more cortisol and other stress hormones in an effort to keep you focused, despite the rising tide of needing rest. The stress response in the Fall is a natural response in your physiological rhythms, but if it persists for too long or deepens, it can have negative consequences that last into successive ultradian cycles and throughout your day. The best thing to do during the Fall is to acknowledge it, finish up whatever you are working on, and take a break to rest and reset.

Several factors can trigger faster and more intense ultradian Falls. If you didn't get enough sleep the night before or are generally sleep deprived, you may notice that you are more susceptible to quicker stress responses and less able to control your emotions, leading to increased fatigue and irritability (see chapter 9, Rest). If you are hungry or have not been fueling your body with the right nutrients, you may also experience a faster and more intense Fall (see chapter 8, Eat). Chronic stress, anxiety, stressful events, negative thoughts, arguments with others, tight deadlines, not taking enough breaks, and attempting to push through the Fall can exacerbate stress responses throughout your day. People often report that their early afternoons feel like a perpetual Fall—they are irritable, find it hard to focus, feel peckish, want to take a nap, and can't get much done.

You shouldn't try to push through a Fall because it's a critical ultradian physiological response that gives way to the Valley period of healing, rest, and replenishment. As such, it's valuable in itself as a period of flux where the brain (and all its neurons, waves, hormones, and regions) switches gears from the high performance of the Peak to the required restorative processes of the Valley. During the Fall, the brain and body shift from cognitive production and metabolic resource consumption to repairing and fixing cells and neural networks, as well as replenishing the necessary metabolic resources. This represents a 180-degree shift in the system's activities and requirements from peak performance. This downshifting can be physically, psychologically, and cognitively challenging—often feeling disappointing for high achievers—and consequently can lead to misguided efforts to deny, thwart, or compensate for diminishing returns, output, or productivity.

A Peek Inside: What's Happening in There

During the Fall, some predictable neurochemical and hormonal activities happen.

- Most notably, cortisol, the hormone released by the adrenal glands in response to stress, suddenly increases, leading to an increase in heart rate and blood pressure. Cortisol also helps mobilize energy stores (glucose levels in the blood) and suppress the immune system to divert resources to areas where they are needed for the immediate response. Cortisol is the best known of the glucocorticoids, but it isn't the only one circulating during the stress response phase. Other stress hormones circulating during this time may include corticosterone, cortisone, DHEA, DHEA-S, 11-Deoxycortisol, and aldosterone, as examples. An increased number and amount of these can increase the perceived speed, harshness, and duration of a stress response.

- When your body experiences stress or an uptick in stress hormones, the adrenal glands and sympathetic nervous system release epinephrine and norepinephrine. These neurohormones cause your alertness, heart rate, blood pressure, and respiration rate to increase while also helping to mobilize energy stores in your body. These prepare you for an immediate reaction to the stress response itself (e.g., taking a break) or to your need to keep working on something, and they contribute to physical and psychological manifestations of stress (e.g., irritation, muscle tightness).

- When the body enters a stress response, the levels of excitatory glutamate in the brain rise, resulting in heightened neural activity, neural communication, and alertness, often including negative emotions (e.g., anxiety).

- When the brain experiences stress, levels of calming gamma-aminobutyric acid (GABA) decrease, which can cause negative feelings, anxiety, or increased stress perceptions.

The Fall phase can be associated with low beta, gamma, alpha, and theta waves. Lower beta waves signal the transition from peak cognitive performance, focus, and attention to a more relaxed state. Gamma waves—responsible for executive functions and memory at the Peak—are likely to be present at the outset of the Fall, petering away as you get closer to the Valley. Alpha waves characteristic of the Valley appear, which also denote a transition phase from high alertness and cognitive activity to a more relaxed or resting state. Failure to heed the Fall may result in excessive beta wave activity, which block more relaxing alpha waves and can lead to perceived anxiety, stress, or frustration (a phenomenon known as "alpha blocking"). Prolonged beta wave activity during the Fall can also cause physical symptoms such as headaches, muscle tension, or increased heart rate—more reasons to take a break when the brain and body are asking for it. Theta waves characteristic of the Valley appear during the Fall—especially nearing the end of this phase—as they represent a shift from conscious, active, alert awareness and thinking toward lower alertness, subconscious or emotional processing, fatigue, and relaxation.

The body's ultradian stress response features increased inflammation, the accumulation of toxins, waste and cellular debris, increased blood pressure and tension, and slight activity in the sympathetic nervous system. These can signal to the brain that potential emergency measures may be necessary (should a break not be possible or taken, for example). Hormonal disruptions and imbalances in blood sugar can occur, leading to increased cravings—especially for salt, fat, sugar, carbohydrates, or caffeine. These cravings are often coupled with a decreased ability to delay gratification, self-regulate, maintain emotional stability, or make good decisions. The body's immune function may also decrease slightly during this phase.

If you ignore or try to push through the Fall, this series of physiological events can deepen, causing the sympathetic nervous system (SNS) to increase its activity and stress response. Neurotransmitters may become imbalanced, such as when higher levels of epinephrine and norepinephrine in the brain and body make you feel jittery, anxious, or overwhelmed at first, giving way to feelings of being wiped out or exhausted. A stress response that is deepened or prolonged may also lead to a decrease in the production of serotonin (the happy hormone), dopamine (the get-it-done hormone), and BDNF (brain-derived neurotrophic factor—the learning, knowledge, memory hormone) contemporaneously or in successive cycles.

How It Feels: Common Fall Challenges

As a result of all this internal activity, during a normal Fall there is a decline in sensory abilities (e.g., hearing, seeing), and the ability to retrieve information or memories, as well as increased difficulty reading, learning, or retaining new knowledge. Mental capacity and patience decrease, as do motor skills and physical coordination. Emotional volatility and reactivity increase while emotional regulation and stability decrease. Communication, objectivity, executive functioning, information processing, and reasoning all decline. There is also a measurable decrease in decision-making abilities, thinking accuracy, and problem-solving skills. Here are some quick ways to identify if you are in a Fall.

- **Sudden or increased difficulty paying attention, focusing, or concentrating** because the various internal systems are distracted by having to respond to the internal "threat" of diminished resources, building waste and debris, and increased stress hormones.

- **Decreasing physical abilities** because of the body's focus on responding to the Fall.

- **Increased anxiety, irritability, or emotional instability** (such as HALT sensations) due to an increase in stress hormones and response.

- **Physical symptoms** such as headaches, eye fatigue, muscle tension, hunger, thirst, cravings, or needing to use the restroom.

- **Decreased motivation, energy, willpower, or stamina** for the tasks at hand or work in general.

There are also some common—and unsurprising—challenges during the Fall that most people encounter from time to time.

- **Attempting to "power through"**: In modern work culture, we have been conditioned to push through our own discomfort and prioritize productivity at all costs. Although it may seem like a good idea to power through and override the natural urge to take a break, doing so can cause the body to produce and circulate higher levels of stress hormones, leading to a deeper, stronger, or longer stress response. All of which means that pushing through typically backfires.

- **HALT sensations:** The Fall may be when HALT sensations surface. You might want a snack, especially one high in salt, fat, or sugar ("hungry"). You may have a sudden, unexplained uptick in negative emotions like anger, hostility, frustration, or irritation ("angry"). You may suddenly feel as if you are alone in a task or project, doing more than your fair share, or in need of more support from others than you are getting ("lonely"). You might feel physically and mentally exhausted ("tired"). You may feel suddenly parched, especially for a beverage with sugar or caffeine ("thirsty"). These stress response by-products can be easy to overlook or misplace, but they can affect many aspects of your life, including your longer-term health and social relationships. Often a break will help diminish or eliminate these sensations.

- **Interpersonal friction:** Because your emotional regulation and social skills can take a hit during this phase, you may find it harder to interact with others in a positive, gracious, or prosocial manner. It might be more challenging to cooperate, collaborate, compromise, or coordinate with others during the Fall, when the alarm bells in the brain and body are sounding and maintaining a positive attitude or good-humored cadence feels much harder.

- **ANTs may creep in:** In this case, ANTs stands for automatic negative thoughts, not insects. During this phase ANTs may start to creep in because your ability to inhibit, ignore, or thwart them is decreased. There are three main types of ANTs: all-or-none thinking ("I'll either succeed completely or fail entirely at this"), "should" statements ("I should have done all this completely differently"), and distorted discounting of the positive aspects ("Who cares that I'm 90 percent done—I'm still not finished"). Your ANTs "attack" you first ("I'm no good at any of this"), others second ("They're no good at any of this"), and the situation third ("This whole project has been set up to fail from the beginning"). Left unchecked, ANTs can also contribute to a slew of other challenges, including catastrophic thinking (a cognitive distortion of worst-case-scenario spiraling), negative comments or interactions toward others, or scrapping an otherwise worthwhile and successful project, as examples. Negative thoughts and distortions further quell executive functioning, emotional regulation, reasoning of all types, mental acuity, social skills, self-efficacy, motivation, productivity, and performance, just to name a few. Avoiding ANTs, HALT sensations, and more extensive SNS activation requires adequate rest, breaks, downtime, replenishment, and heeding each Fall.

More Functional Falls: How-Tos

Heed Each Fall

Everyone experiences ultradian stress responses differently, so it is important to listen to your brain and body and honor your natural impulses. If you feel hungry, eat; if you are thirsty, drink water; if you think you may need a break, take one. Your brain and body can perform at their best only if you are attentive to their requirements. Your brain is a remarkable supertechnology, performing millions of calculations every second and asking for very little in return. The Fall is a sign that your brain needs something. Respect these requirements and you will regain your composure, motivation, and productivity faster. Don't try to keep up with or work like others, either—their physiology is different from yours. Listen to your own needs so that you are working with your natural energy cycle, not against it.

Think of Negative Emotions as Informative

Negative emotions such as irritation, exhaustion, frustration, and anger can be uncomfortable, but they are designed to provide you with insight into how to take care of your internal, mental, and physical states. The discomfort of emotions (most of them experienced are negative) is in fact the point: *negative emotions and sensations are designed to make you feel uncomfortable enough that you will do something about them.* However, if these negative emotions go unchecked or unmanaged, they can spill over and create friction in your life and work. Part of a functional and well-managed Fall is acknowledging your own needs and negative emotions and containing them long enough to take a restorative break.

    It is relatively common to experience negative emotions during the workday, during the Fall, or in the workplace. In general, emotions should be considered helpful, functional, and a message from within. They are there to motivate actions and behaviors and provide insight into your own inner needs and workings. Typically, the best way past uncomfortable emotions is through them: recognize them for what they are (indicators that you need to take action, a pause, or a break) and use them to make functional, conscious, or more rational decisions about how to manage your time, thoughts, energy, behaviors, and tasks. This self-awareness can help you move through the ups and downs of your day more seamlessly, with less friction, and return to a productive and emotionally stable state of mind faster. For regulating your emotions through the Fall, it may also be helpful to revisit your to-do list, take time away from others, or reprioritize your tasks for the remainder of the day's efforts. By acknowledging and managing your emotions and energy, you can engage more fully in the Fall and the Valley and get back to being productive sooner.

Develop your own self-awareness and emotional regulation so you can thwart or transform negative emotions into more prosocial, constructive behaviors.

Give Yourself a Smile and Laugh

What is one way to ensure you are feeling more positive and happier at any point in your workday? Smile, even if you don't feel like doing it. Smiling facilitates the release of small amounts of serotonin, dopamine, and endorphins, which together help your brain perceive that things are good and you are happy. This works even if you are alone and smiling only to yourself, and to some extent even if you are just visualizing smiling and not actually doing it. Laughing works in much the same way. It is a helpful cue for your brain that all is well, the mood is light, negative emotions need not take over, the nervous system can ease any tension, positive neurochemistry can recirculate, and you are in a good place. Research has shown that both smiling and laughing improve neurochemistry, thwart stress response and inflammation markers, and help you cope with whatever ails you psychologically and even physically. There is scientific evidence to affirm the old adage "laughter is the best medicine."

Of course, real smiles are better than forced, fake, or imagined ones. If you need a pick-me-up, think about something that brings you true joy and makes you authentically smile or laugh (your kids, a joke, a funny part in a movie). Do what you can to infuse joy, humor, smiling, and laughter into your workday as much as possible—it will be to your ultimate benefit.

"Right-Size" Expectations of Yourself

During the Fall, it is common to experience a decrease in self-confidence, self-satisfaction, self-efficacy, or self-concept (remember ANTs attack you, too), which can lead to what's known as expectancy violations about yourself. An expectancy violation is exactly as it sounds—you expected one thing (huge progress on a project) and got another (underwhelming progress on a project). When we set too-high expectations for ourselves but cannot accomplish everything we wanted to, the resulting disappointment—which on its own is bad enough—also triggers other negative emotions and thought distortions, including self-berating, self-doubt, or a reassessment of our own perceived abilities. To avoid this, try setting more conservative goals and expectations for your accomplishments during any given work stint. Being more realistic about what you can get done in an hour, for example, will help you avoid negative feelings and self-criticism for not achieving your expectations, and will help you pleasantly surprise yourself if you are able to achieve more than you originally expected. Positive expectancy violations—when you overachieve or do more than you set out to—lead to increased satisfaction, confidence, self-concept, momentum, and work-related enjoyment.

Stand Up for Your (Neural) Needs

Sometimes people struggle to take breaks during their ultradian Fall because those around them are not experiencing the same moment or their work culture discourages anything but the appearance of uninterrupted high productivity. It is important to prioritize your brain's needs and take a break when it is necessary for you, even if it means excusing yourself to go to the restroom, faking a phone call, or offering to grab coffee for others. By honoring your own neural and physiological needs, you will be more productive, find it easier to maintain good humor and mood, and feel better overall. If you need a break, chances are others around you do, too. Ultimately, your performance will speak for itself when you take more breaks and honor what your system needs.

It is important to treat yourself with the same consideration and compassion as you would your spouse, kids, friends, and pets. If the Falls are coming too fast and feel like too much, don't berate yourself for taking more or longer breaks through the day (especially in the super Valley of the afternoon). Breaks aren't just great examples of healing time; they also signal self-care and spark positive neurochemistry for replenishing. While the next chapter deals with breaks specifically, the point is that you allow yourself to take a load off, ease the tension, and be kind to yourself during the Fall instead of the opposite, which is often characteristic of this phase, especially for high-achievers.

Wondering How Much Is Too Much?
Take a Perceived Stress Test

The Fall is characterized by a stress response that under normal circumstances is helpful, functional, useful, and not too invasive or long. However, this shouldn't be confused with abnormal, heightened, or chronic stress you may experience at work. If you find that you often feel defensive or overwhelmed at new tasks or requests, are having more than your normal negative emotions during the workday, are slipping into non-optimal performance on the Yerkes-Dodson curve, or are experiencing persistently higher anxiety, you may want to investigate further.

The way you experience stress will be different for you than for others—it's perceptual and based on one's own allostatic abilities (physiologic changes to meet environmental demands). Your colleagues may appear cool, calm, and collected while you are freaking out, but they may be better at hiding it, perceive things differently, have more practice, carry a lower allostatic load (cumulative effects of chronic stress), or manage their stress more concertedly. Your relative stress levels will also vary over the course of your life, with each role you hold in your career, and with what's going on in your personal life.

You can take a perceived stress scale (PSS) test to figure out your stress levels at work. PSS scores range from 0 to 40, where 0 to 13 is low stress, 14 to 26 is moderate stress, and 27 to 40 is high stress. A quick online search will reveal several free resources for you to begin to assess this on your own. This can help you get a read on how much stress you are experiencing in general every day, and therefore what you likely need to do about it.

Knowing where you are in terms of your stress load can help you navigate your day, schedule, tasks, and expectations—with both yourself and others. When you have done the homework and figured it out, having this information can also help you be more articulate about where you're at, what you need, and what is causing you undue discomfort, anxiety, or stress. You can't effectively communicate your boundaries or needs to others if you don't know what they are yourself.

6

The Valley

Breaks can lead to breakthroughs.
RUSSELL ERIC DOBDA

THE VALLEY, also known as the ultradian healing response, is likely the most important of the four phases, though it may not feel like it. It is a natural period of rest, recuperation, restoration, replenishment, and preparation for action. It should feel easy, peaceful, and calm in general. High achievers may be impatient with this phase or try to override this necessary resting period to get more done. This backfires and produces negative results in the form of increased stress hormones, autonomic (sympathetic) stress response, unproductive neurochemistry, and potential burnout.

Isaac Newton is famous for the concept that "what goes up must come down in equal and opposite proportions." Peak performance isn't possible without taking some time to rest and heal. Furthermore, your highs will be in direct proportion to your lows: you can only expect your Peaks to be as productive as your Valleys were restorative. Think of the Valley as preparation for the Peak. Ideally, the Valley lasts from 12 to 20 minutes under normal, healthy conditions, which is highly efficient considering how much needs to happen during this relatively short period.

Unbeknownst to you consciously, there are important things to accomplish during the ultradian healing response. It is critical to organize your breaks each day in a way that allows for optimal healing and recovery. The ultradian healing phase gives your brain time to replenish, restore neurotransmitters, reset synaptic clefts, and do some waste clearing, all while restoring metabolic resources.

A Peek Inside: What's Happening in There

When we enter the Valley, our brain and body collaborate to assist with recovery and healing. The autonomic nervous system (part of the peripheral nervous system attached to the brain and central nervous system) is divided into two branches: the parasympathetic nervous system (PNS) and the sympathetic nervous system (SNS). The PNS triggers the body's rest-digest-repair response, while the SNS triggers the fight-flight-freeze response. Under normal conditions during the ultradian healing response, the PNS is dominant, allowing the brain and body to repair and restore themselves. Under duress, extreme uncertainty, or chronic or pervasive stress, the PNS won't be able to do its job because the SNS may suppress and override it.

During this phase, the body undergoes changes in physiological, nervous, neurochemical, and electromagnetic activity. Ideally, these changes result in a shift toward a more relaxed and calm state of replenishment for a little while. The body also experiences an increase in hormones and neurotransmitters that promotes relaxation and restoration. This phase is crucial for the whole system to recover from the stress and demands of previous phases of Peak performance as well as prepare for the next cycle of activity.

During the Valley, some predictable neurochemical and hormonal activities occur.

- **Serotonin** levels may rise, resulting in an overall increased sense of well-being, stabilized mood, tranquility, contentedness, calm, and ease.

- **Endorphin** levels may rise, which helps alleviate any pain and enhance positive emotions, including a sense of well-being and relaxation.

- **GABA** may rise and contribute to decreasing stress, anxiety, and neural activity while also promoting calmness and restorative rest.

- **Acetylcholine** levels may increase to support relaxation and the parasympathetic nervous system, and to aid with rest, recuperation, and recovery.

- **Growth factors (GFs)**—proteins that help cells in the brain and body develop, maintain, repair, restore, and replenish—are especially active during the Valley. They play a role in learning, memory, neuroplasticity, brain development, immunity, healing, maintenance—and, as their name would suggest, new growth of tissues, neurons, connections, and networks. Some examples of GFs are brain-derived neurotrophic factor (BDNF), insulin-like growth factor 1, transformation growth factor beta, platelet-derived growth factor, and fibroblast growth factor, among others.

This phase is associated predominantly with alpha and theta waves. Alpha waves help you feel more relaxed, even during wakefulness. They are prominent when the mind is calm and at ease, promoting a restful and restorative state that aids with the healing response. They are also present during periods of focused attention and creativity, which is likely why many people report having "eureka moments" during the activity of the Valley. Theta waves are also typically present, and help with deep relaxation, meditation, and calmness. They are also often present during periods of creativity, emotional processing, and subconscious thinking—as when you are daydreaming or your mind is wandering.

During the Valley, the brain's plasticity may be more active, as new pathways or connections can start forming. These changes occur mostly during sleep, which can be thought of as a deeper Valley of sorts (though ultradian cycling is happening all night, as well). Whether during waking or sleeping hours, the Valley provides a crucial opportunity for neural wiring to occur—assimilating newly acquired information into neural networks as knowledge and learning. The default mode network (active when your brain isn't working on anything specific) is often active during this phase, allowing for a period of contemplative thinking, mind wandering, daydreaming, emotional processing, and readiness for eventual action. The activity required for real learning, knowledge retention, and memory formation can be energy intensive, which is why replenishment and neuroplastic change happen most often during the brain's rest periods (especially sleep). Synaptic connections can also fatigue or desensitize, and require breaks in the action sometimes. The Valley is the perfect opportunity for the electrochemical signaling between any two neurons to take a break before re-establishing connection. The ultradian Valley serves as time for metabolic replenishment, synaptic rest, and transmitter synthesis, so that the brain can build, learn, grow, and be even more effective in successive cycles. Suffice it to say, there's a lot happening during this relatively short but critical phase.

How It Feels: Common Valley Challenges

During the Valley's healing response, your brain isn't just recuperating from the last cycle of productivity, it is also preparing and priming the system to get ready for the next one. Here are some common challenges with this phase.

- **Wanting to return to work:** You may feel impatient with yourself or the ultradian process during this phase. High achievers are especially prone to wanting to override or shortchange their breaks to get back to work and continue making progress.

- **Not wanting to return to work:** Sometimes the opposite happens, especially if a break stretches on too long or eats into your brain's natural impulse to engage in the Climb again. You may feel break inertia or already be too far removed cognitively from the work you were doing to go back to it. For this reason, except for a longer midday break (when you would likely eat lunch), breaks shouldn't be longer than 20 minutes, and preferably somewhere around 12 to 15 minutes. Breaks that stretch longer may cause you to lose your train of thought or work drive, lose your momentum, and ultimately decrease your progress and productivity.

- **Worrying about optics:** Colleagues or managers may indicate that they think you are slacking when you take a break, or you might simply worry that they will think so. Despite how it might feel or look to an outside observer, the quality of your brain's rest directly impacts the quality of your work, output, performance, and uptime, so you should take the rest you need and worry less about how it may look to others.

More Victorious Valleys: How-Tos

Lean In to Break Time—There Are No Peaks Without Valleys
Everyone needs downtime. Even the highest performers. Even you. It is important to take many breaks throughout the day to allow your brain to rest and recover. The good news is that taking breaks and allowing yourself a proper ultradian healing phase will actually improve your overall performance and productivity. The better quality and right quantity of rest you get, the better you will be able to perform at your peak. Experiencing the highs of performance requires doing the requisite lows of healing and resting. Rest should be seen not as a reward for hard work but as essential preparation for it.

Rest should be seen as both reward and essential preparation for your work.

Take breaks as many times as you feel you need to every day, and certainly every 90 minutes or so. Ensuring that you schedule purposeful breaks throughout each day is critical for optimizing your productivity and performance. Do not structure workdays without scheduled, regular breaks in your calendar. This can backfire and promote burnout.

Ensure Break-Time Activities Are Restorative

While structuring your downtime sounds paradoxical, it is not enough to schedule your breaks regularly—you should also plan what you will do during a break for it to be optimally restorative. It is all too easy during breaks to slip into answering emails, scroll on blue-light-emitting screens, let others pull you into a meeting, mindlessly eat too many snacks, or start working on something else. The discipline to actually take a break—or, more specifically, do things your brain will find restful and replenishing—often requires some amount of deliberate planning, especially in busy workplaces or if you are otherwise stressed during the day.

Best practices for breaks include engaging in light physical activity, even if it's just gentle movement; rehydrating yourself by drinking water; playing with kids or animals; chatting with friends and socializing; meditating, praying, or visualizing; doing some yoga or light stretching; being in nature, breathing fresh air, and getting real sunlight; closing your eyes; reading (preferably a book, not from a screen); daydreaming; listening to music; journaling; or taking a short nap.

Breaks that give your brain time and distance from your work tasks and technology will help your recuperation. Try not to engage with more tech on these short breaks (e.g., staring at your mobile device) or eat or drink at every break (e.g., drinking more caffeine or snacking). Not everything that relaxes others on their breaks will work for you (and vice versa), so you must determine what allows you to best relax and replenish. Once you figure this out, plan to incorporate it into regular, scheduled increments throughout your workday.

Use Breaks to Declutter, Reset, Reorganize

Valleys are a prime time to organize yourself for the next work stint. During this time you might revisit your to-do list, organize your calendar further, and reset your physical space by organizing or decluttering. There is nothing less helpful as you embark on your day, a challenging project, a work stint, or another task than a bunch of physical (and therefore mental) clutter. Decluttering your physical space can help you look and feel more organized, facilitate your task-prioritizing efforts, help you focus later, and contribute to your daily productivity. Some organizing time is ideal during a Valley—it is physical, low-intensity, non-task-related, and contemplative. The satisfaction and completion of a more organized task list, drawer, shelf, or desk can also elevate neurochemistry for productivity, through little surges of serotonin, dopamine, or endorphins.

Do Something Physical—Take a "Movement Snack"

"When the going gets tough, the tough get going." Sitting for long periods of time (e.g., over an hour) is posited to be just as bad for your health as smoking. Memes everywhere indicate that "sitting is the new smoking." As we will discuss in chapter 7 (Move), to maximize the value of your Valleys and let your brain rest and recuperate through your ultradian cycling, you should move around whenever possible. Physical activity is a key component not just of physical fitness, but also for maintaining positive physiological processes, neurochemistry, mental wellness, and cognitive performance. It can be helpful to do anything physical during your Valleys—like taking little "movement snacks"—instead of forcing yourself to sit, stay put, or continue working. Every time you find yourself in a Valley or taking a planned break, move around at least a little. As far as your brain is concerned, no movements are wasted—it loves them all. Try getting up and going for a walk, changing your environment, talking to someone, shaking out your limbs, dancing at your desk, or getting some fresh air. This can help your brain replenish valuable chemistry, boost your creativity, and increase overall productivity.

Whether it feels like it or not, your brain craves some consistent low-intensity movement to aid with recharging, rejigging, and replenishing.

Restorative break activities include moving around, socializing, avoiding more screens, breathing fresh air, and getting real sunlight.

Find a Way to Greet Mother Nature

Whenever possible on a break, go outside, breathe fresh air, and get real sunlight—especially if you are already walking, moving, or exercising. Some researchers dub this "green exercise." Studies show that movement and exercise in nature (or at least outdoors) catalyzes health, wellness, and productivity benefits, including increased positive mood, mental wellness, energy levels, cognitive functionality, and creativity. This is because fresh air, sunlight, and natural surroundings trigger higher circulating levels of valuable neurochemicals (dopamine, serotonin, endorphins, GABA, noradrenaline) while also increasing the quality of blood flow and relative oxygenation levels. The brain loves all these things and can perform better as a result.

If you can't get outside during the day, work near a window whenever possible so you can at least see the great outdoors from your desk. Research shows, for example, that patients who have a hospital bed next to a window feel better, heal faster, and are released sooner than fellow patients who weren't close to a window during recovery. (Perhaps this could be dubbed "green healing.") Similarly, workers report being happier and more productive if they can see out a window while working and/or are surrounded by plants in their office space. We might call this doing "green work," and it should increase your sense of wellness, balance, and productivity.

Spend Some "Time In" Your Mind

The contemplative cognitive states of practices such as mindfulness, meditation, introspection, visualization, daydreaming, mind wandering, and prayer facilitate a period of advantageous brain activity and mental rest that include many of the same advantages as deep sleep, despite being quite different. While these states, sometimes referred to as spending "time in," are also different from one another and can be used for different ends, they all require you to focus inward and pay attention internally, to your mind (as opposed to the external world). Engaging in such practices has been shown to reduce stress, anxiety, discomfort, stress response, and cortisol levels, while also improving mood, dopamine, serotonin, physical health, pain management, quality of sleep, mental wellness, and a sense of psychological balance. Taking "time in" also helps with well-being, self-awareness, and happiness, which has been shown to improve performance in just about everything, including cognitive, mental, physical, and interpersonal tasks.

The following list covers most of the commonly understood time-in practices. When we take some time for ourselves to relax, reflect, and recharge, we are better able to cope with stress, obstacles, and challenges, and we are more likely to be productive and successful in all areas of our lives.

- **Visualization:** Creating mental images of events or desired outcomes and the actions required to get there. It can be used to achieve a variety of goals, such as improving performance on athletic or cognitive tasks, boosting confidence and creativity, and reducing performance anxiety.

- **Meditation:** Taking time out from the activities of daily life and focusing your mind on the present moment to achieve calmness and clarity. It can be done in a variety of ways, such as by focusing on breath, attempting to think about nothing, repeating a mantra, or simply observing your thoughts and feelings. Meditation has been shown to reduce anxiety and depression, improve sleep quality, and increase focus and concentration.

- **Mindfulness:** Paying attention to the present moment and the content of your mind without critical assessment or judgment as you go through your ordinary life. It can be applied to all aspects of life, from eating and drinking to walking, talking, and working. Mindfulness has been shown to reduce stress and inflammation and improve self-awareness, emotional regulation, balance, and calm.

- **Prayer:** Communicating with a higher power, deity, and/or the spiritual self. It can be used to express gratitude, ask for help, or simply reflect on your life. Prayer has been shown to increase hope, optimism, mental health, physical health, and positive emotions, and reduce hopelessness, helplessness, unhealthy lifestyle behaviors, and feelings of loneliness.

- **Introspection:** Reflecting and looking inward, focusing on your mind and body, and generally being contemplative, aware, and present with yourself. It can be a component of the practices listed here, as well as include other activities such as contemplative reading, journaling, reflexive thinking, or being aware of yourself in various environments or nature (e.g., extrospection). Introspection can improve cognitive functionality through better self-awareness, although it has also been linked to the introspection illusion—an interfering cognitive bias in which people falsely believe they have direct and accurate insights into their unconscious mental states and thought origins.

- **Daydreaming:** Daydreaming is not so much a specific practice, but just exactly as it sounds—it's like a brief, daytime, wakeful moment, when your brain engages different networks and has a little eyes-open dream during the day. During this time, your brain may be accomplishing similar tasks to nighttime dreaming during REM (rapid eye movement) sleep: e.g., negotiating a neural pathway, rejigging a neural network, or assimilating information into networks. While you are daydreaming, your brain is thought to be coming to a conclusion, processing an emotion, making a decision, solving a problem, or developing new ideas. Don't berate yourself for daydreaming or zoning out; it's your brain's way of giving your mind a break from direct engagement and taking the time it needs to regulate emotions, formulate new ideas, or problem-solve. Daydreaming in moderation has been shown to reduce stress, improve motivation, and increase creativity and innovation. It is during daydreaming when most people report having had their eureka moments. In chapter 9 (Rest) we will discuss the science behind night dreaming as well as daydreaming in further detail.

- **Mind wandering:** Letting your mind wander and your thoughts meander wherever they might in free association in the absence of other required or assigned tasks (e.g., task-unrelated) or occurrences (e.g., stimulus-independent). This is the typical experience or outcome of your brain's resting state and default mode network activity, which may also include inner narratives or a self-referential internal monologue. While mind wandering can be a sign of fatigue or poor attentional control, it can also bear the benefits of perceived mental refreshment, reduced fatigue, better emotional balance, and restored cognitive resources.

PART III

YOUR WORKDAY BRAIN AT ITS BEST: THE MERIT FRAMEWORK

Let no one rule your mind or body.
CHRISTOPHER PAOLINI

7

Move

*If you don't make time for exercise,
you'll probably have to make time for illness.*

ROBIN SHARMA

WE HAVE now covered many specifics of what's important to know about your brain's functioning throughout your workday—that your brain operates on an ultradian rhythm all its own, how each phase may feel for you, and some of the key tactics for optimizing each phase for higher motivation, productivity, and performance.

To further optimize your workday brain more generally and sustainably—as well as over a longer career arc—we must also consider the bigger-picture factors that affect you and your brain, physiology, psychology, productivity, performance, and well-being.

Many factors that can affect your neural functioning, cognitive performance, or workday productivity aren't under your control. Things like society, politics, laws, corporate culture, regulations, genetics, past experiences—as just a few examples—are simply not up to you, at least not directly, consistently, or absolutely.

However, the good news is that there are other universal factors, supported by research, that arguably affect your brain and its functioning even more significantly, and that *are* under your direct control. I have labeled each of these five domains to comprise my "MERIT Framework." Everything you can control and do for yourself to make a difference in your brain's functioning and workday performance falls into one of these five categories:

1. **Move:** Physical activity, movement, exercise, and fitness
2. **Eat:** Diet, food choice, eating, and nutrition
3. **Rest:** Sleep quality and quantity, downtime, rest, and breaks
4. **Interact:** Positive social interactions and standing, quality connections, interpersonal relationships, and social support
5. **Think:** Mentality, thought processes, attitude, and mindset

We're going to look at each of these factors in further detail, one at a time, in the coming five chapters—starting with the value of physical activity, movement, exercise, and fitness for optimizing workday performance.

Movement Is Magic for Health and Wellness of Every Kind

I sprained my ankle doing nothing. It was such a senseless misstep (literally)—I took a step the wrong way, rolled my ankle, and writhed in pain for half an hour afterward. When I went for an assessment, the visiting ER doctor—a sarcastic but pragmatic guy—said to me, "Next time, break it. At least then I could cast it and someday it might be as good as new. There's just about nothing I can do for a sprain, and it will probably be weak and prone to injury forever. See ya."

As predicted, the sprain never healed fully. Now it's my Achilles' heel. Almost literally. I often reflect on that physician's prognosis and my inadvertent mistake, because I am quite active most days and feel the echo of the ache from time to time in random movements or as a storm descends—my very own weathervane.

The ankle sprain was the incident, but not the whole story. The story is this: for managing the pain, swelling, healing, and rehabilitation, nothing traditional seemed to help. Not painkillers; not tensor bandages; not raising it; not resting it; not icing it the recommended 20 minutes on, 20 minutes off. Just an unrelenting ache for hours every day until my eyelids finally drooped enough to get some sleep. Meds made my face puffy and my mind slow, while my ankle continued to ache. Ice made my skin blotchy, and while the swelling subsided for a few minutes, the pain stayed. Raising it also helped the swelling but did nothing for the ache or the rate of healing.

It all seemed ineffective and useless until, out of sheer frustration, exasperation, and willful denial, I did the opposite of what you might feel like doing in that situation: I exercised. The first exercises didn't involve putting weight on my ankle, which would have been unthinkable. Instead, they were rehabilitative, inspired by yoga and Pilates. I devised these exercises myself, based on what didn't hurt too much. I also exercised more than the ankle itself, focusing on strengthening, stretching, and increasing mobility, flexibility, and stability.

I found these exercises also helped me focus and concentrate better, I had better range of motion, and I started to wear regular shoes again to work. Movement, as it turned out, did what painkillers, ice, elevation, positive thinking, rest, and doctors' orders could not. The pain subsided, the swelling went down, the healing noticeably accelerated. I'm a fan of rest, ice, elevation, and meds when you need them, but physical movement was the magic in this case when no other advice, intervention, or prescription had worked.

My methods weren't novel but well documented in the relevant physiotherapy, sports medicine, lifestyle medicine, and mind-body research. I had simply been a successful guinea pig in my experiment of one. As it turns out, movement of all types (including formal, functional, physiotherapy, and rehabilitation types) has been shown time and again to be one of the best forms of preventative and rehabilitative treatment we have at our disposal. And here's the thing: movement is not *just* beneficial for physical performance, pain, injury, disease, or recovery, either. It also works amazingly for cognitive, mental, psychological, and non-physical ailments. Movement has been documented to improve many other things like anxiety, stress, hormone imbalances, mental disorders, mood disturbances, sleep problems, forgetfulness, and learning issues, to name a few. All the above benefit from moving the physical body, as part of a formal exercise program or otherwise.

Christopher Palmer asserts in his book *Brain Energy* that effectively all mental disorders can be thought of as metabolic disorders in the brain. If this is so, that which increases the metabolic activity and functioning of the brain—such as increasing blood flow, oxygenation, physical capabilities, and metabolic activity in the body by moving it—must also benefit your mental health and well-being. The corollary to Palmer's assertions is that if you want your brain to function optimally, you should seek to maintain or improve its metabolism. Levers for improving brain metabolism are captured by the MERIT framework: adequate physical activity, proper nutrition, adequate quality sleep, mental wellness, and deep breathing, among others.

The further into the research you look, the more ubiquitous the findings become: second only perhaps to the magic of sleep (see chapter 9, Rest), physical activity also works something like magic in the brain and body. Movement is critical for health of every kind (mental, psychological, physiological, and, of course, physical), for healing, and ultimately also for peak cognitive performance. We are highly physical beings first, and intellectual, psychological, and mental beings second. It follows that mental health, psychological wellness, and cognitive performance *must* be highly tied to our physical state, fitness level, and bodily health.

What's interesting for me is the resistance I see to this message in my talks, training, and practice. People will happily listen to the insights about food and nutrition, nod their heads along, and vow to put it into action—citing they can't wait to get out there and "eat the rainbow." They typically accept that high-quality sleep is critical for performance and productivity, acknowledge that they probably aren't getting enough of it, and let on they often just needed permission to shut down earlier, go to bed sooner, or invest in a better mattress. But tell them about the exceptional merits of exercise or that more, consistent physical activity will improve their mental health and work performance? This is where I often lose them. People regularly say, "How can I possibly put together a consistent workout routine after my very long workdays? Do you know how demanding my job is? Do you have any idea how my evenings with a young family go? I can't stomach another item on my daily to-do list. How could I possibly do more exercise while also working this schedule *and* go to bed earlier—there aren't enough hours in my day!"

I get it, of course. It seems impractical to ask someone who is already extremely busy and perhaps stressed to ensure more physical activity as a to-do item most days. And yet, that's exactly what I'm advocating, because the science is in: concerted physical activity won't detract from your day, energy, mood, or productivity; it will add to it. If you find the time to move, time—in the form of higher efficiency and bolstered energy, stamina, and motivation—will find its way to you. You will feel more balanced, better capable of coping with your responsibilities, calmer, and able to get items on your to-do list done faster with less friction. Physical activity doesn't have to happen exclusively within a formal exercise routine: you can engineer your day to include moderate, consistent movement that will ultimately serve to replenish you and your workday efforts.

Feeling stressed? Even five minutes of continuous physical activity has been shown to alleviate stressful thoughts, cortisol production, stress response, and sympathetic nervous system activity. Feeling overwhelmed? Moving around even a little bit will help you breathe better and feel more able and willing to face the tasks of life by improving your mental resources, emotional regulation, and coping mechanisms. In moderate pain? Movement can decrease your pain perception, increase your pain tolerance, improve your neurochemistry, and lessen the brain's natural protective instincts over the area.

Contrary to what you might hear from a personal trainer, fitness model, or elite coach, for professionals' mental workday performance the advice differs: when it comes to physical activity for professionals, more is not necessarily more, although less is less.

You should not max out on exercise every day—or engage in too-intense or too-long workouts—unless you are training for something specific under the watchful eye of a certified coach or trainer. As we will discuss, balance, variation, moderation, consistency, and rest in exercise routines are the keys to health and wellness optimization for the modern working professional.

Rest is just as important as exercise for health, wellness, and performance—to benefit from one, you need the other. Rest, breaks, quality sleep, and downtime are considered critical in any worthwhile exercise routine (see chapter 9, Rest). You may modify or consciously limit formal exercise on a workday that is especially long or stressful. The goal should be to keep moving and keep enjoying that movement so you'll return tomorrow and not to overdo it to the point of injury, exhaustion, or further stress. Too much exercise without rest often leads to a deeper stress response, lowered immunity, burnout, injury, and/or illness. Similarly, a sedentary lifestyle increases risks of disease, disorder, and dysfunction.

Movement is magic for your brain, body, and health. Keys to physical activity for mental and cognitive performance are consistency, moderation, balance, variation, and rest.

When considered and approached moderately, physical activity shouldn't feel like a burden added on top of your already very long day—yet another to-do item on your list. Instead, it should be incorporated into previously scheduled activities, perhaps thought of as "me time" or meditative time, and a valid method of recuperation for one extended or shorter periods each day. You don't need a membership, a gym, or a bunch of equipment, either. Think of movement as something you *get to* do for yourself each day, not something you *have to* do. Find ways to incorporate more movement into your day however possible—it doesn't have to be as part of a formal exercise program, necessarily. Physical activity isn't just good for you: when you do it the right way for you, you are going to really enjoy it, and it will help prevent or lessen physical and mental issues for the years to come. Consistent, varied, moderate movement is a best practice for ensuring peak mental performance, achievement, and success.

For many who read this, and indeed many in my audiences, this is preaching to the choir. You already know all this, believe it, and have proof from your own life that it works, because you have already incorporated purposeful movement into every day. Whether you are convinced already or not, a closer look at the science will help you really understand this phenomenon and the magic of movement (and rest) for mental, psychological, and cognitive health, wellness, resilience, and peak performance.

The Physical Can Recharge the Mental

There are only so many resources in your system to go around. While your brain does most of the "budgeting," it must share oxygen, energy, and nutrients with your body. While the body is in motion, using many system resources, the brain won't—and shouldn't—do its heaviest lifting or biggest work. It saves that for when the body is at rest during sleep and everything else in the system is calmer or less demanding. As we will discuss more in chapter 9, your brain is doing its biggest rewiring work of the circadian cycle while you're dreaming and your body is temporarily paralyzed (to both conserve energy and stop you from acting out your dreams). Conversely, when you are in motion during exercise, to help protect the body from injury or damage, the brain is more cognitively idle, focused on the brain-body connection, monitoring movement, assessing internal resources, and watching your physical space. Next time you're sprinting, try also doing an algebraic equation. Point proven.

You likely have had this or a similar experience: You head to the gym after a long day, feeling frustrated, irritated, anxious, or stressed. The whole way there and through the doors you are grumbling, restless, and thinking of all the ways you could shorten this workout—or, better yet, cancel it. Soon into your routine, however, you zone out, let your mind wander, and focus on the moment you are in and the exercises at hand. By the time you leave through those same doors some 50 minutes later, you are in a much better mood; you feel better physically and psychologically; you are uplifted and feel more mentally balanced, resilient, and capable of coping with your stressors; and you likely have at least partial answers for the things that were bothering you. This is why we often say that you can't let your mood going into your workout decide whether you do it or not. Whatever comes of the session (if you were able to complete all of it or performed well), you will likely be glad you tried and will feel physically and mentally better when leaving than when you arrived.

While it is more challenging for some people when first starting out (which is why it's important to start small and slow and be patient), a benefit to regular physical activity is that it gives you the perception of having more energy, motivation, ability, and bandwidth back—you feel more positive, capable, upbeat, energized, and buoyed in general because of the neurochemical, metabolic, and physiological by-products of movement. While physical activity is effort, burns calories, and may cause slight soreness, it gives your brain a little reboot, rejigs and changes your neurochemistry, and ultimately makes you feel better as opposed to more mentally or physically depleted.

There are a few mechanisms by which this works. First, exercise excites the mitochondria in each of your cells while also increasing their production (something called mitochondrial biogenesis). You have approximately 100 trillion mitochondria active at any one time in your body, and each is like a mini energy factory for your cells. Especially when you do aerobic exercise, for example, your mitochondria are ecstatic—they produce more energy for the cell they occupy while new mitochondria are also being created. Mitochondria research increasingly implicates them as principal regulators of overall metabolism—which is important for everything from weight maintenance to mental health and wellness to cognitive performance.

Second, exercise increases the rate of blood volume circulation as your heart rate goes up (supply quantity) and the flow improves the delivery of oxygen and nutrients to all the cells in your body (supply quality). This has obvious benefits for every part of your body, especially the brain, which is highly receptive and susceptible to even slight fluctuations in oxygen and nutrient levels (more on that in chapter 8, Eat). Physical activity and its metabolic outcomes benefit your brain and body physically, chemically, and physiologically, as well as your mental (e.g., mindset, psychology, emotional regulation) and cognitive abilities (e.g., thinking, reasoning, information processing, decision-making) as a result.

Third, when you exercise, you jump-start or catalyze a symphony of feel-good, health-promoting, wellness-inducing neurochemistry and hormone production—compounds such as endorphins (mood boosters, painkillers), enkephalins (painkillers, stress relievers), oxytocin (social bonding, stress reliever, mood booster), dopamine (the get-it-done, reward hormone), serotonin (the happy, focused, contented hormone), GABA (mood booster, stress reliever), and norepinephrine (stress reliever, the "pay attention" hormone), to name a few.

In other words, your post-gym high is physical, metabolic, physiological, neural, psychological, cognitive, mental, *and* endocrinological. Think of exercise as inducing a collective of many dancing cells, receptors, and chemicals in your brain and body, literally buzzing, bouncing, working, excited, energized, and happy. You would be hard pressed to find any health, wellness, or productivity metric you care about that physical activity doesn't facilitate, catalyze, or solve in some way. Here are just some of the things that exercise has been shown to improve when done consistently and moderately.

- **It improves your sleep quality and quantity** by decreasing stress, the amount of time it takes to fall asleep, and the number of times you wake up in the night. It also aids your melatonin production and the length of time you spend in deep sleep, resulting in faster recovery and perceived refreshment.

- **It improves your muscle strength, tone, and endurance,** which can help your mental stamina, physique, and cognitive abilities, as well as motivation to be consistent with your exercise routine.

- **It increases your energy levels and reduces fatigue,** which can make it easier to get started on tasks, stay focused, and get things done.

- **It reduces inflammation** in the body and brain, which prevents a myriad of disorders, dysfunction, and disease.

- **It improves weight management,** which has been shown to increase many things, including self-esteem, stress management, psychological wellness, mental health, and happiness.
- **It increases blood flow to and metabolism in your brain,** which brings oxygen and nutrients to the brain cells and aids overall brain functioning, wellness, and health.
- **It increases production of brain-derived neurotrophic factor (BDNF),** as well as other growth factors and proteins that promote the growth, repair, and survival of all cells, including neurons, neuroglia, and neural networks.
- **It increases neurogenesis and neuroplasticity,** which increases learning capacity, knowledge retention, memory stores, resilience, and cognitive flexibility.
- **It improves your cognitive function,** including information-processing, thought processes, executive functioning, reasoning, and decision-making.
- **It increases your focus and concentration,** which can make it easier to stay on task, pay attention, avoid distractions, and be productive.
- **It increases your self-confidence and self-efficacy,** which can make it easier to take on challenges, persevere in the face of obstacles, and succeed in your endeavors.
- **It increases your creativity,** which can be helpful for problem-solving, innovativeness, divergent thinking, resilience, experimentation, and coming up with new ideas.
- **It improves your mental health** by helping reduce stress, anxiety, or depressive thoughts, while also increasing feelings of joy, happiness, satisfaction, and contentment.

Varying Your Physical Activity— Different Components of Fitness

Real fitness is more than hulking muscles or the ability to run exceptionally long distances uninterrupted. Most fitness experts agree that fitness has three main components (which are sometimes broken down further into six or more):

1. **Aerobic cardiovascular fitness**—the ability of your heart and lungs to deliver oxygen to muscles and cells while exercising. Some example exercises: jogging, brisk walking, running, biking, rowing, swimming, using an elliptical machine.

2. **Muscular strength and endurance**—the ability of your major and minor muscles to generate force and perform repeated contractions over time. Some example exercises: lifting weights, resistance training, load-bearing exercises, working with resistance bands.

3. **Flexibility (range of motion, coordination, agility, stability, balance, neuromotor ability)**—the ability of your joints, tendons, ligaments, stabilizer muscles, and fascial tissues to stretch, bend, balance, and provide a full range of motion without limitation, pain, or injury. Some example exercises: yoga, Pilates, tai chi, barre, functional exercise, stretching.

To optimize mental, psychological, and cognitive functionality, health, and wellness, you'll want to vary your exercises each week to include each of these components of fitness. You will achieve better cognitive benefits *and* physical fitness improvements if you cycle between the various exercises or include some of each type most days. When someone works on one component to the exclusion of others (e.g., only lifting weights, only running every day), imbalances, injury, burnout, boredom, and dysfunction crop up more quickly. This of course has negative effects on a person's ability to feel good, get motivated, concentrate, or get things done anywhere—in the gym but also at work.

The American Council on Exercise (ACE) recommends at least 150 minutes per week of moderate-intensity exercise (approximately 50 percent heart rate reserve) or 75 minutes a week of vigorous exercise (approximately 70 percent heart rate reserve) outside of the general activities of daily living. Moderate intensity will vary by person, but it might include brisk walking, jogging, moderate rowing, doubles tennis, or cycling below 10 mph (e.g., the aerobic cardio exercises on the previous page). Not included in the minimum time recommendations of 150 minutes (2.5 hours) per week were two sessions a week that "overload the muscles" for strengthening all major muscle groups (e.g., the strength-training exercises on the previous page). The recommendations indicate that flexibility or neuromotor activities should take place five to seven days a week and would also be above and beyond the 150 minutes of moderate intensity (or 75 minutes of vigorous intensity) and two strength-training sessions.

While ACE used to require that exercise sessions be 10 minutes or longer to be counted toward the weekly totals, it has eliminated this, acknowledging that exercise in shorter bouts counts toward the weekly minimums and can be just as beneficial (great news if you plan to do physical activity during workday Valleys). More recent research has spurred a movement to amend these guidelines further and suggests that it's better for people to move at least 60 minutes a day every day doing a combination of moderate-intensity (e.g., jogging, cycling, rowing, weight lifting) and/or light-intensity activities (e.g., walking, gardening, yoga, housework)—either all at once or in increments throughout the day—than to have some days in the week with little or no physical activity. While these guidelines are open to interpretation and will vary by person, the gist is clear: more, consistent, moderate, varied physical activity each day is better for health and wellness outcomes than intense or repetitive workouts followed by sedentary days.

By cycling between different types of activities, you increase muscle confusion, microtrauma, and microtears (little tears in muscle fibers), which force your muscles—and also joints, ligaments, tendons, fascia, and other tissues—to adapt, grow, repair, and change faster in response to new, unpracticed, or challenging physical movements. Muscle microtears after strength training, as an example, take approximately 72 hours to heal fully, which means you should separate strength training of a particular muscle group by as close to 72 hours as possible for maximum healing, growth, and benefit (e.g., don't do legs two days in a row—not that you would likely be tempted). Novel movements increase heart rate, oxygen requirements, and metabolic activity, as well as both mental and physical exertion—all of which can benefit you in many ways by improving mood, health, wellness, sleep quality, and cognitive function. It may feel psychologically harder to vary your workouts, but the benefits are proportionate: the minute an exercise feels easy psychologically or physically, the incremental benefits have tapered off. Varying your workouts also has physical benefits of looking better (e.g., more muscle definition, lower BMI) and feeling better (e.g., better overall fitness, better quality sleep, higher immunity, relative increases in feel-good hormones).

Move More, Breathe Consciously

What is something you do 22,000 times a day, is critical for staying alive, and yet you very rarely think about? You guessed it: breathing.

The oxygen you breathe is in fact the most critical input for the brain (even above critical water, sleep, and food, in at that order). Only four minutes without oxygen can lead to irreversible brain damage or death. Your brain gets all its oxygen from an iron-possessing protein called hemoglobin that binds to oxygen and can be found in the cytoplasm of your red blood cells, which make up about 45 percent of all your circulating blood volume. Red blood cells collect oxygen from the lungs, which synthesize it from the air (21 percent oxygen) you breathe. Each red blood cell can carry up to 1.12 billion oxygen molecules. Multiply that by the 35 trillion red blood cells thought to be circulating at any one time and you see just how important oxygen is to human life and therefore how important breathing, breathwork, and fresh air may be for your health and well-being.

Movement is great for your brain also because it necessitates an increase in your rate of breathing, resulting oxygenation, and overall metabolism. Focusing on your breath and practicing proper breathing techniques are central tenets of yoga, meditation, Pilates, and mindfulness for good reason. Consciously and intentionally thinking about your breathing activates part of your brain that can decrease your stress and anxiety levels, increase your oxygenation levels, and improve your overall functionality and performance at any point in your day. Go ahead, try it right now: close your eyes, take a deep breath in, exhale slowly, and repeat this a few times. For even more stress relief, exhale for longer than you inhale. We will look at formal breathing techniques that can help bring you back to the present moment (e.g., mindfulness practices), increase your vagal tone (e.g., activate parasympathetic nervous system activity), calm your nervous system stress response (e.g., sympathetic nervous system activity), and help optimize your daytime mental and cognitive functioning.

Rest Is an Integral Part of Fitness

As we discovered in Part II, your mental performance at the Peak is directly proportionate to the quality of rest during the Valley. Similarly, savvy athletic trainers put a premium on sleep, rest, downtime, and recovery days for powering peak performance. No one with a true understanding of the human brain and body recommends exercise, movement, activity, or fitness routines without also addressing planned and purposeful rest.

Deliberately resting the body goes hand in hand with exercising. One without the other is a recipe for disaster. As we've discussed, rest without exercise or purposeful movement (e.g., sedentary lifestyle) increases your risk of just about all known disorders and diseases. Exercise without rest can also lead to more chronic stress, anxiety, burnout, injury, exhaustion, depression, or illness.

Working hard physically accelerates the body's use of valuable resources like hormones, chemicals, nutrients, vitamins, minerals, water, salt, glycogen, and energy, while simultaneously increasing the production and circulation of stress hormones like cortisol. As the Yerkes-Dodson law teaches us, some stress is helpful, but too much can activate the fight-flight-freeze sympathetic nervous system (SNS), which can put your whole body into overdrive or survival mode. If this happens, you can do yourself more harm than good, because circulating stress hormones (and others they trigger) will work to deplete muscle mass, increase fat stores, trigger a deeper stress response in your body, and set off the alarm bells in the brain. All of this serves to decrease your mental, cognitive, and physical well-being. Therefore, deliberate, purposeful, restorative rest is a critical part of any exercise or movement routine toward achieving true fitness as well as peak cognitive performance.

Moving for Workday Performance: How-Tos

Be Moderate in Intensity and Timing—Especially at First

The temptation of many high achievers is to work hard, play hard, work out even harder. This isn't advisable. If you are training for something specific, incremental adjustments to your training schedule are key for ensuring an injury-free progression toward your goal. Follow the advice of certified coaches. Otherwise, overdoing it in the gym (or track or studio) has the potential to increase your stress response and activate the SNS, counteracting the good you were trying to do in the first place. Instead, be consistent, conscientious, and moderate in physical activity—especially if you're just starting out, or starting again after an injury, illness, or time away from exercise. Upshift slowly and incrementally in your exercising. Incorporate more physical activity into regularly scheduled tasks wherever and whenever possible. Pat yourself on the back for every set of stairs, every extra step, every pound lifted, every twitch you made. While your pants size might not decrease immediately, your brain will love it—from your brain's perspective, every twitch counts—it loves movement. For bigger training goals, rest assured, you will get there, but key to physical health, wellness, and fitness are consistency, variation, balance, rest, and moderation.

Here are tactics you can use to ensure you keep moving through a workout, are less tempted to quit, and are less likely to trigger a stress response:

1. **Slow.** If things start to feel too difficult, decrease your treadmill speed or slow down the reps. This allows you to keep moving and not quit but decreases the intensity meaningfully so you can catch your breath, calm down, and stay the course.

2. **Modify.** Not all exercises or movements are right in the moment or for every person. Modify exercises that cause pain or discomfort. Modification is not evidence you are incapable or lazy, but rather that you know what's best for you and are willing to stand up for yourself and your body in this moment.

3. **Smile.** It may sound simplistic (and irritating)—and will likely be the last thing you want to do while you're exerting yourself—but when you smile, a part of your brain is triggered to perceive that all is well and there's no cause for undue concern or a stress response. Smiling calms the SNS and decreases cortisol production (any time of day, not just during a strenuous workout). If smiling to yourself at the gym feels socially inappropriate, simply thinking about smiling will have nearly the same benefits: both physically smiling and visualizing it trigger the brain to calm down, relax, and enjoy more.

4. **Breathe.** Paying attention to your breathwork and breathing rate has many advantages. First, it brings you squarely into the present moment so you can situate yourself in the here and now and really listen to your body—increasing

your mindfulness and mind-body connection. Second, it helps oxygenate your brain, muscles, and cells and ensures you're not holding your breath (tempting when you feel acute strain or exertion), which helps you feel calmer, more relaxed, and more capable of continuing.

5. **Stop.** This is a viable option. There's no shame here, especially if you feel any real pain (more than a moderate burn). Stopping does not make you weak, undisciplined, or a failure. It is evidence you know your body's limits and boundaries and are prepared to stand up for your needs in the moment (which is important in every aspect of life, not just your workouts). Stopping needn't be terminal for the session, either—it can also be momentary. If you stop for a moment or two to catch your breath and recenter yourself, this can help you get back into the exercise more readily and allow you to keep going with your workout.

I have often heard from people who say they won't try for anything physical in a day if they don't have a full hour to dedicate to it. This mindset is a mistake and evidence of the cognitive distortion of "all or none" thinking. Anything is better than nothing when it comes to moving for neural, mental, and cognitive wellness and health. Also, once you get going, exercise momentum and inertia will typically get you through a reasonable-length workout for the day. Especially at first or for the busy working professional, the sweet spot is right in the moderate, balanced middle: spend some time each day doing physical activity you enjoy.

Another "all or none" moderation mistake especially beginners often make is to go too hard, too long, too soon, which quickly stunts consistency, progress, a sense of wellness, or health. You know you aren't overdoing it in the gym or with physical activity if you can come back tomorrow without too much stiffness, pain, discomfort, exhaustion, procrastination, or having to really talk yourself into it. Do only as much each day as will allow you to come back tomorrow (three to six days a week). Even your rest days should include some light physical activity—no days should be totally sedentary. It's more important that you consistently engage in some physical activity every day at least a little bit, instead of going so hard on your workout days that you're prone to being completely sore, tired, or immobile the following days. Strive for physical moderation each day over an all-or-nothing approach to exercise.

Variation Is Key—Switch Up What and When

The same old routine may be comfortable, but it can lead to boredom, fitness plateaus, and risk of injuries, all of which decrease the probability that you will reap maximum benefits and be motivated to exercise consistently. Keep your movement routine fresh by trying new things. Remember that fitness has (at least) three main facets (cardio, strength, flexibility) and it is best to engage in all three weekly. While routines can lead to habits and habit formation helps us stay consistent by facilitating our autopilot, there is such a thing as too much of the same thing, especially if it leads to a stale, boring, unmotivating routine. No matter your physical, mental, or fitness goals, you should have fun with movement—switching it up can help with a sense of play, curiosity, and enjoyment. Including all three types of fitness activities in your weekly routine is one way to ensure variation and better overall fitness.

Another way to ensure variability in your movement routine is to separate your rest days. The temptation is typically to take the entire weekend off, having two rest days in a row, although this is often not the ideal schedule for health, wellness, gains, or cognitive optimization. Instead, think about separating your recovery or active recovery days (e.g., yoga, a long walk) by about 72 hours. For example, more than one trainer I have worked with prefers to set recovery days as Wednesdays and Sundays. The logic here is that (a) no two days in a row are recovery or sedentary; (b) workout days are as few as possible in a row each week (because too many together can more readily lead to injury, fatigue, demotivation, or burnout); and (c) strength-training workouts are separated by as close to 72 hours as possible, given that this is the length of time muscle microtears take to heal, typically. For the working professional, remember that more isn't more where exercise duration, intensity, or contiguousness are concerned—although less is often less. Accordingly, the resulting exercise schedule for a busy professional might look like this: Monday and Tuesday as workout days (e.g., one aerobic cardiovascular workout, one strength-training workout, both including some flexibility or neuromotor components (such as during warmup and cool down); Wednesday as active recovery (e.g., yoga, tai chi, long walk); Thursday, Friday, and Saturday as workout days (e.g., two aerobic cardiovascular workouts, one strength-training workout, all including some flexibly or neuromotor activities); and Sunday as a recovery day (e.g., stretching, housework, gardening, laundry).

Bonus tip: No matter what type of exercise or component of fitness you are about to engage in, make sure you warm up properly before your workout to avoid injury, and don't skimp on the post-workout stretch. The harder the workout, the more time you should allocate to cool down and stretch afterwards. The benefit of stretching properly after a workout is to help clear lactic acid and prevent its buildup so you won't be as sore in coming days. I swear by my post-workout stretching routine as the number-one way to ensure I can show up the next day. I have noticed that whenever I skimped on my post-workout stretching, the tightness and lactic acid build-ups have gotten ahead of me, which then required a successive recovery day instead of the typically planned active one, messing up my weekly schedule and fitness goals.

Consistency Is Key—Find Your "Why"

I hear this type of question often: "I know it's great for my productivity, happiness, physique, and health, but no matter what I do, I can't seem to stick with an exercise routine. How do I?" or "Why do I start off strong in the first couple of weeks but then lose motivation and quit?" The short answer to these questions is that they are not exercising for their own right reasons: they haven't found their real "why."

One of the main reasons people give up regular exercise is that they don't see desired physical changes in their body, either not at all or not fast enough. They dive right in, go too hard, too fast, which can lead to injury, disappointment, demoralization, and sometimes hits to the ego. The right reasons to exercise will vary from person to person, but the amazing benefits to your cognitive and mental health are likely to be among them—the physical or esthetic are often not enough to motivate you consistently, especially given how long it takes to witness results. If you are new to exercise or a fitness routine, you will likely need to start slowly, which you might find underwhelming, demotivating, or even disappointing. Remind yourself that the exercise trainers, athletes, and fitness models you see on glossy magazine covers or Instagram have been working at their physique typically for decades, not days. Further, for the beginner, overexertion and injury are easier and more detrimental than you might anticipate.

You might be able to spot someone who exercises regularly and consistently because they would likely score high on obvious vanity metrics. To the outside observer, they probably look toned, trim, attractive, happy, relaxed, and healthy. However, if they are honest with you, they will likely tell you that what keeps them coming back to the gym, mat, studio, track, or treadmill is something more than these desirable outcomes. Instead, you might hear: "Because it helps my mental health." "Because it's the only time in my day that's just for me." "Because I sleep better." "Because I want to be strong enough to protect myself." "Because I never want to lie in that hospital bed again." Vanity alone wouldn't keep them coming back day after day, rain or shine, hell or high water—and it's that level of commitment to consistency that's required for real and ongoing fitness, as well as its resulting physique.

As with so many other things, exercise also works on the inverted U graph of hormesis—moderation is best, and performance and benefits *reverse* if you overdo or underdo it. If you want to achieve something amazing (e.g., run a marathon) or ambitious (e.g., lose 50 pounds), you're going to need a long runway to gear up, put in the work, and train properly—it shouldn't be expected to happen quickly. When you overexercise, do too much too soon, don't take adequate time to rest, or don't fuel for your exercise routine properly, bad things happen. Overdoing exercise is a good and fast way to see negative mental, psychological, physical, and cognitive effects while also increasing the chances you get injured or sick.

For daily exercise motivation and consistency, sometimes it's helpful to give yourself a fitness goal to work toward (20 reps instead of 10, lifting 30-pound dumbbells instead of 20 pounds, registering for a 10-km family fun run, training for a half-marathon, etc.). Conscious fitness goals will keep you motivated and moving while also improving deliberate practice, mind-body connection, and exercise mindfulness. If you miss a workout or two, don't let it slow or stop you. Pick up where you left off in the following days and continue. The overarching goals should be to make time every day for physical activity that is challenging yet enjoyable for you. Whatever your "why," nothing you do should tax you so much you can't easily and happily work and work out again the next day, or maintain your weekly schedule. You know the right schedule or routine is in place when you are consistently ready, willing, and able to exercise three to five days a week without undue strain, pain, stress, emotional dysregulation, or demotivation. In general, you'll want to exercise for a reasonable length of time at moderate intensity, for your own right reasons.

Exercise When Your Brain Needs a Break

While many people think they should work out first thing in the morning (and sometimes that's helpful when first starting out or trying to create the habit of exercising), depending on the type of work you do or your typical schedule, this might not be best for your cognitive output. It may mean you spend your freshest brain, motivation, stamina, willpower, and energy of the day on the treadmill, for example, instead of doing your toughest mental tasks or getting your most important cognitive work done. Instead, try matching exercise timing with cognitive dips in your day: move your body when your brain needs a break. In chapter 6 (The Valley), we discussed the value of engaging in shorter bouts of physical activity (e.g., a short walk, dancing at your desk) during your daily breaks—like "movement snacks" that re-energize you and your mind throughout the workday.

Similarly, it might be more beneficial for you to do formal exercise during lunch hour, the mental dip of the afternoon, or at the end of your workday, when your hardest tasks and thinking are over for the day and you are keen to rest and reset the brain for different tasks (e.g., administration, emails, driving, yard work, making dinner). With cognitive work accomplished for the day, your brain can switch gears into neutral, take a breather, wander, and daydream (great for eureka moments) while you do your exercise. (For me, so many ideas would come during my daily 4:00 p.m. workout that I started taking a pen and notepad to my gym so I could jot them down as they occurred to me.) Afternoon or end-of-day workouts may also give you a boost for the remainder of your workday or evening. In the neuroscientific view, exercise facilitates ultradian healing, easing stress, and promoting a sense of cognitive and mental well-being from surges in beneficial neurochemistry, all of which can help you shift gears from the heightened cognitive activity of the day into a more relaxed evening and bedtime routine.

That said, given that consistency is key, you should exercise whenever you like to, so you stick with it. Many people prefer the morning, when they feel the freshest, most motivated, or best energized, and they often report that it helps propel them psychologically through their workday. There are neurochemical, physiological, and hormonal advantages to exercising anytime—including first thing. The post-workout high (burst of dopamine, norepinephrine, serotonin, endorphins, enkephalins) can certainly help power you through the demands of a stressful workday or cognitively demanding task list.

Move to Improve Sleep

As we will discuss in greater detail in chapter 9, sleep is also magic for the brain and critical for every one of its systems, processes, and functions. Regular exercise helps you feel more tired earlier in the evening, build melatonin (the sleep hormone) more readily throughout the day into evening, and regulate your body temperature more effectively, all of which help you fall asleep faster and stay asleep longer. Regular physical activity improves both quality and quantity of sleep. For example, exercising helps you stay longer in the deep sleep phases, including REM, which enables better learning, knowledge stores, memory, vivid dreaming, emotional processing, and regulation, as well as mental, psychological, neural, and physical repair and readiness for the next day. It also decreases your stress levels and reduces SNS activity, both of which can disrupt your sleep. Moderate, consistent physical activity means faster, longer, deeper, uninterrupted, better-quality sleep and therefore cognitive and mental repair, readiness, wellness, and health.

Bonus tip: Working out too rigorously or too late in the day can interfere with some of these benefits by increasing heart rate, blood pressure, muscle tension, body temperature, stress response, and cortisol levels later in the day. If you exercise too close to bedtime, you aren't likely to be as cool (literally) or relaxed as you need to be by bedtime (which will then likely get delayed), and you might find it interferes with your ability to fall asleep or get enough sleep that night. As a general rule, don't exercise within at least three hours of your intended bedtime, and preferably longer than that.

Special Benefits of Exercising Socially and Outdoors

Whether you are having trouble sticking to a schedule or not, you might want to try having an accountability partner or gym buddy, or pair physical activity with social time. Take a class, engage in team sports, or find a way to make your physical time fun and social on a schedule that can then become routine for you. Exercising socially has all the neurochemical benefits of any workout and can also increase your oxytocin surges, a feel-good neurochemical that improves social connections, bonding, emotional regulation, mood, trust, empathy, social skills, and prosocial behavior.

As discussed in chapter 6, green exercise is also a best practice. Exercising outside has all the benefits of regular exercise, plus the added benefits of interacting with nature, real sunlight, fresh air, organic scenery, and outdoor terrain, and has been shown to further decrease blood pressure, stress, and anxiety, while increasing breathing, oxygenation, vagal tone, PNS activity, mental wellness, emotional regulation, cognitive abilities, and focus. So do what you can to exercise outdoors with others whenever possible. Combining green exercise with social time has additive physical, physiological, mental, and cognitive advantages.

Breathing Techniques Can Help Regulate Your Nervous System and Stress Response

Breathing techniques—and attention to your breathwork anytime, including and especially during exercise—have been shown to be tremendously helpful for decreasing hormonal and nervous system stress response; increasing your oxygenation, energy, and affect; improving mental wellness, emotional regulation, and balance; improving your psychology and happiness; improving sleep; and increasing cognitive functioning and clarity. Engaging with your breath, doing breathwork, or practicing formal breathing techniques are especially advantageous because they can be done almost anywhere, anytime.

- **Diaphragmatic breathing** is a type of deep breathing that involves using the diaphragm, the muscle that separates the chest from the abdomen. To do diaphragmatic breathing, sit or lie down in a comfortable position and place one hand on your chest and the other on your stomach. Breathe in slowly and deeply through your nose, allowing your stomach to rise and your chest to remain still. Breathe out slowly through your mouth, allowing your stomach to fall and your chest to remain still. Whenever possible, allow your exhalation to last longer than your inhalation, which improves vagal tone and vagus nerve signaling to increase PNS activity (rest, digest, relax) and simultaneously decrease SNS activation (fight, flight, freeze).

- **Box breathing (or square breathing)** is a type of breathing that is taught to Navy SEALs, first responders, and patients trying to work through a panic attack. To do box breathing, sit or lie down in a comfortable position and close your eyes. Breathe in slowly and deeply for four counts, hold your breath for four counts, breathe out slowly for four counts, and hold your exhale for four counts. Repeat this cycle at least four or five times to start, then as long as you want.

- **Alternate nostril breathing (also known as Nadi Shodhana)** is a yogic breathing technique in which you breathe in through one nostril and out through the other. To do alternate nostril breathing, sit or lie down in a comfortable position and close your eyes. Place one finger or thumb on each nostril. Close your right nostril with your thumb or finger, breathe in slowly through your left nostril, close your left nostril with your finger or thumb, open your right nostril, and breathe out slowly through your right nostril. Breathe in slowly through your right nostril, close your right nostril, open the left nostril, and breathe out slowly through it. Repeat this for as many cycles as you like, or until you feel calmer and more balanced.

- **Pranayama** is another class of yogic breathing. There are many different pranayama techniques, but some of the most common include *ujjayi* breathing, which is to make a soft hissing sound as you inhale and exhale; *kapalbhati* breathing, which is forceful exhalations followed by passive inhalations; and *bhastrika* breathing, which involves forceful inhalations followed by forceful exhalations. All are designed to help you center yourself, improve your mind-body connection, feel calmer, and be more mindful.

The vagus nerve helps regulate many things in your body, including your ability to cope and your overall stress response, and is particularly sensitive and responsive to changes in your breathing. It is the longest and most important nerve in the peripheral autonomic system (made up of the fight-or-flight sympathetic and rest-and-digest parasympathetic branches). Sometimes referred to as "the wandering nerve" because of its extensive reach to most parts of the body, the vagus (or tenth cranial nerve) originates in the brainstem and branches out to all the major organs, including the heart, lungs, stomach, and intestines. It is either responsible for or involved in a wide variety of functions in the brain and body, including but not limited to heart rate, digestion, breathing, blood pressure, immunity, and regulation of mood, as well as some swallowing, coughing, talking, tasting, and pain perceptions. Slow and deep breathing techniques such as outlined on the previous page help activate your diaphragm and increase your heart rate variability (HRV), which is a sign of a healthy and responsive autonomic nervous system (ANS). Purposeful breathing techniques, attention to your breath, and conscious breathwork—especially that with a longer exhale than inhale—allows heart rate, blood pressure, cortisol, adrenaline, and SNS activity to decrease, while HRV, oxygenation, vagal tone, and PNS activity should increase. All of this produces a sense of calmness, relaxation, and balance. By practicing more purposeful breathwork and breathing techniques, you decrease your currently perceived stress while also increasing your nervous system's ability to cope with and regulate your allostatic load—the cumulative effects of chronic stress in your life.

Bonus tip: Especially as you engage in breathwork or breathing techniques, think about the quality of the air you are breathing. It sort of goes without saying that you should avoid pollution in the air you breathe as much as possible, including and especially from immediate smoking or vaping sources. It's no surprise that breathing polluted air has been shown to put downward pressure on your cognitive, mental, and physical functioning and doesn't facilitate optimum health, wellness, or performance.

8

Eat

*Tell me what you eat
and I will tell you what you are.*

G.K. CHESTERTON

F OR THE LONGEST time in my practice, I avoided discussing nutrition with people. I figured others out there—nutritionists, dietitians, sports coaches, primary care physicians (PCPs)—were better to advise folks on their food and nutrition. However, people kept asking questions that directly implicated improper nutrition or poor eating habits for the brain and its functioning. Over time it became apparent that in order to talk to people about neurons, neurochemistry, brain function, brain health, and brain optimization, I also had to discuss the building blocks: food sources and nutritional habits that support all of these.

People often ask questions they think are solely related to their brain, not realizing that the answers have much to do with what (and how) they are eating (or not eating). Here are some examples.

"I feel super tired every day around 1:15 p.m. and can barely keep myself from napping at my desk."

- I mean, who isn't tired in the afternoon? After a couple of questions it became obvious what this person might have been doing wrong from a diet and nutritional perspective: they were skipping breakfast and more than making up the calories at lunch (thanks to ghrelin and rampant hunger cues) with a much too large high-glycemic meal, which sat heavy in their system and made them even more lethargic in the afternoon. Their dietary choices and timing were exacerbating an already significant dip in their cognitive alertness in the early afternoon.

"I'm peckish all the time. I'm gaining weight, and this constant low-level hunger impedes my focus and ability to concentrate."

- While other hormonal factors were also likely at play, this person was chronically dehydrated, not sipping enough water throughout the day and misinterpreting their thirst signals for hunger. At too many periods in the day they were consuming vending machine snacks (processed; high in salt, fat, and sugar) or sugary, caffeinated (diuretic) energy drinks instead of water, which was exacerbating their inflammation, dehydration, hormonal dysregulation and ruining mealtimes.

"I'm so jittery and nervous in my job. I am often paralyzed by indecision, which is worst in the mornings."

- This person didn't know they were a slow metabolizer of caffeine—nor that such a thing existed. They were experiencing caffeine-induced anxiety every morning because they were drinking too much coffee as their breakfast, which was interfering with their morning mood, emotional regulation, and executive and cognitive functioning, and had spillover effects for the rest of their workday, ultradian cycling, and nighttime sleep.

Over the years, hundreds of similar examples cropped up. People were sometimes surprised when I asked about what or how they were eating, because they didn't realize their dietary habits were relevant to their brain, psychology, feelings, or cognitive performance. Many thought diet and nutrition primarily affected the body, not the brain. Despite being easy to overlook, the link between diet and brain function is well established, and it's an exciting, active area of inquiry.

Diet, eating, and nutrition are (usually) choices you make for yourself each day—a performance lever under your control—and for this reason is the second lever in my MERIT framework simply labeled "Eat." Food choices have a huge effect on your cognitive and mental abilities each day and are typically under your direct and consistent control. Often equally important is what you *don't* eat, or what you make sure to avoid consuming. Fueling your brain (and body) for peak workday performance involves many inputs beyond just food (e.g., moving, breathing, sleeping, resting, interacting, mindset)—all of which we have covered or will discuss. Despite weighing only about three pounds, the brain is the most energy-consuming organ in the body. It accounts for only about 2 percent of the body's overall weight, but it can use up to 20 percent of its calories and oxygen daily. Any system expected to provide quality outputs should be given quality inputs. The ultradian cycle is a physiological rhythm that requires lots of metabolic and nutritional resources to proceed optimally, so how you fuel yourself is critical for optimum neural, mental, cognitive, and psychological performance. Understanding your brain and its functioning allows you to fuel it more precisely and effectively. Because your diet and nutrition relate so significantly to the brain's metabolism and functioning, let's start with a tiny history lesson to understand some links between the brain and its nutritional requirements.

What Was Once Scarce Is Now Abundant (and Often Altered)

What our brains need is partly determined by what they were made for and from. We truly are what we eat. Our brains are said to have been about 500 million years in the making—evolved from early mammals into primate form and then to Homo habilis and Homo erectus and later to Homo sapiens. The human brain experiences an evolutionary lag in the modern context because it was designed for a past era, a time biologists call the "environment of evolutionary adaptedness" (EEA). The EEA is thought to have lasted from the time of early hunter-gatherers to the development of agriculture about 10,000 years ago, so you might think of your brain as best adapted to life and circumstances of at least 10,000 years ago.

The most significant challenges during the EEA were finding food and shelter, avoiding predators, and raising children (not contending with hypercompetitive global markets, battling cyber-attacking AI, or dodging rapidly mutating superbugs). To meet these challenges, humans evolved a number of cognitive abilities and intelligences, such as more advanced problem-solving (including how to find, grow, and prepare food), social intelligence (including how to get along with others, work together, and survive), language (e.g., how to communicate for problem-solving and division of labor), and theory of mind (including how to imagine the thoughts, feelings, and needs of others), among many others. Individuals who were better able to cooperate with others, solve problems, and understand the thoughts and feelings of those around them were more likely to grow and survive long enough to reproduce. You are the genetic product of thousands of generations of ancestors who were good enough at all of this to survive at least long and healthily enough to have healthy, surviving children of their own—quite a feat, and evidence of some very strong genetics.

This also means that our preference for certain foods over others is far from accidental; much of it is coded in our genome. What our ancestors naturally (read: genetically) preferred eating and were motivated enough to find was a matter of life and death for them. There were no nutrition guides to steer them in the right direction; no hospitals, medical practitioners, or surgeons to right the ship if their choices proved to be nutritionally or medically wrong. In an era of scarcity, ancestors who developed a preference for fat, sugar, animal protein, water, and salt (and an aversion to poison, toxins, allergens, bacteria, and rot) must have fared better during famine, drought, and strife than those who preferred other things. Relatively high-calorie, proteinaceous, fatty, sugary diets resulted in body mass, muscle tone, adipose stores, blood composition, and mental clarity enough to carry them through when drought, famine, or resource scarcity was inevitably occurring. Preferring a fatty, fibrous avocado to a lettuce leaf, for example, might have given early humans better energy, more stamina, meatier fat stores, healthier neuronal myelin, flourishing gut microbiota, lower inflammation, heightened neuroplasticity, and therefore better cognitive functioning—including higher emotional, intellectual, or interpersonal intelligence. Such preferences would have allowed them to keep foraging for longer or run faster, think more quickly, help more readily, and be perceived as fitter or more attractive. The EEA humans with genetics for low-protein, fat-free, low-carb diets might have felt more readily depleted, exhausted, moody, weak, or sick sooner. In an era of scarcity, appetites for higher-fat, more caloric food items allowed them to build a productive and reproductive life: more resources, stronger shelters, sharper tools, innovative weapons, more energy for socializing, higher-quality relationships, and better mates—like the original upward cycle of prosperity—partly due to better nutritional choices in the circumstances.

In the modern-day, late-stage industrial-food complex (IFC), however, these inborn dietary preferences often lead us astray, especially given how most of our food is now made and the depleted soil in which most of it is grown. We now have such easy access to an abundance of fatty foods, processed items, animal products, sugary drinks, and salt-laden everything that it makes it all too easy to overconsume what were once the right food items to value. Westernized food cultures have seen a startling uptick in all the "diseases of affluence" in recent years (e.g., heart disease, type 2 diabetes, high cholesterol, obesity, cancer, alcoholism, gout, hypertension, cardiovascular diseases), partly as a result of our inborn dietary preferences coupled with availability of these foods. These preferences were critical during a time of supreme scarcity, but they can be harmful (even potentially fatal) in our era of IFC abundance.

The EEA and ancestral genomes are only a couple of factors that shape your brain and its inborn preferences. Your individual proclivities, experiences, culture, thoughts, microbiome, and social environment all contribute, too, though a basic understanding of the biological background of humans lends important insight into what we need to consume, are hardwired to want, and should avoid—as well as why.

You (and Your Brain) Are What You Eat

You have heard it before, but as we look to dietary choices for optimizing cognitive functioning it bears repeating that you are what you eat. Very simply, you and your brain are made up of what is put in your mouth from birth onward. Your brain is a combination of nerve tissues (consisting of fat and protein), glial cells, blood vessels (which contain salt, water, and glucose), and connective tissue (made of water, proteins, and some fats). In total, your brain is mostly fat (60 percent), followed by a mix of water, protein, salt, nutrients, and some carbohydrates. All these components are surrounded by protective and cleansing cerebrospinal fluid (CSF, a water-electrolyte-micronutrient solution), which circulates through the meninges (outer layer of the brain), ventricles (cushioning sacs of watery CSF inside the brain), and spinal column. Your CSF is replaced about every seven and a half hours and is made of 99 percent water and about 1 percent amino acids, vitamins, electrolytes, salts, glucose, and proteins. Water is critical in the human brain, given how much of it the brain uses for everything—to cleanse, nourish, and safeguard the brain and the meninges that surround and protect it. In the brain, water is a resource, a catalyzer, a nutrient carrier, and a building block.

Everything you eat and drink may become essential fuel or building material for your 37 trillion cells. Starting from birth, the macronutrients (fat, protein, carbohydrates), micronutrients (vitamins, minerals, antioxidants), and water you consume contribute to your neural and physical makeup, turning over regularly until the day you die. Every day you make and replace billions of cells and are said to be "all new" approximately every seven years—although there's a lot of variability to that (skin and red blood cells replace every few weeks, while skeletal muscle cells may take up to 15 years or so) and some cells never "turn over" throughout your life (e.g., spinal cord cells). That said, given the importance of what you eat for building who you are, how you look, and how you function, let's take a look specifically at macronutrients for fueling your peak performance.

See the Nutritional Reference Lists at the back for examples of amino acids (protein building blocks), fats, carbohydrates, and micronutrients, as well as their typical functions and some example dietary sources. Consult your nutritionist, naturopath, dietitian, or PCP for exactly what proportion might be right for you to consume each day—every brain and body has unique needs for various reasons.

Prized Protein

The brain uses proteins and amino acids as critical building blocks for neurons, connective tissues, hormones, and neurochemicals. Amino acids are the building blocks of proteins and can be synthesized to make neurotransmitters and hormones, which help regulate most things about you, including your emotions, psychology, physiology, cognitive functioning, and mental health. There are nine essential amino acids—"essential" meaning they must be eaten. These amino acids that you can only get from your diet are critical for building and repairing brain (and body) tissue; producing enzymes, neurochemicals, and hormones; and transporting nutrients.

In the EEA, protein came from many sources, but the primary one was thought to be animal meat. Because hunting wouldn't have been successful every day and the highest-ranking members of the tribe would likely have had first dibs on available meat, protein was highly valued and relatively scarce in most humans' diets.

In a Western, post-agrarian, IFC setting, getting meat to eat is no longer difficult or scarce (if chemical-laden and expensive). However, getting enough healthy, unaltered dietary protein can be challenging still, because of (a) the emphasis on carbohydrate-based meals and sugar (e.g., sandwiches, pasta, cereal, toast, candy); (b) the abundance of fatty food options; and (c) the focus on processed or red meats, which are often infused with harmful additives like antibiotics, hormones, preservatives, compounds, and fillers designed to improve perceived taste, appearance, shelf life, and marketability. Heavily processed proteins typically have lower nutrient density, higher saturated and trans fats, higher sodium and sugar content, and higher advanced glycation end products (AGEs, harmful molecules formed when protein or fats are exposed to sugars and oxidized during processing, causing inflammation, cell damage, oxidation, and aging, and contributing to degenerative and chronic diseases).

All the above help company profitability initiatives but hurt you, your various systems (including your gut microbiota), your brain, your overall health, and resulting performance. Because proteins are foundational building blocks and form the basis of so many things, including all your neurochemistry, you have the challenge of getting enough protein each day without effectively poisoning or hurting yourself. Finding lean, unaltered proteins that are as close to their original form as possible to maximize your brain's functionality, health, and performance is the challenge each day. The most likely solution to this ongoing challenge is to find it from (a) the source (angling, hunting, farming, growing); (b) unaltered sources (e.g., wild, organic, or free-range); or (c) plant proteins that are as close (if not exactly) to their original form as possible.

While weight loss isn't the focus of this book, another advantage to prioritizing protein in your daily food intake is that protein helps you feel full more quickly and for longer, so you are less likely to overindulge (therefore eating fewer overall calories) or experience cravings, while fueling your body and brain with materials they can readily use. Maintaining a healthy weight, decreasing cravings, and snacking less will also foster better hormonal regulation, improve physical health, decrease inflammation, and improve mental focus, concentration, and productivity throughout your workday. Prioritizing eating unaltered protein at every meal is a triple win: (1) you feel better and are healthier on the inside mentally and physically (with less inflammation and fewer hormonal imbalances, insulin surges, etc.); (2) you look better on the outside because of improvements in physique (especially over time); and (3) you get more done because of resulting improved mental, neurochemical, and cognitive functioning.

Like so many things in health and life, there's a hormetic or inverted U-shaped curve to this. Too little protein is detrimental, but more isn't always better, because too much can tax your adrenals, slow your gastrointestinal (GI) tract, and cause inflammation, among other things. You shouldn't eat protein (or meat) to the exclusion of all else—despite what some fad diets or extremists might assert. Moderation and pairing with the other macro- and micronutrients are key.

Functional Fat

The brain and nervous system's fundamental unit is the neuron, which sends signals throughout the body, enabling us to think, move, feel, and perceive the world. Like any human cell, neurons are made of protein, water, compounds, and a very significant amount of fat. A neuron consists of a cell body (protein, water, fat), dendrites (branches that receive messages from other cells), and a long thin fatty fiber that sends messages from the cell body to other neurons, which is called an axon. Myelin is the fatty substance deposited all along the outside of the axon, which facilitates electromagnetic signals and is the primary transmission line for all communication inside your brain. Consuming fat is critical for brain functioning, energy, cellular repair, network building, and health, as well as cognitive and mental performance.

Fats have unfairly gotten a bad rap. People often report thinking that if they eat fat, they will put fat on their body—the (colloquial) words are the same. On the one hand, since fats pack a caloric punch (nine calories per gram, as opposed to four calories per gram for proteins and carbohydrates), it does need to be consumed in the context of your daily caloric requirements. Healthy fats are nutritionally critical, not just tasty, and are key for the proper functioning and building of various parts of the brain. Contrary to popular belief, dietary fats are not stored (preferentially, at least) as fat on the body: that is more typically the case with consuming too many carbohydrates (especially simple ones) or daily calorie overconsumption. In moderation, good fats are used as energy and for critical tissue building, cell growth, tissue repair, and an energy source. Consuming dietary fat also serves to slow down the intestinal absorption of the carbohydrates you eat, which levels out glucose variations and insulin surges. Most micronutrients (critical vitamins and minerals) are fat-soluble, meaning you get the benefit of having consumed them (e.g., introduced into your cells as opposed to eliminating them through the bladder or GI tract) only if you eat them with fat. Therefore, eating good fats is also helpful because your brain functioning is particularly sensitive to fluctuations of blood levels of sugar and nutrients, which the dietary fat helps to facilitate and level out.

Critical Carbohydrates

Depending on who you talk to or what diets you may have been exposed to, carbohydrates have sometimes also been cast as the bad guys of food, but they, too, serve a critical role and function in your physiology and performance. Carbohydrates are critical to life and indispensable for brain metabolism; you just need to make sure you get the right amount of the right ones. Your liver makes two critical compounds from the carbohydrates you eat: glucose (immediate fuel) and glycogen (storable fuel). Your brain gets approximately 50 percent of its energy requirements from glucose in the bloodstream through a network of blood vessels called the cerebral circulation, which carries glucose to the brain. This blood serum glucose is manufactured from the carbohydrates, fats, and even proteins that you eat. The remaining 50 percent of the brain's energy requirements comes from glycogen, which is stored in the liver, skeletal muscles, and the brain's astrocytes, a type of glial cell that supports a myriad of brain systems and functions.

The brain doesn't use carbohydrates as building blocks in the same way it does with protein and fat molecules. And because of its reliance on blood glucose for energy, it is very sensitive to even slight changes in blood sugar levels. Consuming too few carbohydrates in general might leave you confused, light-headed, or unable to concentrate, which could make you sluggish or unproductive. Too-high consumption can produce harmful free radicals, cause oxidative stress, facilitate systemic inflammation, disturb hormonal and metabolic balances, and even damage brain tissues. Insulin spikes resulting from consuming too many carbohydrates can decrease your ability to focus or concentrate. Consuming too many carbohydrates (in even one sitting) can lead to their conversion into adipose tissue on the body—e.g., "love handles" you may not love so much.

Unfortunately, overconsuming carbohydrates is easy to do given their prevalence in the Western diet and through the IFC. Consuming too little is also a problem because neural and cognitive functioning can dip quickly and dramatically. Here again, an inverted U-curve is the rule of thumb: moderation and combination are key. Each of the three macronutrients has a critical role, function, and use. None should be discounted or eliminated in a healthy diet. Carbohydrates can vary in their digestion time—depending on if they are simple or complex—and are not all created equal when it comes to delivering benefit to you.

Magic Micronutrients

Although macronutrients are essential building blocks and fuel, micronutrients play a crucial role in neuroanatomical structures, chemical reactions, bodily processes, neurochemical synthesis, and energy production for all brain and body systems. Examples of macronutrients include proteins, fats, and carbohydrates; examples of micronutrients are vitamins, minerals, antioxidants, and salt. Micronutrients are needed in only small amounts, and not consuming enough can cause big problems. While it is possible to overconsume micronutrients (e.g., when taking supplements), toxicity is far less common than deficiency, because many of our foods have micronutrients inadvertently stripped off during farming, peeling, processing, precooking, stabilizing, or packaging, as examples.

Most micronutrients are also antioxidants, meaning they have cellular protective properties that decrease the rate of cell decay and oxidization (read: aging) and help every cell, including neurons, stay "younger" and healthier for longer. Looking at the micronutrient density of foods is important for determining which foods to prioritize in your diet and which to avoid. For example, gram for gram, white bread and pasta are low in micronutrients and higher in calories, while a hard-boiled egg, purple cabbage, or a piece of steamed broccoli are high in micronutrients and lower in calories per gram. Eating for micronutrient density (as opposed to calories or macro-nutrient composition, as examples) increases how quickly you feel satiated and is helpful for moderating caloric intake appropriate to your fluctuating needs. Again, while the focus here isn't on weight loss, micronutrient-dense foods keep you fuller, faster and for longer, which helps you regulate how much you eat, gives your body what it actually needs, and helps to decrease cravings. Eating micronutrient-dense foods can also help with cognition, emotional regulation, concentration, and focus because your brain gets more of the vitamins and minerals it needs to facilitate neural, cognitive, and mental processes and is less likely to spur the hunger pangs, insulin spikes, or lethargy that can interfere with your ultimate productivity. The How-Tos section has insights for how to identify if you are looking at micronutrient-rich food or not. See the Nutritional Reference Lists at the back of the book for examples of some essential micronutrients (e.g., must be eaten), their typical functions, and some typically healthy dietary sources.

Water Is Brain Food, Too

Though it became evident earlier in this chapter, it bears repeating: water is critical for your brain. Water serves many purposes: fueling, cleansing, cushioning, and creating compounds within your brain. You need to consistently drink clean, fresh, preferably uncarbonated water throughout your day to maintain the health, protection, and replenishment of your brain through its various systems (e.g., the ventricular, sinus, and meningeal systems), as well as through your bloodstream, which transports essential macro- and micronutrients for all systems and functions.

Micronutrient-dense foods are typically colorful to the human eye—strive to "eat the rainbow" every day.

Here's a key detail, however: by the time you feel thirsty, you are already dehydrated at the cellular level, and by the time that happens, your brain has given up as much valuable water as it possibly can to facilitate your body's operations and the cells' metabolism while compromising its own optimal functioning. Even mild dehydration (as little as one to two percent loss of body water) can impair cognitive functions, including attention, memory, reasoning, and decision-making. Severe dehydration can lead to confusion, delirium, and even loss of consciousness. Therefore, to keep your brain properly hydrated, don't wait until you feel thirsty to drink water. Sip water continually throughout your day at regular intervals—not enough that you have to run to the restroom inconveniently often, but enough that you never actually feel really thirsty. Not only is brain dehydration a problem for optimal brain functioning and performance, but very often, thirst gets mistaken for hunger pangs and can cause snacking urges, electrolyte imbalances, mood disturbances, or hormonal fluctuations. If you have eaten enough recently, unexpected or uncharacteristic hunger cues may be thirst rather than an actual need for food. Given its importance in every physiological, neural, and bodily process, try drinking small amounts of water throughout your day before you reach for a snack.

Your Microbiome: A Critical Link Between Dietary Choices and Brain Functioning

A critical link between our nutritional choices and cognitive functioning is in our gut; specifically, our gut's microbiota—often referred to as our microbiome. The microbiome is a collective of trillions of microorganisms living in your digestive tract, including bacteria, viruses, fungi, and other microorganisms. The composition and diversity of the gut microbiome are significantly influenced by diet because microbiota get hold of your food before you do, and grow, thrive, survive, or die depending on what you eat. Microorganisms in your gut often partly digest your food for you, eliminate or kill food-borne pathogens, or convert food to something you can more readily digest and use (the compounds that ultimately enter your bloodstream and cells are often the waste or output from your microbiota). They are part of your first line of immune defense and a conversion mechanism from eaten food compounds to usable nutrients, so the health of your microbiome is important for yours also—they're inextricably linked. The microbiome has more recently garnered attention because of findings regarding its influence on various bodily functions, including digestion and immune response, as well as brain functioning through something called the "gut-brain axis."

The gut-brain axis is the bidirectional, complex communication network that involves various mechanisms and links the gastrointestinal tract to the brain (and vice versa). For example, the vagus nerve acts as a direct communication highway between your gut, its microbiota, and the brain. Gut microbiota can influence the immune system and produce or modulate neurotransmitters like serotonin, dopamine, and GABA (which regulate mood, anxiety, and happiness, among other things). The microbiome can also affect the hypothalamic-pituitary-adrenal (HPA) axis, which controls many things, including largely the body's allostatic response (physiological changes in response to demands) and the resulting allostatic load (effects of cumulative stress on mental and physical health). A balanced microbiome can help regulate cortisol levels, facilitate an allostatic stress response, and help reduce the adverse effects of chronic stress on the brain and body.

What you fuel yourself with affects your physical, mental, neural, and cognitive performance and well-being in direct proportion to how it builds, diversifies, maintains, changes, or destroys your microbiome. In the How-Tos we will discuss dietary choices for optimizing your microbiome's functioning, diversity, and health.

New research emerges daily linking your microbiome's diversity, composition, health, and functioning to your brain's health, functioning, and performance.

Where Neurotoxins Hide

You probably don't need to be reminded that toxins are bad. They are bad for everything: your body, your microbiome, your brain, your cognitive performance, and your mental wellness. While the blood-brain barrier mostly protects your brain, it is still susceptible to some toxins and contaminants, as well as pathogens such as viruses, prions, fungi, and bacteria.

Unfortunately, toxins can hide anywhere in the foods available to you and in many systems of the body once they are inside you. Because of this, it is incumbent on you to pay close attention to what you are consuming. Along with the genetically modified and bioengineered foods that are increasingly common (and whose effects have yet to be documented fully), your food can be contaminated with chemicals (pesticides, herbicides, fertilizers, artificial additives, industrial pollutants, animal growth hormones, antibiotics), biological bodies (viruses, bacteria, protozoa, parasites, fungi), and physical contaminants (plastics, heavy metals, insects), among other things, all of which can negatively affect your nutritional levels, brain function, health, and daily performance.

Cigarettes, alcohol, and illicit drugs are also known to be neurotoxic, and they don't provide benefits from the brain's perspective, even in small quantities. The best you can hope for is that the inflammation, free radicals, toxins, and other harmful effects they cause don't result in any severe or long-term damage for you—although with repeated use these risks increase.

Assuming that since you are reading this, you are already in pretty good command of your overall mental and physical health, have had access to public health announcements circulated in the last 50 years, know how to read warning labels, and therefore don't (or no longer) smoke or do drugs, nothing more really needs to be said about this. Alcohol, however, is another matter because of its prevalence in our culture and a very effective alcohol lobby around the world.

The reminder that alcohol has no health benefits is often unwelcome. While many of us love a glass of wine occasionally, there is bad news: in basically any amount, alcohol is not good for the brain or the body. *Some* red wines have been shown to have the same quantity of polyphenols (one of many heart-helpful compounds) as a handful of almonds, but that's it. Of course, you are better off eating the almonds packed with other micronutrients and brain-helping good fats than drinking the sugar-laden, chemical-ridden wine.

Like any manufactured or processed food, there is also increasing evidence that fermented bottled and commercialized alcohols can have harmful levels of added sugar, contaminants, pesticides, herbicides, heavy metals, toxic chemicals, and other noxious compounds on top of the harmful effects of the ethanol itself. At the time of this writing, in the US alone, for example, wine producers can legally include almost 80 FDA-approved additives without having to disclose it on the label (things like purple dye, sulfur dioxide, dimethyl dicarbonate, and many other compounds). Clearly, these possible additional chemical toxins would negatively outweigh any potential benefits of a small amount of polyphenols.

More Fuel for Thought: How-Tos

Eat Every Macro—Perhaps in This Order

If you are what you eat, you should eat what you are made of (or want to become). While body composition will vary from person to person and even day to day, you are mostly made of fat (approximately 20 percent on average), protein (approximately 20 percent on average), and water (approximately 60 percent on average), and it's helpful to think about your nutritional choices in context of this.

That said, because of how macronutrients are metabolized, how long they take to absorb, what they do to blood sugar levels, and how critical they are in your system, it's a great idea to try to eat your meals in the following order: protein first (e.g., salmon fillet), fat simultaneously or second (e.g., avocado, yogurt), micronutrient-rich foods second or third (e.g., steamed broccoli, vegetable medley), and carbohydrates last (e.g., brown rice, mashed potatoes).

You will probably notice that if you eat in the above order, you will more likely feel full before the whole carbohydrate portion can be consumed. This is beneficial for ensuring that (a) you get all the most critical macros first; (b) you feel properly satiated; (c) you are ingesting all the micronutrients on your plate; (d) you aren't stuffed first and foremost with insulin-inducing carbohydrates; and (e) you are more easily able to maintain portion control. You may more naturally feel satiated more quickly if you prioritize eating in this order. This works because both proteins and fats are slower to absorb through the intestines than carbohydrates, they even out your blood sugar, and they leave you more satiated for longer than carbohydrates can (even fibrous, complex ones).

As mentioned previously, while they've unfairly gotten a bad rap, there are a couple of things to keep in mind when it comes to carbohydrates. First, especially simple carbs are easy to consume in too-high quantities compared with the proteins and fats in your meals. They are cheap to produce, easy to manipulate in labs, tasty, and convenient to get through the IFC, so they are often easily accessible everywhere you go. They are also hidden everywhere. Because they are tasty and addictive, sugar and simple carbohydrates are added to a huge number of food items, including to most sauces, dressings, processed meats, breads, cereals, and anything manufactured or processed (e.g., chips, crackers). When food has been processed in a factory, plant, or system, its nutritional density is typically decreased, as there is a higher chance that additives (and often more carbohydrates, sugar, and salt) are included. While you already know to avoid simple sugars (e.g., sweets, sodas, candies, chocolate), typically, even complex carbohydrates (e.g., rice, grains, whole wheat bread) can pose a challenge if you consume too much, because these, too, can have additives, cause insulin spikes, trigger inflammation, make it harder to concentrate, exacerbate mood swings, and contribute to cognitive waning throughout your day.

Eat for Micronutrient Density— Strive to Eat the Rainbow Every Day

You often know you are looking at micronutrient-rich foods because they are colorful and typically appealing to your human eye. In the EEA, your ancestors who thought colored, micronutrient-packed vegetables—like broccoli, tomatoes, peppers, and beets—looked beautiful and therefore appetizing did better than their peers. Consuming these colorful vegetables meant they had a more diverse microbiome, stronger immunity, better growth, faster healing, more strength, better stamina, and better cognitive functioning. So, your genetics now code for this and your visual cortices are wired as such.

You have likely heard dietitians tell you to eat the rainbow every day, and there's a reason for this. Most micronutrients that are critical for all your functioning, microbiota, neurochemistry, immunity, physiology, hormonal regulation, and emotional systems are typically colorful and pretty. Micronutrient-dense foods are usually grown in nature, relatively low in calories, complementary to one another (e.g., have mutually catalyzing effects) and constitute items you might think look both esthetically pleasing and appetizing when on your plate. Think of a beautiful salad with a range of ingredients, reflecting a kaleidoscope of color. Typically, the more colorful a meal is, the more micronutrient-dense it is and the more useful it is to your various systems. Your health, wellness, stress coping, and ability to perform at your best are directly proportionate to the availability of these foundational nutritional components in your diet and bodily stores. As a rule of thumb, try to include as many naturally colorful foods as possible in every meal. Eating the rainbow isn't the whole solution to your daily dietary needs, but it is a quick guide for determining if a meal is likely nutrient-dense or not.

To give you an idea of the benefits, for example, the anthocyanins in berries, grapes, cherries, apples, plums, and purple cabbage have been shown to be antioxidant (decrease harmful free radicals or cell damage), anti-inflammatory (decrease the risk or severity of arthritis, asthma, and cancer), brain healthy (improve cognitive functioning, learning capacity, and memory while simultaneously decreasing risk of dementia and Alzheimer's disease), eye healthy (protect against age-related macular degeneration), and heart healthy (improve blood flow while simultaneously decreasing cholesterol levels and risk of heart disease). That's some heavy lifting for a simple plum. You will get more, similar, and varied benefits from other plant colors.

Eating the rainbow helps ensure you get the compounds you need, avoid the ones that aren't good for you, stay fuller for longer, and decrease your cravings, while also improving brain functioning, cognitive performance, mental wellness, microbiome diversity, emotional regulation, body composition, and physical capabilities.

Feed Your Microbiome Properly—
It Loves Color, Fiber, and Variation

A more diverse microbiome contributes to overall health by enhancing metabolic functions, supporting immune and gut health, protecting against pathogens, reducing inflammation, influencing mental health, and providing dietary adaptability, among many other functions. Foods rich in dietary fiber such as fruits, vegetables, legumes, and whole grains act as prebiotics, nourishing beneficial gut bacteria. These bacteria ferment the fibers, producing short-chain fatty acids like butyrate, propionate, or acetate, which have anti-inflammatory and neuroprotective effects. Consuming fermented foods like yogurt, kefir, sauerkraut, and kimchi introduces live beneficial bacteria into the gut, helping to maintain a healthy balance of gut flora, while foods rich in polyphenols, such as berries, tea, and almonds, can support the growth of beneficial bacteria and enhance cognitive function by reducing oxidative stress and inflammation. Conversely, diets high in saturated fats and refined, simple sugars can promote the growth and colonization of harmful bacteria while also reducing overall microbial diversity, leading to inflammation, lowered immunity, disorder, disease, cognitive decline, and degenerative diseases.

In general, your microbiome loves fiber and variation because these contribute to the health, functioning, and diversity of helpful microbiota. An ideal meal for your microbial diversity is one that is highly colorful (eat the rainbow), heterogeneous (calories come from many different food types (e.g., a salad), as opposed to just two or three on the plate (e.g., steak and potatoes)), and particularly high in fiber (aim for 50 grams per day).

Avoid Processed Foods

Food that is highly altered or processed—comes through a lab, factory, or processing facility—typically has higher levels of additives, preservatives, chemical or physical contaminants, bad fats, sugar, salt, and other things that are not at all helpful for the brain or body. Examples of these foods are factory-processed bread, pasta, hot dogs, deli meats, and snack foods. Additives can increase your toxic load, inflammation, and oxidative stress while putting added pressure on your liver, kidneys, and immune system. Processed foods also work against micro-biota health and diversity, as well as neural and physiological functioning (e.g., insulin spikes, increased inflammation, more free radicals, cell damage, oxidative stress).

The health and functioning of your brain and body are aided by variation in color of good food choices, lots of fiber, and proper hydration.

In general, it is a good idea to avoid foods that are highly processed or have had too many steps removed from their original form. While your grandmother didn't necessarily have all the scientific facts, data, or research to back her advice, she was right: if a food label lists things she didn't recognize or wouldn't have used in a recipe, you probably shouldn't eat it. The closer in form and format the food item is to God's original creation, the better it likely is for you. Eat food in its whole form, or as close to it as possible—e.g., from the ground or off the tree. Whenever possible, do things like making your own sauce with fresh tomatoes instead of using processed, jarred tomato sauce—and bonus points for using tomatoes you grew yourself in rich soil. This will help ensure you get the intended nutrient density and micronutrient content of the foods you put in your mouth.

Your brain and body were developed in the EEA, which didn't have organized, sophisticated, mass-produced, profit-driven agriculture, let alone foods processed in factories. If the food didn't exist a few thousand years ago, it probably isn't ideal for you. While there are exceptions (e.g., some isolated proteins or medicines), as a rule, the more humans or machines have tampered with food or drink, the less nutritious it is for you.

Whenever Possible, Cook Your Own Food at Home
An emerging field of research about culinary education as medicinal prevention and intervention suggests that the more often people cook for themselves, the better quality of food they consume, the better nutritional choices they make, the more nutrients they absorb, and the better they are able to moderate how much they eat (contributing to better health outcomes including the obvious—weight maintenance). It follows that your best possible chance for knowing what is in your food (as well as how it was selected, stored, and prepared) and being able to make informed decisions about what goes into your body is to prepare it yourself. Even then, the farming and growing practices aren't always knowable to you. Still, you mitigate many risks by selecting your own food at a grocery store and preparing it yourself at home (and all the better likely if you can also grow, catch, raise, or farm it yourself).

While you already know that fast food restaurants are infamous for their low-quality, inflammatory ingredients and cooking procedures (not to mention sometimes deplorable kitchen hygiene and cleanliness), higher-end restaurants are also guilty of making dishes that are high in fats, salts, sugars, preservatives, additives, and fatty animal meats—all so that the food tastes delicious and you might return. Their loyalty initiatives and profit maximization typically come at the direct proportionate expense of your nutritional needs and overall health (not to mention your wallet). While restaurant meals will likely have a time and place in our lives, forewarned is forearmed here. There's mounting evidence that your brain and body health and optimal functioning will improve now and in the future in direct proportion to how often you grow, select, store, clean, prepare, cook, and eat your own food, at home (though picnics are great, too). There's a caveat here: what you buy, stock your fridge with, and keep in your pantry eventually make their way into your body (or those of your loved ones)—so don't put into your grocery basket what you know shouldn't end up in your mouth.

Bonus tip: Try to eat with people whenever possible—friends, family, spouse, roommate, or kids—and preferably at the dinner table at a consistent time each evening. This has been shown to improve mealtime enjoyment, happiness, satisfaction, brain-body connection, food choices, digestion, nutrient absorption, cardiovascular health, and stress management.

Try This: Fuel for Desired Cognitive Outcomes

If you have ever visited a naturopath, nutritionist, or dietitian (and I'm a fan—if you ever have a chance or your insurance covers it, do go), you find out quickly that they are a wealth of information about many things, including and especially food choices for specific conditions or desired outcomes. Their recommendations go beyond tastes and preferences and get to the chemical basis and interactions of food compounds to consider the catalysts or building blocks for specific outcomes. While they are also helpful for weight maintenance, athletic performance, and improving disorders, these specialists would also be able to advise on required precursors (e.g., amino acids) to build neurohormones for desired cognitive outcomes. Do you want to feel better and more able to focus? You might want to add foods with the serotonin-building amino acid of tryptophan to your diet, while also doing what you can to please your microbiota (e.g., fiber, variation), which are responsible for most serotonin production, for example. Foods high in tryptophan include but are not limited to salmon, turkey, and tofu. While there is no promise that eating more turkey will necessarily net you higher levels of serotonin, for example, you are further ahead both mentally and physically to think holistically about what you eat, understand that your nutritional choices have real life (not just bodily) consequences, and select foods with intention based on your desired outcomes. There's debate as to whether Hippocrates said it or not, though the wisdom holds: "Let thy food be thy medicine and thy medicine be thy food." Eat (and drink) according to your desired health and life outcomes.

Water Your Brain Properly
Water gets to the brain through the bloodstream. While many people try to correct thirst (dehydration) by drinking a lot of water at one time, this fails to optimally rehydrate the brain. Suddenly drinking a lot of water can dilute the delicate balance of salt, glucose, and electrolytes in your bloodstream, making you light-headed, dizzy, or peckish, and you might find it harder to concentrate and focus. When you chug water suddenly, the digestive tract routes excess directly to the kidneys, bladder, and urinary tract, not necessarily to the systems that need hydration. For this reason, sipping water consistently throughout your day—even before you feel real thirst—is ideal because it means your body is consistently hydrated and your brain can function at its best. Drinking too many liquids before bed can also be unhelpful because it can disrupt your sleep cycles if you have to get up to use the washroom throughout the night.

What is the right amount of water to consume and how should it be consumed? That will vary from person to person and day to day, depending on activity, sleep, the weather, stress, your health, and even hormone fluctuations. Currently, according to leading authorities, the recommended amount is approximately 3.7 liters a day for men and 2.7 liters a day for women. Or you can use this rule of thumb calculation: take your body weight in pounds and drink half that number in ounces (so a 200-pound person should consume 100 ounces a day, or about 3 liters). You will have to figure out the amount that is right for you through trial and error, but here's a way to help you determine this: sip water consistently such that you never feel thirsty but are also not running to the restroom or feeling peckish or light-headed. While doing this, keep track of how many glasses or refills you went through each day, so you have a handle on your typical hydration requirements. Keeping the brain properly hydrated is important because of water's significant role in all neural, mental, and cognitive functioning. You should try to think as purposefully and strategically about hydration throughout your waking hours as you do about food and nutrition.

A common question asked is about carbonated or flavored water. While hydration is better than dehydration, the preference is always for plain, uncarbonated, filtered (if fluoridated), no-sugar water. Carbonation comes from infusing carbon dioxide into water sources to form carbonic acid. While the doses are low, some researchers posit that exposure or consumption of carbonic acid (which is implicated in decay of bone tissues, such as in dental cavities and osteoporosis) should be limited when possible. While scientifically the jury is out on carbonated water alone, the jury is in on what often accompanies it: sugar, additives, colorants, and chemicals, which need to be avoided and shouldn't be in the water you drink for hydration.

Give Yourself Permission to Eat More Intuitively

What follows might differ from the advice of athletic trainers or weight-loss coaches because it is geared toward brain optimization and high cognitive performance at work, not on weight loss or athletic attainment (although it may incidentally help with both). A set daily calorie limit fails to take into account that (a) every brain and body is different in terms of the fueling it needs; (b) caloric needs will vary day to day, week to week, and over the life course; (c) proper nutrition is about much more than calories or macronutrient breakdown; and (d) body weight and composition are not always great indicators of neural, mental, or cognitive functioning and nutritional needs.

While it's important to ensure you aren't regularly consuming more calories than your body needs or can use (overloading your systems has many downsides, including weight gain, inflammation, and oxidative stress), this shouldn't necessarily require that you count every calorie or track every bite. It's good to have a general idea of your calorie requirements for your size, age, and sex (a quick online search will net you many such calculators) so you don't inadvertently over- or undereat. However, it is just as important to develop the skill of listening to your (properly hydrated) body, being mindful about your system cues, triggers, and needs, as well as developing your mind-body connection. Some days you may be more or less hungry. Some days you may need or feel like consuming more or less of certain foods. Under normal, healthy circumstances, this is natural and something you should heed instead of trying to override, evade, ignore, or control. Your brain and bodily systems have limited ways of telling you what they need more or less of or are missing, so it's functional to learn to listen to all the cues you can.

In place of calorie counting, then—especially as it pertains to optimizing your brain's functioning each day—permit yourself to engage in what's called intuitive eating. The idea is that if you are equipped with the right information, your mind-body connection is strong, and you are mindful when you eat, you can make informed yet differing nutritional decisions each meal based on how you feel, what's available, or what you can sense your system needs. As you practice intuitive eating, over time you will get both more comfortable with it and better at it (feeling satiated without overconsuming, not gaining or losing weight, eating fairly consistent calories each day despite not counting beforehand). Especially as you focus more on how you feel and function after each meal, you'll become less inclined to adhere to weaker metrics (e.g., calorie-count or macronutrient composition) for desired mental outcomes, as they will likely prove to be less helpful, predictive, or informative for what you're trying to achieve each workday.

Eat Mindfully and Slowly

One way to eat intuitively with confidence is to be mentally mindful while you do it: eat slowly and deliberately, while actively listening to your own internal signals. Just as being conscientious about *what* you eat is important, so is *when* and *how* you eat. Mindful eating helps you eat only when you are legitimately hungry (not just because it is mealtime or because you are tired or bored, etc.) and stop eating as soon as you're full (no matter what's left on the plate). Research shows that people eat more in a sitting if they aren't paying attention specifically to the activity of eating, such as if they are also watching TV, reading a book, or working on something else. Eating without looking at the food you put in your mouth or without being mindful decreases your mind-body connection and how satiated you feel. If you feel less satiated, you are also more likely to overconsume, make worse nutritional choices, and snack later on. Eating mindfully also slows down chewing and consumption, which has been shown to increase your food enjoyment, nutritional choices, digestion, and nutrient absorption, while decreasing stress and overall calorie intake. It's good to eat at a table, away from your work or television, paying specific attention to your food, the activity of eating, and the signals your body sends. You will be more able to fuel yourself properly and eat more intuitively (read: what's right for you right now) if you pay attention to how the foods you put in your body make you feel.

Practice *Hara Hachi Bu*

The philosophy of *hara hachi bu* originated in the ancient blue zone of Okinawa, Japan, and is still widely practiced. *Hara hachi bu* is the philosophy that you would eat until you are only 80 percent full because of the emphasis on respecting food, bodily health, hunger cues, and community resources. *Hara hachi bu* translates to "belly 80 percent full," but it is part of a more encompassing philosophy about food, nutrition, abundance, community, and wellness. This best practice is to eat slowly and mindfully, typically in the company of others, and to stop eating when you feel your best estimate of 80 percent full. The principle is designed to prevent overeating and the health problems that result from it (e.g., diseases of affluence), and it has been shown to help with digestion, energy levels, weight maintenance, health, mental acuity, and aging processes.

Skimp on the Snacking

You are likely to crave a snack occasionally—especially during the Fall and Valley phases of the ultradian cycle, and even more so if you haven't eaten for a while—and that's fine. Nourishing yourself properly during the workday is crucial, though snacking constantly (or at every break) can backfire. Snacks of the prepackaged variety are often heavily processed and high in salt, fat, sugar, or other additives, which can cause performance-flattening outcomes (e.g., insulin spikes, inflammation) that hinder many things, including motivation, focus, and concentration. Ingesting and digesting food is an energetic, inflammatory process that shouldn't be done continuously throughout your day. Snacking interferes with meals, metabolic processes, growth hormone secretions, and the parasympathetic nervous system's ability to rest, digest, and repair your systems. Conditioning yourself to snack at every Valley, or whenever HALT sensations rear their heads during your day, is not helpful conditioning or habit formation, and ultimately not likely to help you perform at your best. Snacking or eating too late at night can interrupt critical growth hormone (and other necessary) secretions during your sleep, which are important for healing, development, repair, growth, cellular metabolism, learning capacity, memory, and neuroplastic change.

While it may be tempting or encouraged in your office, conditioning yourself to snack often during your day can result in unhealthy consumption practices. To combat this, it's important to devise alternative activities to snacking, such as going for a walk, socializing, changing your environment, or drinking water. All of these alternatives are beneficial for you and your brain—especially during the Fall and Valley phases, for example, when temptation to snack may be higher.

Fasting Sometimes Is Fine

After the *what* and *how* of eating, what about the *when*? What schedule should we eat on? Should it be three square meals a day?

In fact, it likely wasn't until the agrarian revolution of the seventeenth and eighteenth centuries that people started to eat three set meals a day: one in the morning after the fast overnight (breakfast), one during the day to fuel grueling farm labor (lunch), and one after the workday was over (dinner). In the twentieth-century developed world, as families settled into post-agrarian and industrialized systems where food (especially grain and cereal products) became more abundant, three-meal days became even more possible, popular, and culturally normative. Normative as it now may be, it may also be a departure from both the EEA and how your brain and body are best suited, adapted, and built.

In recent years there has been a growing popularization of something called intermittent fasting or IF. IF is more about *when* to eat and less about what (all the same advice applies) or how much (typically the same amount as ever). IF limits the eating windows to schedules that cycle between voluntary fasting and non-fasting over a given period. IF schedules include alternate-day fasting (e.g., eat one day and not the next), periodic fasting (e.g., fasting for a couple of days each month or year), and daily time-restricted eating windows (for example, a 16:8 schedule, where you eat during 8 hours of your day and fast during the remaining 16).

While IF has been criticized by some as a contemporary fad diet in its prescriptive and structured form, our prehistoric ancestors were likely forced to live in similar—and less organized or predictable—circumstances quite regularly. Hunters may not have been able to kill for many days in a row; gatherers may have hit a dry spell with no new berry bushes or birds' nests found. In some groups, lower-ranking or non-hunting people may have been forced to fast when food was scarce. Even if the food was relatively abundant, depending on the group, priority in feeding may have been given to the energy-expending hunters, growing children, or pregnant and breastfeeding women, as examples.

Dehydration is especially impeding for the brain and its functioning. Sip water continuously throughout the workday.

While this is not an endorsement of any specific diet or rigidly prescriptive formats of IF, the research shows that our brains and bodies are biologically quite well adapted to some periods of not eating—and it can sometimes even be quite helpful. From the perspective of neural functioning and optimal brain performance, if you miss a meal, either by accident or because you are genuinely not hungry, there's nothing to worry about. In fact, this can sometimes help your brain, cells, and the parasympathetic nervous system (rest, digest, repair) do their respective work, unencumbered by insulin surges, nutrient influxes, variations in blood sugar, inflammation, or disruptive digestive and metabolic activity. If you strive to eat naturally colorful foods when you are legitimately hungry and listen to your body while you do, don't panic if you miss a meal or have days when you eat very little, either accidentally, because of circumstances, or because you intended to. This might be considered natural from a biological perspective and also part of eating intuitively. Like so many things in our workday, society, and culture, it's easy to be conditioned to things (e.g., three large meals a day) that are not necessarily natural or required for our unique brains and bodies, which is why it is important to assess these norms for yourself, based on your specific needs and resulting performance.

Another plug for water: the same principle does not hold true for water consumption. There are no IF-type benefits to intermittent dehydration. Dehydration sets in at the cellular level in a matter of hours and is detrimental to proper functioning of all your systems, including and especially your brain.

Skip the Supplements (Probably)

Questions about supplements always come up: Should you? Shouldn't you? Which ones? The short answer is that generally, for healthy people (e.g., no known deficiencies, sensitivities, illnesses) under normal conditions (not training for something specific, under supreme stress, postoperative, etc.), it's probably best to skip the supplements.

The longer answer is: it depends.

On the one hand, the science is getting better, supplement technology and testing continue to improve, and most companies mean well when they put their items on the market (we hope, anyway). Some supplements can be lifesaving when prescribed by your physician for known disorders or deficiencies. Unfortunately, on the other hand, just like any processed or manufactured food, supplements often have profit-maximizing inclusions that are not as benign as we might like. Additives such as coloring, flavoring, and preservatives can include known allergens and undisclosed or unregulated ingredients. In this case, the best you could hope for is that the supplements go through you without any issues (meaning you have just spent a lot of money on the composition of your urine). However, at worst, they are toxic or harmful to you. Despite your best efforts, it may be near impossible on your own to detect evidence of often unlisted potentially harmful heavy metals (even trace amounts), fillers such as magnesium stearate (included for bulk texture), artificial colorants, artificial sweeteners, sugars, preservatives, shelf-stabilizers, or microplastics. Next time you are tempted to purchase a supplement, look for third-party testing, and check the product label, manufacturer reputation, and with your PCP or a registered dietitian for any contraindications, potential interactions, side effects, or harmful inclusions.

Several commonly taken supplements can have adverse effects if consumed in unregulated or excessive amounts. Sometimes dosage information is misleading or hard to understand (e.g., mcg, mg, g, IUs, etc.), or the amount printed on the label is not actually what is in the product (especially if they don't do third-party quality assurance and testing). It's important to know that most supplements are typically offered on the market without FDA review or approval. Also unfortunate is that to date, the supplements I have found to be helpful and arguably performance-enhancing are also quite expensive—out of range for most people's grocery budgets. The supplements industry is worth some $100 billion annually in United States alone at the time of this writing, and for the most part it's *caveat emptor* for consumers, basically.

Rest assured, however, that you should be able to get everything you need from a well-balanced diet that is rich in micronutrients and scarce in processed goods (including alcohol). The body will also be more likely to have an easier time recognizing and using a micronutrient in its original form (e.g., an apple) than in supplement form (e.g., a powder). Because most vitamins and minerals are fat-soluble, it is also typically better to eat your micronutrients in food form in combination with other foods and macronutrients (e.g., an avocado) so they can be properly absorbed in the gastrointestinal tract. Enzymes, microbiota, and cells will recognize nutrients more readily, which will allow them to be more readily absorbed and used. You probably aren't familiar with and couldn't easily identify exactly what is inside a supplement (nor the outcomes or side effects of consuming each compound), and because of the strange form (e.g., pill, powder), you can't count on your intestinal tract doing so, either. Also, even if the supplement is of the highest quality and does wonderful things, if it is used in a substituting fashion (consciously or otherwise), your overall attention to proper diet and nutrition may suffer and you may inadvertently consume less than requisite amounts of other compounds. You don't want to rely on supplements as a crutch or substitute in your diet or nutritional plan.

Consume Caffeine in Moderation

In moderation, caffeine has been shown to help focus and performance among fast metabolizers. According to proponents, caffeine in moderation can cultivate the internal resources, energy, and willpower necessary for getting into—and staying in—a higher-performance mode for longer periods.

Coffee has a half-life (how long it stays active in your system and takes you to eliminate) of anywhere from 1.5 to 9.5 hours, with the average said to be around 5 hours or so. Slow metabolizers of caffeine (people with only one copy of a gene called CYP1A2) will have elevated levels in their bloodstream for longer (e.g., a half-life of 9.5 hours), and are therefore more likely to experience caffeine-induced anxiety, jitters, elevated blood pressure and/or heart rate, and sleep disturbances because of this. For example, a slow metabolizer who has one 200 mg cup of brewed coffee at 8:00 a.m. might still have about 100 mg in their system come 5:00 p.m., and as much as 50 mg or so still by 2:00 a.m.—while they toss and turn in their bed, not knowing why. Fast metabolizers, meanwhile (two copies of CYP1A2), process and eliminate caffeine more quickly (e.g., 1.5 to 5 hours), allowing blood levels to drop sooner, so they are less likely to experience negative effects and more likely to experience the performance-enhancing effects of caffeine.

You know whether you are a fast or slow metabolizer based on how caffeine makes you feel when you consume it. If you experience negative effects of caffeine, cut back or eliminate it from your routine. Even for fast metabolizers caffeine consumption follows the hormetic curve: more isn't more, less can be less, and there's some ideal moderate, optimal level that may be hard to get exactly right, day to day, depending on other things like hydration levels, hormones, and sleep quality. Because of the varying results, side effects, and some coffee bean procurement practices, people are increasingly turning to alternative options that may use adaptogens, mushrooms, matcha, nootropics, or other compounds instead of caffeine to stimulate cognition, alertness, and daytime performance.

No matter how you metabolize caffeine, it remains a known diuretic (leaching your whole system of water through the kidneys and contributing to faster dehydration), addictive compound, and sleep disrupter (affecting sleep quality and quantity). If you consume it at all, it is best to stick to a maximum of 400 mg per day if you are a fast metabolizer and much less or none if you are a slow metabolizer (perhaps investigate the aforementioned alternatives). Also, many caffeinated beverages (e.g., energy drinks, bottled beverages, fancy coffees) are high in sugar, additives, and other undesirable compounds that are also best limited or avoided. Further, the half-life of caffeine means it is a great idea for everyone to avoid caffeine later in the day—think any time after about 2:00 p.m. or so—so as not to disturb your bedtime routine and sleep quality. You know you have had the right amount of caffeine when you can feel motivated, energetic, and focused and can fall asleep readily at night at a reasonable time. You know you have had too much if you are sweaty, jittery, overstimulated, talking too fast, frequenting the restroom, or finding it hard to fall asleep at night.

Here's a quick guide for how much caffeine is in popular caffeinated beverages:

- Brewed coffee: 95 to 200 mg per cup
- Espresso: 64 mg per cup
- Instant coffee: 63 mg per cup
- Decaffeinated coffee: 2 to 5 mg per cup
- Black tea: 47 to 90 mg per cup
- Oolong tea: 30 to 50 mg per cup
- Green tea: 25 to 45 mg per cup
- White tea: 15 to 30 mg per cup

Avoid Alcohol

Unfortunately, mounting evidence shows that consuming alcohol not only doesn't have any of the previously touted positive qualities, effects, or outcomes for your health and wellness, but that the opposite appears true: even in very low doses it bears some level of health risk. As the research amasses, it seems the best we can hope for with alcohol consumption is that it is neutral in our systems—a toxin that came in and was effectively evacuated without notice or collateral damage to our digestive, circulatory, neural, or renal systems. From the brain's perspective, the ethanol in alcoholic beverages is effectively a harmful, simple-sugar neurotoxin. Ethanol is also dehydrating, strips you of vitamin-B stores, pillages micronutrients in your systems, alters your microbiome, induces hunger, spikes insulin, slows metabolism, and disrupts sleep, among many other disadvantages. Psychologically, the odd elixir here and there might feel relieving, but actually the short-lived perceived benefits typically backfire, causing higher anxiety, stress, and emotional dysregulation ultimately. It likely goes without saying, but alcohol is also not the most functional way to cope with stress, boredom, social anxiety, or sadness.

Alcohol is especially bad for sleep, which is the topic of the coming chapter—Rest. It interferes with just about every valuable process that is supposed to happen while you sleep (melatonin production, growth hormone secretion, neurochemical processes, cell repair and regeneration, dreaming, hormonal allostasis, neuroplastic change, etc.). Normally, melatonin production slowly increases throughout the day, reaches a peak at night, and helps you fall and stay asleep. When alcohol interferes with melatonin production (and almost all other neurotransmitters as well), you may find it harder to fall asleep and stay asleep (although you may be too intoxicated to truly notice this). This disruption often results in fragmented sleep, which means you don't get as much restorative deep sleep, have as much growth hormone secretion during slumber (important for repairing all tissues, building muscle, healing, and immunity), or spend as much time in REM sleep (important for neural network building, learning capacity, knowledge stores, and memory). Alcohol consumption has been shown to decrease how much overall sleep you get, not just because you wake up more often and may find it hard to fall back asleep, but also because you may be tempted to go to bed later and may take longer to fall asleep once in bed. It has also been shown to increase the number of nightmares or disturbing dreams you experience, which can be psychologically troublesome.

As previously mentioned, another aspect to consider is the sugar content and additives in alcoholic beverages. It's best to think of alcoholic beverages as neurotoxic, simple-sugar, micronutrient-stripping, processed foods that tax every bodily system while also causing undesirable inflammation, hormonal dysregulation, oxidative stress, and cancer risk. When you do, you have what authorities increasingly assert is a more accurate picture of where alcohol consumption should fit in your nutritional plan. Sorry to be the bearer of bad news, but at least now you know, and when we know better, we can do better.

9

Rest

*A good laugh and a long sleep
are the best cures in the doctor's book.*

IRISH PROVERB

IN 2016 A SURPRISING story hit the sports highlights and newswires: some elite performance trainers refused to work with even high-profile NFL players who wouldn't sleep as much as the trainers demanded. Around the same time, Gary McCoy, a sports performance consultant, was studying the stress response and sleep habits of NFL players using wearable technology. McCoy quickly concluded that the elite trainers were right: sleep quality was an integral part of a player's stress response and ultimate performance. Teams needed to factor in sleep as seriously as diet, training, and coaching to move the needle on player performance. Fortunately, gone were the days of unreliable self-reports or the clunky, uncomfortable, lab-only polysomnography technology to monitor someone's sleep. With wearable technology, trainers were able to measure players' sleep while it was happening and monitor their bodies throughout each practice, during gym training sessions, and while they were on the field on game day.

Asking athletes to take sleep as seriously as sport was considered unconventional back then, even among the highest-performing athletes who had made a life and fortune pushing their bodies to their limits every day playing the game at a professional level. Announcers balked, fans laughed, coaches sneered, players scoffed. Then the stats came in.

Players who did as the sleep-science revolutionaries advocated—slept more and took the quality, quantity, and concept of sleep seriously—played better for longer; posted better numbers; healed more completely; were out for shorter durations; reported feeling better and happier; rebounded more quickly; avoided illness, injury, and burnout; had more strength and stamina; demonstrated higher mental acuity on the field; and by all accounts dealt with stress and strain better. Despite being chronically and systematically overlooked, it turns out that sleep was as (or more) critical as nutrition and training for how these players performed, both physically and mentally. Studying these training outcomes, coach Brett Bartholomew said, "What was once seen as a weakness is now known to be a strength. Rest is a weapon in sport."

Like brain research, sleep research continues to advance, and we learn new things every day. But the jury is in on this: sleep has undisputed, near-magical value for you and especially for your brain. Whether you have sleep-monitoring technology or not, everyone can now consider more closely their nightly sleep patterns and sleep hygiene—not just professional athletes who use their bodies for work every day, but also professionals who use their brains for work each workday. Here are just some of the things adequate, high-quality sleep is known to fix or improve (basically everything):

- Immunity and overall health, including decreases in chronic diseases
- Stress response and allostasis, including lowered cortisol and SNS activity
- Mental health, wellness, and emotional balance
- Alertness, awareness, and mindfulness
- Cognitive function, including information processing, decision-making, reasoning, and executive function
- Learning capacity, knowledge stores, and memory
- Creativity, problem-solving, resilience, and communication abilities
- Intelligence (as measured with IQ metrics)
- Hormonal health, balance, and regulation
- Athletic performance, recovery, strength, and stamina
- Neuromotor abilities, including flexibility, stability, coordination, and balance
- Nutritional choices, digestion, and nutrient absorption
- Metabolism, physique, and weight management
- Overall attractiveness (as reported by self and others)

Sleep hygiene has (all too slowly) gained mainstream popularity of late as an important factor in brain performance for everyone: athletes, executives, managers, decision-makers, movers, shakers, and everyone in between. You can go only minutes without oxygen, hours without water, a day without sleep, and potentially weeks without food before your brain is seriously affected or damaged. Sleep is near the top of the list in terms of importance for how and how well your brain functions.

The quality of your nighttime sleep directly dictates the quality of your mental (e.g., mood, psychology, mentality) and cognitive (e.g., thinking, reasoning, decision-making) performance the next day, as well as just about everything else about you. If you have ever experienced insomnia or been unable to get a good night's sleep, you know that no amount of food, water, deep breathing, or positive thinking is going to fix how awful you feel the next day (and potentially think, behave, and look). Sleep isn't for the lazy, thoughtless, or hedonistic. It's now accepted as a key practice of the highest performers.

Adequate, high-quality sleep has been shown to improve just about everything you likely care about, from immunity to intelligence to attractiveness. It's considered a key practice of the highest performers.

It cannot be stressed enough: no matter who you are or what you do, it benefits you in boundless ways to get as much high-quality sleep as you can every single night. For this reason, sleep, rest, napping, daydreaming, and daytime breaks—all collectively referred to in my MERIT Framework as "Rest"—are considered the third key domain you can control and should think conscientiously about for optimizing your workday, mental performance, and cognitive functioning.

What's Happening in There

The pineal gland regulates the production of the hormone melatonin. Melatonin levels increase consistently throughout your day and into the evening to promote sleep. Feeling sleepy, actually falling asleep, and staying asleep are all the function of elevated melatonin levels. Nathaniel Kleitman introduced the concept of the brain's ultradian cycle when he discovered the brain produces different types of waves during various phases of sleep. The timing of the different stages of sleep varies throughout the night but is cycling continuously. In the first half of the night, relatively more time is spent in NREM 3 (non-rapid eye movement sleep) or deep sleep. In the second half, relatively more time is spent in REM (rapid eye movement) sleep. Here are the stages of sleep that you cycle through all night long:

- **NREM 1** (5 to 20 percent of total sleep time, 5 to 30 minutes): Prepares the body for sleep. Brain waves are alpha and theta, slowing down from wakefulness levels. Muscles are relaxed. Heart rate and breathing slow down slightly. You can still be awakened easily.

- **NREM 2** (45 to 55 percent of total sleep time, approximately 4 hours during the night): Prepares the body for deep sleep (NREM 3). Brain waves are theta, sleep spindles, and K-complexes; brain waves slow down further. Muscles are more relaxed; body temperature decreases. Heart rate and breathing slow down further.

- **NREM 3** (15 to 25 percent of total sleep time, approximately 2 hours during the night): Known as deep sleep or slow-wave sleep. A time of physical restoration of muscle, tissues, and bones; memory consolidation; emotional regulation, management, and control. This is when helpful growth hormones and many other growth factors (e.g., BDNF) may be secreted. Brain waves are mostly delta waves, very slow—which is why it is sometimes called slow-wave sleep. It is usually more difficult to wake someone from this stage of sleep. Muscles are very relaxed. Heart rate and breathing are at their slowest. This is the stage that helps you feel most refreshed and replenished in the morning.

- REM (20 to 25 percent of total sleep time, approximately 2.5 hours during the night): Time for vivid dreaming, learning, neural network repair and reconfiguration, memory consolidation, and emotional processing and regulation. Initially occurs about 90 minutes after falling asleep, with subsequent REM stages becoming longer throughout the night. Brain waves are predominantly beta (typically associated with wakeful arousal, attention, awareness, and active engagement), with some sawtooth waves, reflecting higher brain activity. Alpha waves may reappear, but they are much slower than when you are awake. The brain speeds up from NREM 3 rates. Muscles are mostly relaxed, although heart rate and blood pressure may increase to near waking levels. This is when there is rapid eye movement, and muscle paralysis occurs (so you don't act out your dreams).

A full sleep cycle, from NREM to REM, lasts about 90 minutes. During a typical night, an individual typically goes through four to six sleep cycles, with the length of time spent in each stage changing throughout the night. Early in the night, more time is spent in NREM 3 than REM, while later in the night, REM sleep phases become relatively longer while NREM 3 phases become relatively shorter. The amount of time spent in each stage of the sleep cycle varies from person to person, but the general pattern is the same. Infants spend more time in REM sleep than adults, while older adults spend more time in the lighter stages of sleep. Several factors affect which brain waves are more active during sleep, including:

- **Age:** Brain waves slow down as we age.

- **Hormonal fluctuations:** Circadian cycling is altered by hormonal fluctuations, menopause, andropause, and pregnancy.

- **Blue-light exposure:** Blue light can interfere with your brain's normal circadian cycling and the pineal gland's ability to manufacture melatonin, which is required for feeling sleepy and falling and staying asleep.

- **Sleep deprivation:** Ironically, being sleep deprived can hinder your ability to fall and stay asleep even further—like a negative cycle. Sleep deprivation can lead to a chronic increase in beta waves (awake, anxious) and a suppression of the necessary alpha, theta, and delta waves (sleeping, relaxed). It's as if your brain gets out of practice at falling or staying asleep, which has drastic, negative consequences for both sleeping and waking hours.

- **Medical conditions:** Many conditions, including and especially sleep disorders (e.g., insomnia, sleep apnea), can negatively affect brain waves during sleep, interfering with sleep quality and duration.

- **Drugs:** Some medications, caffeine, and alcohol (not to mention recreational drugs) can all negatively affect brain wave activity during sleep, the quality and quantity of sleep, and the content of dreams (e.g., you have more negative content in your dreams after drinking alcohol, for example).

Sweet, Sweet Slumber

While we learn more every day, we still don't have all the answers about why humans sleep. There are many theories. A biologist might say it's to avoid predation, danger, or accidents during the dark hours when our eyes aren't as well equipped to see and monitor our environment. A physiologist might tell you it's to conserve energy, recalibrate your systems, and replenish your hormones and neurotransmitters. A brain scientist might explain that it's to renegotiate neural networks, consolidate learning, build knowledge, and solidify memories. A psychologist might describe how it's to regulate your emotions, improve your mental wellness, and increase your happiness, creativity, decision-making, and problem-solving skills. A physician might say it's to clear the brain and body of toxins and waste, repair damaged tissues, build muscle, increase immunity, protect against chronic diseases, and replenish the various systems.

They would all be right, but even together, they would still be only scratching the surface. While it is all too easy to take for granted, the importance of sleep for your brain and body health—and ultimate daily performance—cannot be overstated. Every morning after a good sleep, you wake up a smarter, better person who has new neural network configurations and therefore knows new things; is probably healthier; is more emotionally stable and happy; and is more likely to look, feel, and behave better than the person who had a bad night's sleep.

I am often asked if there is a way to "hack" sleep—sleep less, sleep in increments, or train yourself to require less sleep. The short answer is no, there isn't. With inadequate sleep comes notable losses in just about everything we can measure, including IQ points, motor coordination, hand-eye response times, problem-solving skills, decision-making accuracy, executive functioning, cognitive processing, emotional regulation, creativity, mindset, interpersonal intelligence, happiness, mental health, immunity, stress response, muscle mass... You get the picture.

The longer answer is that if a person feels the need to cheat, avoid, or shorten their sleep, they may need to update their understanding of the science of sleep and the crucial role it plays in daily human functioning and performance. Sleep isn't an obstacle, a weakness, a waste of time, or a practice of the slothful. While you may not be able to perceive it—because, well, you're asleep—sleep is so highly productive for everything to do with you (your health, psychology, personality, relationships, intelligence, physique, appearance, functioning, performance, prospects in life, and more) that it's about as close as you will come every day to experiencing real magic happen to you.

The Brain-Body Activity Trade-Off

As discussed in chapter 7, contrary to popular belief—and most people's reported subjective experience—the brain does not rest when you do. A paradox happens when you fall asleep. Despite how it may feel, during sleep—when the body is finally at rest with low muscle tension and no planned actions—the brain starts doing or triggering some very big work (even if the associated brain waves are slow).

Although the rest-activity cycle persists, sleep can almost be thought of as a Super Valley. During sleep, the brain performs many critical healing tasks it couldn't accomplish during the Valley in waking hours. It renegotiates neural networks (pruning neural pathways, forging new ones, attending to synapses, etc.), cleans out debris and toxins, fixes broken connections or networks, replenishes and synthesizes neurotransmitters and hormones, and prepares the systems for the day to come and the energy likely to be required.

Why would the brain be so dynamic during restful sleep? Think of it like remodeling a retail store. You wouldn't even think of tackling this construction while you are trying to engage with customers, showcase your wares, and process transactions. Instead, all this work needs to be done outside the business day so that, come opening hours, you can concentrate on running the business, serving your customers, and managing the pressing tasks at hand. Maintenance, administration, repairs, cleaning, clearing, and reorganizing are done when business is closed and no one else is present to interrupt or observe it.

Your brain is active during the daytime as well, of course: it is during daylight that early humans needed to accomplish tasks they needed eyesight for and could not do in the dark. This includes hunting, foraging, cleaning, mending, tending to children, and building, all while avoiding predation, injury, or accidents. Because these critical survival tasks can be accomplished only during waking hours, in the ongoing budgeting process your brain manages for all your systems, it is the physically active body that is given first dibs on most physiological resources (e.g., water, glucose, glycogen, oxygen, minerals, salts, nutrients) during the daytime. The brain gets to do its own heaviest lifting while you sleep and are (mostly) physically inactive.

No Trade-Off: Sleep Quality and Quantity Are Required

A question I'm often asked is, "Should I be aiming for quality or quantity of sleep?" The short answer is that you need both because there really is no trade-off. Typically you should aim for as much high-quality sleep as you can get every single night. As you know from experience, you can't "sleep fast," even under perfect circumstances, nor can you sleep "light but long" and hope for good outcomes. It doesn't work like that. Quality is a must. Lying awake in bed for hours won't facilitate the required restoration and benefits of sleep: you will feel groggy and exhausted the next day. The more quality sleep you get, the better your brain, body, and future will be. Quantity is also a must. You can't speed up the restorative actions of sleep. The brain needs long enough sleep every single night to do the requisite deep work from the day, which makes "catching up" on sleep on the weekends a bit of a fallacy. While it's great to get more then if you can (go for it!), it doesn't make up for lost sleep during the week. What's lost is basically lost in that case, with probable decrements in learning capacity, knowledge stores, memory, fitness gains, and immunity (as examples) to show for it.

That said, the quantity required will vary night over night, month over month, and throughout your life, depending on many factors. New job? All those new faces, places, smells, stimuli, and learning curves will increase how much sleep you need every night for a few months (probably about three). Just moved, got a divorce, experienced a loss, facing illness, going through exams, dealing with volatile or uncertain circumstances? More sleep is needed; plan for more than eight hours a night, because you almost certainly need it. Conversely, if things are going well—you are excited about things happening in your life, you're newly in love, you're happy and healthy overall, your physical routine is moderate, or life is great—you may find that you can get by with a little less sleep than usual, although it should still hover around that eight-hour mark.

Scientists agree that humans need seven or more hours a night at a minimum, and more when you are younger. Here is a general breakdown of how much sleep you need by age:

- Newborns (0 to 3 months): 14 to 17 hours per day
- Infants (4 to 11 months): 12 to 15 hours per day
- Toddlers (1 to 2 years): 11 to 14 hours per day
- Preschoolers (3 to 5 years): 10 to 13 hours per day
- School-age children (6 to 13 years): 9 to 11 hours per night
- Teenagers (14 to 17 years): 8 to 10 hours per night
- Young adults (18 to 25 years): 7 to 9 hours per night
- Adults (26 to 64 years): 7 to 9 hours per night
- Older adults (65+ years): 7 to 8 hours per night

While sleep requirements exist on a spectrum, with some people needing a bit more or a bit less, even those who swear they are the exception are very unlikely to sustainably need only half or two-thirds that amount (e.g., four to six hours a night), statistically and biologically speaking. Some people may need a little less or a little more depending on variables like genetics, lifestyle, activity levels, and health conditions, among other things. However, as exceptional as one might be, there is no hack for sleep. Getting enough high-quality sleep is critical to be your best self at work and in your personal life. (If you find you are an outlier either way—sleeping much more than eight hours, unable to wake after a normal sleep interval, groggier than usual when you do, or chronically unable to get at least approximately seven hours each night naturally—it could be a sign of chronic stress response, mental health issues, or an as-yet undiagnosed medical condition. Please consult your PCP.)

You know you have had enough sleep when you:

- Wake up feeling refreshed and alert—not groggy, lazy, brain-foggy, exhausted, or uncharacteristically slow

- Can concentrate and focus throughout the day—not drifting off, hazy, daydreaming, mind wandering, attempting to multitask, or persistently procrastinating

- Feel good and are in a good mood—not disgruntled, bad-humored, emotionally volatile, or down on yourself and/or everyone around you

- Feel you have enough energy and motivation to get through the day without having to nap—not sluggish, tired, peckish, already looking forward to bedtime again, or wishing the day away

Because the business day waits for no one, it's typically best practice to go to bed early enough in the evening that you get in seven or more hours before you have to wake up. An earlier bedtime will help ensure you are getting through all the sleep cycles (aim for six 90-minute cycles) that your brain needs before your day must start. An earlier bedtime helps you wake up naturally (no alarm) earlier and better rested, which is all the better for you—you avoid any stress response from your alarm clock startling you awake and blaring in your ear. That old Benjamin Franklin saying is neuroscientist-approved: "Early to bed and early to rise, makes a [hu]man healthy, wealthy, and wise."

Desirable Dreaming

Vivid dreaming happens during REM sleep, a stage critical for emotional processing and regulation as well as negotiating knowledge, learning, and memory networks. Some dreams occur during NREM sleep also. Dreaming is a cognitively complex process in which you effectively consolidate the memory of what you learned the prior day into neural knowledge stores. Some memories get solidified while others get all but thrown out. Your emotional centers are often involved in deciding which memories are deemed important enough to keep and which are discarded. It's for this reason that dreaming is often credited with aiding in daytime mood, emotional stability, and regulation. It is likely during dreams that emotional centers also process, negotiate, and deal with many of your emotions in the safety, privacy, and quiet space of the inside of your sleeping cranium. REM gives you a chance to process emotions and think through your potential actions (and social repercussions) before you might do them. A lack of REM sleep and dreaming decreases this processing, allowing emotions to spill over into the next day's mood, interactions, and behavior. You likely know from experience that too little sleep (and therefore REM cycles) leaves you feeling exhausted, emotionally volatile, and more likely to lash out at others the next day—to negative avail, especially at work.

Your neural networks are rewiring and renegotiating mostly during the REM phase. While this is happening, your brain is active and your body is temporarily immobilized, partly to conserve physical energy and partly so you won't act out your dreams and potentially hurt yourself.

If you were being monitored by a neuroimaging machine during your dream phases, we would see that your prefrontal cortex is quite active and involved in executive functioning, problem-solving, higher-order thinking, and decision-making—similar to midday activity. It is very possible that while you are experiencing the movie-like sequence of a dream, some parts of your brain are making decisions, processing information, solving problems, and coming to conclusions. Other parts of your brain meanwhile might be seen to be processing (mostly negative) emotional events from the day, making decisions about necessary actions (remember that negative emotions are designed to motivate your actions), calming any alarm bells, and helping cope with your feelings. Still other areas might be seen to be cleaning, clearing, or building neural networks with information you acquired during the day, so you consolidate memories, develop your cognitive schemata, create better knowledge stores, and learn while you sleep. When you think about it, dreaming is a marvel of a time in your brain: so many areas can be active and accomplishing important things simultaneously while also playing you a movie (that you may or may not remember). Often your heart rate and breathing will become irregular, and your body temperature may rise to match the content or intensity of your dreams.

While dreams can be quite vivid and realistic (or the opposite: vague and nonsensical), neuroscientists don't believe they *mean* anything necessarily. Despite what I've sometimes been asked, there is no scientific evidence that dreams are spiritual premonitions, secret messages, supernatural connections, or alien communications. Dreams could perhaps be thought of as access to the subconscious mind, although not directly or predictably, even if perhaps what you remember may well turn out to be predictive, connective, informative, or insightful. Your brain is an expert at pattern recognition and for this reason, sometimes patterns from your day or life become more evident to you during dreaming and may feel like "premonitions"—your brain correctly identified a pattern and that pattern played out as it predicted in your life. While we know that part of the processing during dreaming allows areas of your brain to conjure or anticipate future potential events in your life—like imagined, ongoing situational analyses—you could never be sure what parts of your dream were logical, informative thoughts or likely potential outcomes, and which were inconsequential, fleeting ideas or images. One thing is for certain: dreaming is awesome for you. If you're dreaming, you're most likely in REM or restorative sleep. Dreaming indicates you're getting high-quality sleep and your brain is doing some necessary heavy lifting: processing emotions, making decisions, solving problems, consolidating memories, adding to knowledge networks, analyzing an imagined future, and helping you learn.

Sleep requirements go up with just about all of life's stressors.

Because vivid-dream REM sleep happens more in the latter half of sleep, those who don't go to bed early enough often shortchange their longer REM cycles because they may have to wake up during them. It takes a while to get to the first shorter REM cycle of the night (approximately 70 to 90 minutes of sleep) and most of the night to get to your longer REM cycles—as the night goes on you spend longer stretches in this phase. If you finally get to the bulk of your longer REM phases and then your alarm goes off, you likely won't have gone through all the REM cycles your brain probably would have desired naturally. REM will also often get shortchanged if you spent more time in lighter or earlier stages in the first portion of the night for a variety of reasons—you are stressed, overcoming illness or injury, training too hard, experiencing a lot of change in your life, or you drank too much alcohol. Under these circumstances, longer duration of sleep is needed to get in all the required REM and NREM cycles. Sleep requirements go up with just about all of life's stressors.

Productive Daydreaming

As it turns out, daydreaming is not the time-waster it might look like to the external observer. While your mind wanders, your brain does micro-tweaks or small edits to neural networks, negotiates some emotions, and helps you think more creatively. Much like during actual dreaming, during daydreaming people often find that suddenly a pattern becomes apparent to them, a solution occurs to them, a new idea emerges, they can more readily deal with nagging emotions, they may have eureka moments, or they have more resolve about a decision they need to make. You have probably had this experience: you labored all day on a problem, paragraph, or pitch deck to little or no avail, only to have the solution occur to you as your mind was wandering on your commute home, in the shower, or on the treadmill. In moderation, daydreaming has been known to increase creativity, information processing, pattern recognition, cognitive flexibility, emotional balance, affect, and memory, and to reduce stress.

If you were being monitored in a neuroimaging machine during your daydreams, we would see activity in your prefrontal cortex—responsible for executive functioning, planning, decision-making, and paying attention—as with nighttime dreams. We would also see activation of the parietal lobe, which is responsible for processing sensory information, such as touch and sight. This is why daydreaming can feel so real or be so vivid. It's as if you are doing the scenario analysis and visualization of actions in your head and immersively considering the experience of doing what you are contemplating. Similarly, the limbic system—responsible for some (but not all!) of your emotional processing and some memory stores—would be more active, which is why these little dreams can feel so charged or even emotional. While it wouldn't be localized to one region, we would almost certainly witness your social networks ignite, as they consider the actions and reactions of others, as well as the consequences of your own potential social actions. Finally, we would likely see the temporal lobe (responsible for much memory and language) activated as well, because daydreaming involves memories, feelings, and stories. Very similar to actual dreaming, during daydreaming we would see your eyes move around and blink, even though you are not looking at anything in particular or on purpose. Your body may relax, your heart rate and breathing might slow for a few minutes, and your brain waves might change—exactly as they do during nighttime dreaming.

Daydreaming can be a highly functional time for most people under normal circumstances. It's almost like the brain's way of saying it has valuable work it must do right now—even though it is midday. As with anything, moderation is important. Some daydreaming can be highly helpful, productive, and performance-enhancing, while too much likely is evidence you need more nighttime sleep; are bored, stressed, or anxious; or have more pressing emotional issues to deal with than the present tasks at hand.

Napping the Day Away

Some people swear by their afternoon naps or "power naps" for improving their motivation, productivity, sense of well-being, performance, and progress. Others will tell you it makes them groggy, nauseous, or disoriented and interrupts the cadence and productivity of their day.

Napping continues to be studied, and the results are varied. On the one hand, a bit like daydreaming, napping has been shown to improve cognitive performance, creativity, alertness, mood, memory, ability to pay attention, and problem-solving and decision-making capacity in those people who benefit from a quick daytime restoring of the brain's energy and neurotransmitters. It can reduce stress hormones and fatigue, and therefore the likelihood of accidents, injury, or errors, and make it easier to focus, accomplish, or learn through the rest of the day.

Excessive napping, however, has also been shown to interfere with ultradian daytime flow, your ability to get back to the tasks at hand or get back into work, and your ability to fall and/or stay asleep at night. Even for those who love naps, if your nap goes on too long, it can leave you feeling groggy, disoriented, or woozy (something called sleep inertia) for the remainder of the usable workday, as well as decrease your sleep drive come night.

The main issue with napping is that it may be inadvertently used as a substitute for lost nighttime sleep or interfere with your sleep for the night to come—especially when done daily or chronically, which can become a vicious cycle. If you use napping as a substitute instead of as a complement to your nighttime sleep, it will leave you with all the disadvantages of a chronically sleep-deprived person. If you notice that you are napping more, finding it hard to fall or stay asleep at night, or are so chronically tired you can't avoid the daytime nap, you should analyze your sleep habits and determine how you could improve the quality and duration of your nighttime sleep. This could involve changing your sleep environment or routines so you get more higher-quality sleep regularly at night. Once you have done this work, if you still think a nap is worthwhile, go for it. Only you can really be the judge of what your brain and body truly need each day.

Better Brain Rest: How-Tos

Reprioritize Quantity and Quality of Sleep

Statistically, you are probably at least a little sleep deprived. Survey data shows most North Americans are, because of long work hours, blue-light emitting devices, noisy urban environments, shift work, electronics and lighting, medical conditions, and stress. Sleep deprivation has been shown to increase many risks, including accidents, obesity, type 2 diabetes, heart disease, and depression, as well as causing impaired decision-making, learning, memory, and cognitive function. This is completely avoidable and within your control, as long as you reprioritize more and better sleep. Perhaps it's mundane and easy to forget, and it might feel unproductive, but sleep factors very highly in most aspects of your functioning: the quality of your learning; knowledge stores; memory; mental, neural, and cognitive performance; as well as physical, mental, and psychological health and overall well-being, now and in the future. If you get more high-quality sleep, you will get better results in life, athletics, and career. It's that simple.

Go to Bed Earlier and Be Rigidly Consistent with Your Bedtime

We enforce it with our kids, but we often forget to do it for ourselves. Science says it's easier to fall asleep (and stay that way) if you are relaxed by bedtime because of expectations and a consistent schedule for both sleeping and waking. You know that if you fail to plan, you plan to fail: this applies to getting enough sleep, too. Your evening routine should be designed to let you slowly wind down from a long day over the course of a couple of hours, and it should be consistent through the weekdays and even on weekends whenever possible. You will find your circadian rhythm and sleep patterns follow your preparations and expectations—you will be naturally more tired, find it easier to fall asleep, and sleep more soundly.

Setting a bedtime is relatively easy: count at least eight hours (or preferably nine; e.g., six 90-minute cycles) backward from the time you have to get up each day. Allow for more sleep time if you are in a stressful or change-ridden period of your life or overcoming illness. While you might not sleep the entire time you are actually in your bed, you definitely won't sleep if you're not there. Starting about three hours before your bedtime, start to wind down and do relaxing things (e.g., take a bath, drink some non-caffeinated tea, listen to calming music, avoid blue light). Because the business day waits for no one and the world is a noisy place once the day gets started, the only way to ensure you get more sleep is to go to bed earlier in the evening. Many authorities indicate you should aim for a 9:00 p.m. to 10:00 p.m. bedtime each night so you have lots of time in bed to properly power down, sleep, and wake up without an alarm—although this of course will vary from person to person, depending on your typical schedule and circumstances.

Based on all the research, here's an ideal routine. Aim for a bedtime of 10:00 p.m. each night (or earlier). As early as possible after dinner (around 7:00 p.m.), start your relaxing evening routine. Lay out clothes for the next day, and make sure everything is organized for first thing in the morning and scheduled for the rest of your day. Review your to-do list: check some things off, delete others, and rewrite it for the next day with the one thing you want to get done (remember chapter 2?). Your sleeping brain can work on and prepare for the things you want to accomplish the following day. Fill a cup of water for your bedside, apply your lotions, start your sound machine if you need one (though do keep electronics away from your head), and get your sleep mask out. By the time bedtime rolls around, an analogous ritual will help you feel that things are clean, calm, and organized, and all your senses should be geared toward sleep time. You should feel relaxed about sleeping and relatively prepared for the next day. You won't necessarily fall asleep right away, but at least you will be in bed, perhaps reading, praying, or thinking at first—but not working, scrolling, looking at technology, or getting any more news.

Your process might not look exactly like that, but the point is the same: your evenings should be as routinized and relaxing as possible, and your bedtime (and likely wake time) should be consistent throughout the week, including weekends whenever possible. A consistent evening routine will help you sleep more soundly and get enough sleep in your life.

Avoid Blue Light Before Bedtime

The use of screen technology—and specifically the blue light it emits—decreases how well your physiological systems, cycling, melatonin production, and brain work. While it can be nearly impossible to avoid if you like to use an e-reader before bed, best practice indicates that we should try to limit screen time and blue light in the evenings, especially leading up to bedtime. Blue light disrupts the circadian rhythm in the brain and body partly because it fools the brain's light-sensitive areas into believing that it's still daylight outside and nighttime hasn't descended yet.

Blue light is known to disrupt the pineal gland's ability to produce melatonin, which is the neurohormone that helps us feel sleepy, fall asleep, and stay asleep. Blue-light glasses and blue-light filters on devices and screens are a couple of ways to cut down on the amount of blue light you get from electronic devices. However, as with so many things, abstinence (especially in the evening leading up to bedtime) is the only way to ensure you aren't getting too much disruptive blue light.

Invest in Getting the Setting and Bedding Right

Think of the ideal sleep space as resembling a cave—cool (68–70°F), very dark, quiet, and not too dry (although wet and humid aren't ideal, either). This environment has been shown to help regulate body temperature, increase melatonin production, increase growth hormone secretion, and improve quality and duration of sleep. Sleep is as important as the quality of food you eat and water you drink—so if you are in a position to do so, invest in the high-quality sleep essentials. Instead of thinking of these items as luxuries, think of them as essentials or tools for sleep. You likely invest in tools for your other life tasks and business, and sleep should be no different. If you can, get blackout window coverings; buy the right night mask for you; invest in a comfortable, non-toxic mattress; wear comfortable, clean, low-dye cotton pajamas; and get high-quality bedding made of non-synthetic materials (e.g., cotton) that are also without heavy dyes (e.g., preferably white or natural colored). If you are to (ideally) spend almost a third of your life in bed, these expenditures won't seem frivolous or inconsequential.

Cut out noise pollution whenever possible as it can disrupt sleep. Make sure to turn off the television, radio, and computer. If you live in a dense urban area, think about using a sound machine to drown out unavoidable or unexpected noises so you won't be unnaturally awakened. Make sure sound machines, alarm clocks, and charging mobile devices are at least three feet away from your head, if not farther (preferably five or more feet). Their electronic field and light emissions are disruptive to your sleeping brain.

If you sleep with partners, young children, or pets, assess how disruptive you find their presence to your sleep—especially during periods of stress, illness, injury, or change when you need more, good sleep. For some people, the comfort of nocturnal company aids their sleep quality and they aren't disturbed by others' movements, sounds, snoring, covers-stealing, scratching, or periodic waking. For others, this is very disruptive and detrimental to their highest quality of sleep. Make sure you prioritize your own best-quality sleep first and foremost. You can't serve others well during your waking hours if you don't first serve yourself restorative, high-quality sleep.

Assess Daytime Napping Honestly

Napping can increase alertness, problem-solving, decision-making, and creativity for some people, but napping for too long can disrupt your ultradian cycling, increase daytime sleep inertia, decrease nighttime sleep drive, and thwart daily workflow. It can also be a sign of other underlying problems (e.g., hormonal dysregulation, depression, anxiety, ineffective coping strategies, medical disorders) for which you should consult your PCP.

To avoid these pitfalls, if you nap midday:

- Limit napping to a single short episode (approximately one ultradian healing response phase—e.g., 20 minutes) in the afternoon, sometime after lunch, when your energy and attention levels naturally drop off anyway.

- Ensure the highest-quality sleep possible for that short period. For example, avoid sugar, alcohol, and caffeine too soon beforehand. As with nighttime sleep, these can interfere with the quality of your nap. Get the environment right (dark, cool, quiet, comfortable) so you can reap the maximum benefits of the nap. If your nap is of low quality, given that it's already (ideally) short, there likely isn't much point.

If you love a good power nap and it works for you, don't fix what ain't broke. But if you are purposefully or inadvertently using napping as a substitute for nighttime sleep, stop. Napping should be a complement (e.g., in addition) to high-quality, adequate-duration nighttime sleep.

Still Awake? Use a Sleep Aid

Questions often come up about sleep aids, sleep tech, apps for sleep, etc. In short, because of the importance of sleep, I am in favor of using any of these if they genuinely help you get more high-quality sleep. If you are jet-lagged, sleep deprived, extra stressed, or having a difficult time falling or staying asleep, get help wherever you can. I myself take melatonin (3 mg, not more, as this is thought to interfere with circadian cycling and subsequent night sleep drive due to the sleep inertia it causes) whenever I need a bit of help with sleep. Consult your physician for recommendations on sleep aids or ask your pharmacist about the non-prescription options available to you. Sleep is so important, you should do (almost) anything it takes to get more of the highest quality of it. Your doctor shouldn't prescribe anything you don't need, so if you are prescribed a sleep aid, don't be a hero—take it as prescribed.

That said, as mentioned before, don't fix what isn't broken or typically works well for you. If you are sleeping fine in general, you wake feeling well rested, injuries are healing, and you feel good overall, don't start tinkering in a misguided effort to hack your sleep. Sleep is a natural, necessary, magical bodily process. It varies naturally to some extent from night to night and should be something you are usually capable of without undue intervention, aid, or meddling.

10

Interact

Human beings are social creatures. We are social not just in the trivial sense that we like company, and not just in the obvious sense that we each depend on others. We are social in a more elemental way: simply to exist as a normal human being requires interaction with other people.

ATUL GAWANDE

Suppose you have the opportunity to visit the headquarters of one of the world's cutting-edge high-tech companies in Silicon Valley. You would be faced with a new kind of office. Once through the double doors, you might be greeted by a receptionist, and the space will look and feel open, airy, and inviting. You would notice all kinds of furniture, too—a plush-looking lounge space, almost like a home living room but vaster and almost certainly more expensive. There might be communal spaces with modular desks that could be grouped or ungrouped; perhaps some desks have been moved outdoors to the courtyard garden. On a tight deadline but need to get the blood pumping? Invite your team to a big yellow conference bike where five of you can pedal simultaneously in a huddle while having a meeting.

Around these parts, all but gone are the standard, boring cubicles, fishbowl meeting rooms, corporate furniture, bland walls, and eerily quiet hallways. It's designed to be a human-centered, avant-garde workspace to get the best possible performance out of the humans who roam these halls. Designers argue it's rooted in human science and all for the important purpose of helping people interact more frequently and meaningfully with others at work—so they may work more productively, be more creative, come up with new ideas and innovations, and advance knowledge in the sector and for the company. These spaces are supposed to give workers opportunities to work with others in a fluid manner—sometimes in small groups, sometimes in larger ones, sometimes alone, or with a buddy. The idea is that mixing and mingling with others in a fluid and dynamic way throughout the workday boosts creativity, efficiency, effectiveness, productivity, bonding, and a sense of comradery during long hours. Workers can feel a sense of improved workplace wellness, commitment, and satisfaction by being connected to colleagues. Real competitive and profitability gains can be made when these designs and activities foster interaction, connection, belonging, and workplace friendships.

As companies like Google, Meta, and Microsoft have proved, employee commitment, engagement, creativity, innovations, and productivity increase when employees interact with other people at work. Research (including my own) attests that social interaction, discussion, cooperation, and collaboration between colleagues can increase things like shared understandings, learning, knowledge, divergent thinking, meaningful brainstorming, and democracy of thought, and thereby increase new product development, innovation, and breakthroughs. Professionals who interact with colleagues readily, positively, and meaningfully are typically more creative, effective, motivated, productive, committed, and satisfied in their job and careers.

No surprise that employees with richer social bonds at work also report being happier at work, enjoy their work more, work more willingly and diligently, and report higher overall satisfaction. Our brains are highly motivated by positive social interactions, connections, and relationships, because these reinforce our own social standing, support, and opportunities. This is likely why savvy companies increasingly encourage some socializing, use of common areas, and communal leisure in office spaces. Google witnessed firsthand the benefit of innovation time off, where employees were free to work together, in groups, or alone, on projects of interest to them. The idea-sharing, time to mind-wander, experimentation, brainstorming, and ad hoc social interactions fostered better innovations that were more readily commercialized (read: profitable).

This is also why office water cooler discussions and small talk are not so small after all. Forging social connections and a sense of familiarity, liking, belonging, support, or friendship registers as a gain in social networks of the brain, increases positive emotions and associations, and is therefore motivational gold for individual work output, productivity, and performance—and a boon for employers as well. Because social interactions are largely under your control, and because of how important they prove to be for your overall mental, cognitive, and professional health, wellness, and performance, "Interact" is the fourth key domain or lever in the MERIT Framework for you to think deliberately about and strive to optimize.

Social Connections and Support Improve Your Health, Wellness, and Work Performance

A major discovery in neuroscience over the past decade has been the prevalence of social information processing in neural networks of the brain. While social processing isn't localized to any one area per se, during social interactions we see more activity in the limbic structures, amygdala, frontal ventromedial areas, and somatosensory areas (particularly on the right). Further, it turns out that most neural networks are involved in either social perception (e.g., interpreting and understanding social information) or social cognition (e.g., contemplating, making decisions, responding to others) in some way.

Social networks are thought to be a series of networks that are comprised of almost all other major networks of the brain. These other major networks include but are not limited to:

- **The executive control network (ECN):** A collection of brain regions that is involved in controlling and regulating cognitive functions, such as attention, working memory, decision-making, planning, problem-solving, flexibility, and inhibition.

- **The default mode network (DMN):** A network of brain regions that is active when the brain is at rest and not engaged in any specific task. It is thought to be involved in a variety of cognitive functions, including self-referential processing (the ability to think about yourself and your own thoughts and feelings), autobiographical memory (remembering your own life experiences), theory of mind (understanding that others have different beliefs and desires than you), mentalizing (understanding the thoughts and feelings of others), and interpersonal understanding (the ability to understand others as well as the dynamics of social interactions).

- **The salience network:** Another collection of brain regions that is involved in detecting and filtering salient stimuli, or stimuli that are important or relevant to the individual at the moment in their work or social environment. It is thought to be involved in a variety of cognitive functions, such as concentration, decision-making, motivations, emotions, and social processing.

- **Sensory networks:** Networks involved in processing sensory information from the environment, such as sight, sound, touch, taste, and smell, and relaying this information to the appropriate parts of the brain for processing.

- **Motor networks:** Networks involved in controlling and coordinating voluntary movements of the body.

- **Attention networks:** Networks involved in alerting, orienting, and focusing attention on relevant stimuli and filtering out or ignoring information that is deemed to be irrelevant, effectively cutting out much of the noise and simplifying perceptions of the physical (and social) environment.

- **Memory networks:** Networks involved in storing and retrieving information, including knowledge stores (e.g., the memory of something you learned about someone).

- **Emotional networks:** Networks involved in feeling, remembering, understanding, regulating, and retrieving emotions.

- **Language networks:** Networks involved in understanding and producing meaning and language for others to understand.

Ultimately, most brain regions are involved somehow, sometime, in social processing (perception or cognition). Social information, decision-making, and action are huge priorities for the human brain because we are, at a fundamental level, social beings of a social species. At any given moment, some portion of the brain is involved in or dedicated to thinking about other people and/or yourself in the context of others. Now that it has been mentioned, you will probably notice how often even your idle thoughts involve social information, contemplating, fantasies or imagining, problem-solving, or decision-making about your social world or the people around you. Because of the importance to our survival, humans commit much time and mental capacity to thinking about other people and ourselves in the context of social interactions, relationships, and situations.

A biological perspective helps us understand why our brains might be so socially oriented. First, we aren't sea turtles who independently glean their resources from nature and the environment around them. Instead, we are born to carers who provide for us until we are old enough to participate in groups that work together to secure resources and capital (food, water, tools, shelter, currency). Except for the fruits of our backyard herb garden (or if we hunt, fish, or farm), throughout our lives we get survival-critical resources from other people, directly or indirectly. Even the resources we provide for ourselves (e.g., from a backyard garden, a farm, or hunting or fishing) are often accomplished with the help, tools, resources, teachings, and ideas of other people around us, past or present.

Second, different again from your average crocodile, sea turtle, or bear, humans are a social tribal species. We exist in packs or tribes and, as individuals, place importance on being included and valued by these groups. In the EEA, if you were ostracized or excluded from the group, you would find yourself alone, unable to rely on help for finding food, building shelter, healing injuries, or fending off predators, as examples. Historically for humans, being excluded from the pack and left to your own devices was a death sentence, so avoiding this situation is now built into your neural architecture and functioning.

Accordingly, your social circumstances, standing, support, and relationships are considered paramount inside your (mostly non-conscious) brain. Contrary to what the renowned 1940s psychologist Abraham Maslow asserted in his now-discredited needs hierarchy—that human needs are hierarchical, with physiological needs at the bottom and social needs closer to the top—social needs can often override physiological, safety, or other survival needs. For example, people will undereat to attain a certain physique to fit in; race motorcycles down the freeway, risking lives to be considered cool by their peers; use dangerous substances to be part of the in-group; or go into a lifetime of debt just to "keep up with the Joneses." In the human brain, social needs don't just often trump survival needs; they are themselves considered survival critical.

In your brain, social needs are considered survival critical.

A growing body of research suggests that social relationships, connections, and support can have a significant impact on your brain functioning and mental health, as well. For example, one study found that people with strong social ties had a thicker cortex—the outer layer of the brain—than those with weaker social ties. The cortex is involved in a variety of cognitive functions, so it is thought that more and higher-quality social ties would therefore improve one's cognitive abilities and performance. Another study found that people who experienced social isolation had a smaller hippocampus, a region of the brain involved in memory formation and moderating some emotions. Many similar studies suggest that perceived positive social interactions, connections, relationships, and support can help protect the brain from damage, senescence, and dysfunction and promote a healthier, more functional brain, which contributes to your mental and cognitive performance—in life and at work.

Here are some of the ways that positive social relationships, connections, interactions, and support at work have been shown to benefit you and your functioning.

- **Social support can reduce stress:** Stress can damage neurons and lead to cognitive decline. Social support, especially at work, can help buffer the effects of stress on the brain, increase your ability to cope, decrease stress response, and improve allostasis.

- **Social interactions can improve your cognitive functioning:** Social engagement can help improve memory, learning, knowledge stores, productivity, creativity, and other cognitive functions (e.g., thinking, reasoning, decision-making) that help your work performance.

- **Social connections can increase your resilience and competence:** Strong social ties and support can help people cope with adversity and bounce back from setbacks, as well as increase self-confidence and self-efficacy.

- **Social interactions and relationships can improve your physical health:** Isolation is a risk factor for almost all disorders—mental and physical. Socially connected people, meanwhile, tend to be healthier mentally and physically and report being happier than those who are less socially connected or feel less socially supported.

For all of these reasons and more, it likely comes as no surprise that social interactions elicit some strong emotions in people, especially at work. To our brains, the social context of work can feel survival critical and thereby emotionally charged. Not only is work where we earn our living (which feeds, clothes, and houses us and our families), but it is also a group to which we want to belong, matter, and be included. It is also where we glean much of our importance, relevance, standing, identity, and position in society. As Lydia Denworth points out in her 2020 book *Friendship: The Evolution, Biology, and Extraordinary Power of Life's Fundamental Bond*, a primary determinant of our emotional state, mental resilience, and physical health is how much we feel connected to and supported by the people we spend the most time with. (Often we spend more time during the week with our colleagues than with our partners, children, or friends.)

Even in a modern context, your chances of physical, mental, and social wellness—and ultimately success as a professional—increase in proportion to the number of people who know you, like you, and willingly interact with you. This is partly attributable to your social status and/or social support: the resources, benefits, and opportunities that you can access through your social relationships, interactions, and affiliations. Higher or more positive social status typically increases your social support, or how many people will have your back when the chips are down, be willing to give you the benefit of the doubt when things go wonky, or be willing to hear you and consider your point of view on something—especially during a conflict.

Because social processing happens in neural networks that are highly linked to emotional processing in the brain, what our brains process as social rewards or threats result in real emotions. This partly explains why we feel positive emotions when something happens that we think will improve our social circumstances, standing, support, or relationships (e.g., you get a promotion, find an attractive partner, make a new friend, earn a compliment, gain admittance to an exclusive group, get many likes on social media) and we feel negative emotions when something diminishes or threatens our social standing, relationships, or support (e.g., your spouse asks for a divorce, you get fired, someone unfriends you on social media, someone shames you publicly). Our emotional states, stability, psychological safety, and mental well-being are closely tied to how connected we feel to others, the quality of our social interactions, how much we feel we belong, and how socially supported we feel. Accordingly, it is important to monitor and nurture social connections and relationships, especially at work, if you want to optimize your mental, cognitive, and professional performance there.

Social Skills and Likability Improve Your Support, Status, and Success

Given that your chances of survival and success are directly related to others—because others are your core source of aid, capital, and resources—it's no wonder you have dedicated networks and neural areas designed to process their actions and motivations, and that social processing is a component of almost all your neural networks in some way. Because you must work with people, how skilled you are at interacting, connecting, getting others to like you, and gleaning their support is predictive of how happy and successful you will be in life and at work. The more others like you, the more they are willing to be near you, interact with you, help you, collaborate, and cooperate with you—as you are with them. This isn't surprising and it's likely something you have experienced first-hand: people like to work with people they like and will be more likely to help, support, and promote them.

Social standing, status, relationships, and support can perhaps be thought of as an original form of capital, one that contributed directly to a person's well-being, resources, survival, and success. Before there were big houses, fancy clothes, or fast sports cars you could amass through financial capital, you accrued social standing and support (or not) through your social skills, likability, and interactions with others. In a modern context, social connections and support can be used to gain financial capital. Knowing the right people can give you a leg up, better information, and quicker access to new opportunities. The more others like you and want to interact with you, the easier and faster it will be for you to mobilize your own agenda, be publicly acknowledged, rise through the ranks of any system or organization, and establish a higher social status. Positive interactions, more connections, high-quality relationships, more social support, and good social standing at work are helpful for your overall career success.

Many studies assert the importance of having friends at work for things like work satisfaction, decreased turnover, productivity, advancement, and a sense of work-life balance. This insight countervails the industrial-era ethos that advocated for individual, focused, repetitive work and sterile, serious work environments. Exit interviews show that talent doesn't often leave *jobs*, they leave people—typically their bosses, but also the group or culture of the organization. Internal interviews reveal that employees don't necessarily stay, work, or perform primarily for the money, but for the colleagues, workmates, and community they care about. Job satisfaction and commitment scores are typically less about extrinsic motivators—things like compensation and benefits—and much more about intrinsic ones, like finding purpose, meaning, belonging, community, relationships, connections, and support, and having *people at work* that make these things possible. When people like and feel connected to and supported by those they work with, innovation, morale, productivity, and performance go up while turnover, errors, safety incidents, and grievances go down. It turns out that it benefits both the individual and the organization for people to make and have friends at work.

Making friends at work and feeling socially supported there is great for your health and wellness, your workday performance, and your probable career outcomes.

Accordingly, it's highly logical, rational, and advantageous for you to put effort into your interactions, connections, and relationships with colleagues both in context of and outside of the actual work you do together. The ideal would be that these professional workmates turn into real friendships, especially because of how much of your mutual lived existence you likely spend at work together and through your career. Getting to know colleagues and having them know you, like you, and support you stands to directly impact your work satisfaction, productivity, performance, and success, as well as overall health and well-being of every kind.

Optimizing Interactions at Work: How-Tos

Build Support by Being Prosocial and Likable at Work

Start building your social support by prioritizing positive interactions, connections, and relationships through prosocial behavior (actions that benefit others) and doing what you can to get along well with people at work—it will benefit you in multiple ways. Striving to develop mutual familiarity and liking also activates both of your brain's social processing and reward centers, will gain you more real friends at work, and will help ensure you have more support getting your tasks and projects done, all of which will facilitate your professional advancement and success—like an upward, cumulative, prosperous spiral.

There are many ways to be more prosocial and likable at work. Here are a few backed by research:

- **Be intentional about building relationships:** If you don't plan for it, it won't happen. Don't wait for relationships to just happen or for people to approach you. Take the initiative to get to know your colleagues, both at and outside of work. You can't hope to build quality relationships, or for people to like you, if you aren't being open and intentional about it first.

- **Listen more:** Research shows that most people will rate a conversation more positively in direct proportion to how much of the speaking they did and how much they believed the other to be listening to them. In other words, if you want people to enjoy conversations with you: to some extent, say less and genuinely listen more. Bonus points if you can ask meaningful follow-up questions and show that you are interested in their thoughts, ideas, or feelings. While active or informational listening can be energy intensive, you benefit from better insights about who people are and what makes them tick, while also ensuring the other person enjoys speaking with you and will want to do it again. If you are an introvert, this may be relatively easier for you (though all types of listening are work!): ensure you're still engaged in reciprocal dialog and actively conversing. If you often dominate conversations, prepare to brush up on your patience and active-listening skills.

- **Find common ground:** People are naturally homophilic, meaning they are more likely to like and spend time with people they perceive to be similar to themselves, because of familiarity effects (that increase their comfort levels). If you can draw someone in with things that are shared or common between you, they immediately have a better mental foundation for feeling familiar with you and therefore liking you (at least more than they might otherwise or than they started with). Commonality can be work or nonwork related. For example, you might highlight that you share the same hometown, root for the same team, have kids in the same school, or both love pickleball. Whatever the commonality or similarity is, their brain will perceive you to be more like them, more familiar, more likable, and therefore preferential to interact, work, collaborate, or even compromise with. We often say that repeated interactions drive familiarity, familiarity drives liking, liking drives trust, and trust drives a willingness to interact, support, or transact with you.

- **Give compliments:** Flattery really will get you everywhere. Everyone likes to receive compliments. Be sincere and specific in your compliments, and don't overuse this tactic.

- **Avoid the four unsocial Cs:** Try to focus on the positive, and avoid complaining, conflicting, condemning, or criticizing other people or circumstances—even third-parties or distant ones. People take unsocial overtures as non-conscious cues about your general disposition and attitudes, as well as what you may say or do behind their back. It's functional if you are willing to look past others' shortcomings or errors, within reason—everyone makes mistakes. To increase your likability, stay above the fray, avoid embarrassing or shaming others, and be generally pleasant to interact with.

- **Demonstrate the four prosocial Cs:** Show a willingness to coordinate, cooperate, collaborate, and compromise with others at work. It's evidence to them that you are agreeable, likable, and perhaps even trustworthy. People are likely to reciprocate these overtures in kind. If you demonstrate a willingness to cooperate, for example, they are likely to be more open to doing the same with you. While you don't always want to bend over backward unnecessarily (and certainly not to the point of compromising yourself), in general a little prosocial sentiment with these four Cs can improve interpersonal interactions and foster your relationships at work.

- **Be genuinely yourself:** People can tell when you are being fake or insincere, and it will be off-putting to them. It is important to be genuine in your interactions with others. Be your true professional self and let your personality shine through. Don't try to be someone you're not—this will ultimately backfire and decrease the quality of your connections, interactions, and relationships.

- **Have a sense of humor:** A good sense of humor can make you seem more approachable, agreeable, open, and likable (some of the "Big Five" desirable personality traits). Be able to laugh at yourself and don't take things too seriously or personally. Make jokes when appropriate and avoid being sarcastic.

- **Use open body language:** Be open and approachable (as opposed to closed off and cagey), stand or sit up straight, be physically present, and make reasonable eye contact with others. This shows that you are interested in what the others have to say; value their time, presence, and attention; and respect them. Body language is one of the loudest forms of communication, despite it making no sound at all. Pay attention to what your physical, nonverbal statements may be conveying to others in the work environment. This extends to your facial expressions also—even when not actively engaged with others, do what you can to wear a neutral expression so you aren't caught inadvertently frowning or scowling.

Use the Halo Effect to Your Advantage

Typically, the first thing workmates will know about you is what you look like. Because of something called the "halo effect" (basing a positive overall impression of someone on a single characteristic), as well as other stereotyping effects, people who are perceived to be good looking or attractive are typically also rated as more likable, intelligent, popular, kind, and successful. These people also tend to gain social connections, support, and standing more quickly than others, all else being equal. Improving your outward appearance can aid how others perceive you, how prone they are to liking you, and therefore how likely they are to give you the benefit of the doubt, help, an opportunity, a promotion, or a raise. Compared with those deemed less attractive, people perceived as more attractive:

- Are more likely to have positive social interactions and relationships, and their relationships tend to be more satisfying
- Tend to receive higher grades and praise, and have more positive relationships with their teachers, bosses, and direct managers
- Are more likely to be hired, promoted, and paid more than their less attractive counterparts
- Are more likely to be perceived as popular, competent, nice, and trustworthy

Even if you weren't blessed with supermodel genes (and even supermodels work at it), here are science-backed ways to improve your outward appearance and be perceived as more attractive by others:

- **Take care of your physical self:** This includes maintaining good hygiene, styling your hair, smelling good, eating well, staying as fit as possible, and getting enough sleep. The old adage applies here: you get out of it what you put into it. Do what you can to be seen as someone who makes an effort—it signals self-respect and triggers respect from others. Your demeanor, confidence, and self-assurance will increase when you feel better and show yourself self-care, which are also perceived as attractive qualities by others.
- **Dress to impress and feel confident:** Choose flattering colors, cuts, and styles of clothing for your body that make you feel great. Iron your clothes. Ensure they are clean, in good condition, and smelling fresh. Polish your shoes and make sure they are in good shape. Your outfits should make you feel confident and look your best. They don't

have to be expensive—you just have to feel awesome in them. Make sure they are comfortable enough so you don't seem ill at ease or stiff. In general, you are dressing to convey the image, standing, and identity you want to occupy in others' minds.

- **Be upbeat:** Others are typically drawn to energized, motivated, positive people. You don't have to bubble over with enthusiasm, but optimism and a positive attitude will make you appear more approachable, attractive, likable, and interesting. As you know from experience, the converse is also true: others don't like, approach, or support the wet-blanket pessimist scowling in the corner if they can avoid it.

- **Smile:** A smile is one of the simplest and most effective ways to make a good impression. It shows that you are friendly and approachable, and it increases your likability and attractiveness. People who smile genuinely and laugh easily are perceived as more comfortable, relaxed, and confident in themselves.

- **Project confidence:** Confidence is one of the most attractive qualities a person can have. When you are confident, you project an aura of self-assurance that is appealing to others. To convey this, stand and sit with good posture. Stand or sit at the front and center of any room, table, seating arrangement, or stage (when appropriate). Don't hide behind a desk, a row of other people, a table, or a podium whenever possible. Strive to see and be seen. Hold your head up high and make eye contact when appropriate. Avoid fidgeting, wringing your hands, or self-caressing, and relax your shoulders down your back. This conscious body language on your part demonstrates to others that you are confident in yourself and believe you are worthy of attention, interaction, connection, relationships, and support. Physical demonstrations of confidence and positive self-presentation cause others to perceive you as more attractive, likable, and respectable.

Control Social Comparisons

Because of the importance of social life, the brain is unfortunately naturally prone to engaging in social comparisons, evaluations, and judgments. Natural as it may be, comparisons will typically hinder your performance. Both upward and downward social comparisons have more cons than pros. In upward social comparison, you compare yourself with someone you perceive to be superior or more successful, and you come away feeling demoralized, envious, inadequate, and potentially demotivated. In downward social comparison, you compare yourself with someone you perceive to be inferior or less successful, and you may experience short-lived positive emotions, but this does little to motivate you, push you, challenge you, or better you in any way.

Even peer or lateral comparisons—when you compare yourself with someone you perceive to be equal—don't net you much value: you are likely to have neutral emotions and find little motivation or insights. What's more, in all of these cases you would typically end up feeling more distant, competitive, resentful, and disconnected than connected, empathetic, and prosocial toward the person in question—the opposite of what you should be trying to achieve in your social interactions and relationships at work.

Social comparisons of every kind also put you in a more negative, non-functional headspace for achieving your own goals. They also bear the risk of creating unhealthy competition or resentment with colleagues in the workplace. In general, our brains underestimate how much energy, effort, time, or labor other people have contributed to things compared with ourselves. What motivates you, how you ensure your own progress and productivity, and how you guarantee meeting your own goals and objectives should and will be quite different from others around you, even if they are in a similar role or position at work. Appreciate your own uniqueness, nix the comparisons, and move to the beat of your own drum. Focus on what you do better and differently than anyone else, keep your own progress scores vis-à-vis yourself, and stay in your own lane—don't try to be or do like others. This approach should help your performance in social, interpersonal, cognitive, and professional facets of your life, among others. Like the popular adage asserts: you do you, let them do them.

Choose Your Companions Wisely
You will want to think concertedly about who you spend your time with in life and at work, because they have a significant impact on you, your health, your workday performance, and your career outcomes. You come to resemble the company you keep. The more time you spend with someone, the more your mentality and cognitions—how you feel, what you think, the opinions you have, the decisions you make—will come to resemble theirs. So, choose your friends, partners, and colleagues wisely. Bad company can change the way your brain works as much as good company can. If you want to do or be better in life and career, you will have to surround yourself with the influences, relationships, and positive social interactions of those you would like to become or be more like (and not those you don't want to be more like or emulate).

You have likely heard the adage, "You are the average of the five people you spend the most time with." While you don't spend all your time at work, typically a couple of colleagues will make the top five. You don't want to start firing your friends, but you may want to have an honest assessment with yourself about whether you are proactively surrounding yourself with the type of person you would like to become.

Avoid Conflict by Right-Sizing Your Expectations of Others

Expectancy violations can be the source of challenges in our social interactions at work. When we expect something of others, we set ourselves up for the possibility of being disappointed. Disappointment results in negative emotions that, when directed at others, often result in conflict and friction between colleagues.

Here's a scenario you've probably experienced something like: you have an idea of what a colleague should have done or accomplished. They didn't do it. This disappoints you (expectancy violation). You have negative emotions that result from your disappointment, and those emotions spill over into how you treat and interact with them. They resent your treatment of them and reflect it back at you, souring your mutual interactions or relationship.

These challenges typically arise because they either don't know what you expected (and are therefore surprised or confused about why you are irritated with them), don't care (so for you to react poorly would irritate them), or don't think your expectations are reasonable (in which case they are likely to be equally frustrated with you in return). Either way, expectations create opportunity for stress, conflict, and friction between colleagues because of the opportunity for disappointment due to expectancy violations.

While you can't control what others do, there are two things that are under your direct control: (1) you can set or "right-size" your own expectations of others' actions and output; and (2) you can clearly communicate your expectations with them beforehand. Changing your own expectations of others can help you regulate your own emotions and approach, smooth your social interactions and relationships at work, and increase the chances that others either pleasantly surprise you (positive expectancy violations) or are willing to collaborate with you to do as you had hoped.

As difficult as it sometimes is—especially when resources are scarce, stress is high, or you just don't like them—for your own benefit you should strive to create as many fans and friends (and definitely not foes) as possible at work. The more positive social interactions you have with workmates, the more they will like you, compromise with you, and want to work with (not against) you, and therefore the more enjoyable and successful your work will be.

Avoid Conflict by Communicating Boundaries Proactively

Often when people are asked what caused a negative emotion, conflict, or interaction at work, the answer is "the other person." When you dig deeper, you might realize that the friction started with expectancy violations or something called boundary transgressions: you had a boundary that they impinged upon.

You have likely experienced some of the following examples: someone emailed you too late, expected too much, asked you to work on the weekend, expected you to complete more than your share, called you to task when you were underprepared, didn't give you enough information with which to make decisions, or didn't give you enough time to complete the work, etc. The list goes on, but you know it when it has happened to you. They asked, expected, directed, said, or did something that you thought was unreasonable or crossed a boundary; your negative emotions flared, and the interaction turned sour.

We sometimes assume that others know our boundaries or expectations when in fact they don't, don't remember, or weren't directly considering them. Because it isn't in their best interest, people generally won't purposefully transgress your boundaries or try to irritate you, and they often don't know or remember your boundaries or preferences. While your preferences, expectations, boundaries, and comfort zones are known implicitly to you, they are invisible to others until you voice them. And while you might think some things should go without explanation, others might not because they don't share your brain, mind, experiences, or circumstances. Other people's brains don't work like yours, and vice versa. Hanlon's razor asserts that we should not attribute to malice what can be otherwise explained by negligence, incompetence, or ignorance (often touted as "stupidity," but you get the gist).

If you let others dictate too much of your time and energy, you will find yourself feeling resentful and angry. Advocate for yourself proactively about how you would like to structure your time, energy, work, workday schedule, and interactions and how you expect to be treated. Do the same with others—inquire about their preferred working styles, needs, barriers, triggers, and boundaries. Determining boundaries and communicating them proactively (and in a prosocial way) will decrease many opportunities for friction in the workplace, allow you to perform better, and improve your social interactions at work.

11

Think

Flourishing and resilience can be promoted by specific interventions leading to a positive evaluation of oneself, a sense of continuing growth and development, the belief that life is purposeful and meaningful, satisfaction with one's relations with others, the capacity to manage effectively one's life, and a sense of self-determination.

GIOVANNI A. FAVA AND JENNY GUIDI

A **FAVORITE FITNESS** trainer of mine frequently instructs: "Whether you think you can or you can't—you're right!" This simple idea gets to the crux of this chapter: our thinking, mentality (e.g., the set of your mind, view, or outlook), and mindset (e.g., an attitude, disposition, or mood) are critical for our performance in everything, especially at work. To succeed at difficult things in life—or even at relatively easy things under difficult circumstances—we have to gather all our mental resources, gumption, and grit to motivate ourselves past the obstacles, face the challenges, and do the work.

There's good news here: being mentally strong, psychologically resilient, and cognitively flexible aren't static traits, but skills. You can control and guide your own thinking to develop a more functional, resilient, flexible mindset. Like muscles, mental abilities get stronger and more prominent when you fuel them properly and work on them deliberately and consistently. Of course, other factors like genetics, personality, upbringing, experiences, opportunity, and formal knowledge (e.g., what you learned in school) also play a role in your life and success, but none of these is thought to carry you as far or be as predictive of success as your mindset is. What you allow your mind to think as you go through the trials and tribulations of life and work is critical for how you experience, manage, and grow through them. You can deliberately rally your mental resources (bandwidth, emotional regulation, attention, focus, concentration) to build your mental capital (critical thinking skills, emotional intelligence, social cognition, coping skills, cognitive resilience) and resulting mindset (e.g., fixed, fragile, antifragile, growth, resilient).

For simplicity, the terms mentioned above—"mental capital," "mental resources," and "mindset"—will collectively be referred to as your "mindset" from now on, but the importance of the composition remains: you can build and hone the mental thoughts, attitudes, beliefs, and abilities you have with some explicit effort, just like any muscle or skill set. While there's some disagreement depending on what you read, "mindset" can be defined as an established, habitual, or characteristic set of attitudes, assumptions, self-perceptions, or beliefs that determine how you will interpret and respond to the world. It is often used in the literature interchangeably with terms like "outlook" or "mentality."

However it is defined, the helpful tenet here is this: you aren't at the mercy of your own wayward thoughts, past experiences, conditioning, current limitations, or existing mental templates. Just about everyone has room to move the needle on their mindset. Developing your mindset is possible, a developable skill, and will help you be more productive and resilient so you can perform optimally and experience greater success at work and in life. For this reason, mindset enters the MERIT framework as the capstone component lever "Think." What you allow yourself to think and how you train your own mind(set) are under your control, and intentionally working on this is critical to your professional performance and success.

We can achieve great triumphs when we put our mind to something, even if obstacles are apparent. Two thousand years ago, the Roman poet Virgil wrote in his masterpiece, the *Aeneid*, "*Mens agitat molem*": "mind moves matter" or "mind drives matter." Here I propose something more literal for our purposes: "mindset moves your (gray) matter." You can accomplish just about anything you set out to do with the right mindset in place. The work you do on yourself and within your mind will pay dividends in how you, your brain, and all its neural networks manifest and function.

As the adage asserts, successful people aren't those who never got knocked down; they are those who got up every time they were knocked down. In fact, they may be considered pros at overcoming failure before they were ever deemed successful. Something had to keep them coming back to continually try, time and again. That something is almost always an inner motivation or drive of some kind, coupled with an ability to get out of their own way—thought processes and a mindset that kept them tenacious, gritty, resilient, and confident enough in themselves to continue to try.

The ability to persevere through the adversity and obstacles we all face in our work comes down to our ongoing willingness, attitudes, and actions for developing our inner world for greater resilience and fortitude—it doesn't just happen, and we aren't just born with it. And it isn't an end or static state; it's an ongoing way of being—a deliberate, considered practice of continually adapting your thoughts, ideas, attitudes, and beliefs—that shape our perceptions, responses, and behaviors for better outcomes.

Fixed versus Growth Mindsets

In her acclaimed 2006 book *Mindset: The New Psychology of Success*, Carol Dweck described the growth mindset as the belief that one's abilities can be developed through effort and learning. She outlines that people with a growth mindset:

- Seek opportunities to learn new things
- Are persistent
- Are resilient
- Believe in working toward skill mastery
- View failures as temporary and as opportunities to learn
- Seek feedback
- Embrace challenges and often seek them
- Feel inspired and motivated by others' successes

Dweck contrasted this growth mindset with that of the fixed mindset, the belief that one's abilities are fixed and cannot grow, develop, or be changed. People with a fixed mindset:

- Avoid learning
- Give up easily
- Are rigid
- Hide flaws, don't put themselves out there

- View failures as personal flaws
- Ignore or take feedback personally
- Avoid challenges
- Feel threatened by and envious of others' successes

While clearly the less desirable of the two, a fixed mindset could be considered rational in itself: there would be no point in continuing to try or expend unbound energy toward something if your belief is that the outcomes are inevitable and you can't learn or achieve new things along the way. Further, it should be noted that neither of these mindsets is considered an end state per se, but a malleable way of being. Exhibiting one or the other mindset may be transitional, or vary by degrees, and subject to contextual cues about different circumstances. In other words, everyone has the potential for each mindset, depending on the situation, and you may find that some circumstances encourage one or the other in you.

Here's an example. I have a friend who is a gifted academician in physics research. He will test and retest hypotheses, review the minutiae of scientific studies for hours on end, tweak his equipment to infinitesimal levels of nuanced differences from one study to the next, submit and resubmit grant proposals until they are perfect and accepted. There is virtually no limit to his willingness to grow, learn, adapt, try new things, consider new perspectives, or be patient and resilient in the face of adversity or obstacles when it comes to his research. Recently, he asked to accompany me to my gym because he had hit "the big 4-0" (his term), and he claimed he felt both physically unfit of late and out of his element when it came to exercising, especially in a gym.

Evidence of his mindset for exercising there became apparent in his initial (self-directed) five-minute treadmill warmup: he was dismayed by how out of breath he was, complained that his shins hurt, and announced that he wasn't looking forward to the rest of the hour of exercise if this was "how bad he was at this already." He didn't last the whole hour. He retired to the change room early in a disgruntled mood. This despite me telling him all the things we discussed in chapter 7, Move: that this was a process; there were techniques he could learn to modify his perceived exertion; everyone has to start somewhere; one's preferred routine requires personal experimentation; fitness is varied, relative, progressive, and personal; feeling comfortable in this milieu was a matter of repeated experiences, developed familiarity, and practice, etc. Despite these suggestions, he wasn't willing to modify his exercises, engage in shorter intervals, slow down through his warmup, take more breaks, focus on his breathing, do the self-talk, be patient with the process, experiment with movement, persist, or listen to feedback.

When we had coffee together later, he chalked up his poor gym performance to genetics that were an ill fit to running, a gym space that didn't suit him personally, and a body that was "never naturally athletic anyway." He believed the outcomes he was experiencing had been inevitable from the beginning and attempts to grow were futile. I sat there quite bemused about the last two hours of my own experience: here was a person with textbook resilience and grit (e.g., growth mindset) when it came to his work and research, and with fragile or static mental attitudes (e.g., fixed mindset) when it came to his physical fitness.

This story has two important elements: (1) it's a case study example of both growth and fixed mindset thinking, attitudes, narratives, and behavior; and (2) even if one's usual approach reveals a resilient or growth mindset, anyone can slip into a fixed mindset under some circumstances—it can be fluid, relative, and contextual. This story also reminds us that our mindset is a skill set and ongoing practice that requires continuous attention, deliberate effort, and honing—you don't just wake up one day with patience, resilience, grit, and a growth orientation. When you consider your own mindset under differing circumstances or challenges you will likely find that you are more confident, willing, resilient, and flexible in some areas of your life compared with others.

A Mindset Beyond Growth Toward "Antifragility"

While having a growth mindset and being more resilient remains undoubtedly valuable, there is perhaps room to move the needle even further. In his 2012 book *Antifragile*, polymath Nassim Nicholas Taleb, a former finance trader and self-described "former professional risk-taker," described the term "antifragility" as the property of a system that increases its ability to operate and thrive with stressors, shocks, noise, or failures. Taleb differentiates between resilience (e.g., growth mindset) and antifragility. "A resilient system is one that experiences and reflects shocks and maintains itself or stays the same, whereas an antifragile system is one that experiences and absorbs shocks to become even better." Accordingly, developing a mindset toward antifragility might be considered the goal for peak workday and career performance.

Evidence of Taleb's concept of antifragility can be found in the natural world, cinema, and mythology. For example, in Greek mythology, the Hydra grows two heads every time one gets cut off—arguably getting more powerful, meaner, and more menacing the more adversity it faces. The most prized wines of the Italian Montepulciano region are said to come from the very grapevines that struggled the hardest to survive—plants thrown into rock and sand with little attention, irrigation, or fertilizer. Marvel Universe's Incredible Hulk gets angrier, larger, stronger, more aggressive, and arguably more "super" with every assault to his body. Your own muscle fibers ripped from a strenuous session at the gym will grow firmer, tighter, and more capable of exerting force in future sessions (with adequate rest in between). Your brain's neuroplastic change accelerates with traumatic or intense events, like childbirth or strife in life—the common occurrence of post-traumatic growth (not stress) after extreme challenges. Your body's ability to maintain homeostasis in many systems is often accomplished through allostasis: internal physiological change and adaptation in response to demands and stressors in life. There are a plethora of such examples in nature, history, and literature; the more something struggles, the better, stronger, and more effective it can become.

While Taleb is referring to systems in his book—not human mindset—how he describes the fragile versus antifragile system can be adapted (with some extrapolation and thanks to Dweck's concept of the fixed mindset) to the context of human mindset.

For example, an antifragile mindset might be characterized by:

- Viewing change as a growth opportunity rather than a threat; leaning into, or seeking to improve continuously through small changes

- Facing the possibility of failure head-on in the interest of "failing fast" or having answers sooner; not avoiding all possibility of failure

- Accepting some disorder, chaos, randomness, or chance in one's endeavors

- Seeking to adapt to circumstances, loosening control over anything but self
- Seeing value in taking small, calculated risks that either pay off or train you for larger ones
- Experimenting, trying new things, seeking knowledge, relishing challenges
- Questioning conventions, institutions, status quo
- Allowing intuition, flexibility, non-linear thinking, some ambiguity in decision-making
- Falling in love with process, being more flexible about outcomes

By contrast, a fragile mindset might best characterized by:

- Resisting all change; seeing all change as negative
- Avoiding the possibility of any failures
- Avoiding disorder, randomness, chance
- Seeking to control everything
- Avoiding all risk
- Avoiding experimentation, learning, novelty, challenges
- Seeking to maintain institutions and the status quo
- Being consumed by data, order, structure, rules
- Being focused on rigid outcomes—believing the end justifies the means

Because your brain is neuroplastic, what you attempt to build in your mind ultimately manifests in your brain both physically (new neurons, connections, neural networks) and functionally (new ways of thinking, developed attitudes, perspectives, thought processes, tools for coping). If you do purposeful learning, do divergent thinking such as brainstorming, try new things, or consider other perspectives, you increase your neuroplasticity, your network complexity, and the ability of those networks to facilitate or direct novel actions and behavior. Taleb's tenets suggest that the latter is necessary for a system—including your mindset and brain—to become antifragile. This holds in the neuroscience: if you attempt hard things, face challenges, attempt to learn and grow, or overcome obstacles in life, you develop the new neural connections, better allostatic response, network development, cognitive schemata, new knowledge, personal wisdom, and more functional attitudes to better deal with future challenges, stress, learning, strife, or shocks. Friedrich Nietzsche's famous aphorism reminds us of an extreme version of antifragility: "What doesn't kill me makes me stronger."

The Power of Internal Narratives

Likely the most powerful, persuasive, and relevant voice in your life is your own. Self-talk is the internal monologue that you have with yourself every day, which is the product of many things, including and especially your thought processes and mindset. Along with some others, the default mode network (DMN) is active when you aren't working, thinking, or doing anything specific, and is often referred to as "speaking to you constantly"—it's credited as the main source of that ongoing narrative voice inside your head. Self-talk is both a cause and consequence of your thoughts, feelings, attitudes, beliefs, and behaviors because it is evidence of your mindset.

Positive self-talk—speaking to yourself in a supportive, encouraging and uplifting way—can help boost your confidence, mood, optimism, engagement, openness, achievements, and productivity. When you engage in positive self-talk, you are more likely to set ambitious goals, take risks, and persevere in the face of challenges—practices of a growth or antifragile mindset. Conversely, negative self-talk—speaking to yourself in a self-critical or judgmental way—can lead to anxiety, pessimism, self-doubt, and lowered self-esteem or self-efficacy. Negative self-talk also more likely leads to setting lower expectations, avoiding challenges, and giving up too easily—all practices of a fixed or fragile mindset.

Of course, it isn't as easy as simply telling yourself to think positive thoughts. For one thing, these narratives aren't altogether under your conscious or direct control—though they can be modified with deliberate practice over time. For another, the brain is designed to help protect and prepare you for what's to come—an unknown future with many possibilities, not all of them positive. You must look at the dark side of things from time to time so you can consider the various potential events that might negatively impact you. That said, how you train and respond to your own internal narratives, self-talk, and thoughts can be deliberate and developed. You aren't at the mercy of existing internal narratives, and even if your narratives are generally functional, positive, and helpful, there is still likely room to move further toward self-talk that fosters antifragility in more contexts of your life. By developing a habit of regularly questioning and modifying your own internal narratives, you can improve your mindset and thereby productivity, performance, and well-being, in every facet of your life, especially in your work.

Optimizing Your Mindset: How-Tos

Embrace Change

Change—though inevitable and constant in life—is generally considered challenging and uncomfortable from your brain's perspective. The bigger the change, the more the discomfort. At the neural level, this is because change involves the rearranging and renegotiating of neural networks, which can feel (and is) both physically and psychologically taxing. But those who embrace change have been shown to benefit ultimately from higher levels of neuroplasticity, creativity, cognitive flexibility, adaptability, and resilience. In turn, all these qualities help prevent premature cognitive aging, negative mental states, low affect, disorder, and disease while simultaneously pumping up motivation, productivity, mental stability, allostatic response, overall health, performance, and career success.

Be Willing to Learn

As you likely know from experience, what you learned in school is often obsolete practically by the time you graduate—and it may never have been relevant to the workday anyway, given that so much of what is required of you at work is learned on the job. Companies that know this (e.g., Google and its peers) now hire for cognitive adaptability and flexibility (psychometric properties that can be tested for) and openness to learning, rather than rote, explicit, formal, or tacit knowledge (things you think you know but find hard to explain, or things you can't explain but can show you know how to do). A willingness to learn new skills, try new things, embrace the unknown, and listen to varying viewpoints increases the qualities of cognitive adaptability, flexibility, resilience, and likely antifragility.

Use the Novelty Effect to Your Advantage

Your brain is hardwired to notice and to some extent prefer things that are new or different, finding them generally interesting or exciting. The novelty effect explains that motivation, productivity, and cognitive performance may all increase initially in the face of novel stimuli, technology, people, or environments—simply because they are new. For example, productivity may go up for a few weeks in an office that had a complete interior redesign. Implementing your own novelty whenever possible allows you to take advantage of this effect. Try traveling to new places, picking up a new sport, reading a different genre of book, using a new technology, buying a new piece of furniture, wearing a new shirt, meeting new people, or eating new foods. New experiences and perspectives in every domain of your life can help you feel renewed interest and curiosity, improve your performance, and move further toward more resilient or antifragile mindsets (or at least away from fixed and fragile ones).

Experiment, Tinker, Be Curious

A willingness to experiment and be curious about how you might improve yourself, your work, your projects, or your skills also improves your mindset. Having a sense of wonder about what you are working on also increases your engagement, creativity, enjoyment, Flow, autotelic experience, motivation, and productivity. You might not want to dismantle processes or methods that are working well—no point reinventing a perfectly good wheel—but where you see an opportunity for something to be improved or more efficient, you might benefit from tinkering or experimenting because it can challenge your own thought processes, beliefs, and attitudes. At worst, you will net out at square one, but the possibility remains that you might improve something, and either way you will also learn. The saying "you either win or you learn" applies here. If you continue to do as you have always done, you will get what you have always gotten. Improvements and professional growth often come at the personal cost of discomfort, experimentation, trying new things, making mistakes, and amassing one's lessons.

Aim to Improve a Little Every Day
The Japanese concept of *kaizen* is the principle of continuous improvement of business processes and personal efficiency. The concept proposes that small, consistent, deliberate improvements each day eventually lead to otherwise unattainable, radical, or more significant improvements over time. Taleb asserts that all systems are dynamic, and change is ongoing and inevitable—therefore you might as well work with these forces than try in vain to oppose them.

You can practice *kaizen* toward an improved mindset by striving for small, deliberate improvements in your projects, skills, and processes. Let go of impatience and any need to move through the ranks faster, advance by leaps and bounds, get rich quick, or be an overnight success. Instead, focus deliberately on the more manageable things you can do each workday to get even slightly better at your tasks, job, or skills. For example, on your way to achieving your fitness goals, each week you might pick up a slightly heavier set of dumbbells (e.g., 12 lbs) than the ones you used last week (e.g., 10 lbs), such that you're building to your goal of completing your exercises with 20-pound dumbbells, but in a slow, deliberate, methodical, continual way. Such small changes might feel insignificant—and perhaps even mundane—but *kaizen* contends that every little bit counts, is cumulative, and results in major improvements naturally over time. Another helpful feature of *kaizen* is also that no magic, radical changes, or heroics are required. The only prerequisites are a willingness on your part and a small amount of concerted attention or deliberate practice toward your goals each workday.

As you consciously attempt to learn, grow, and adapt, you usher in antifragility and allostasis of mental, cognitive, and physical systems.

Question the Status Quo

Fostering your own resilient, growth, or antifragile mindset also means being willing to consider alternatives to existing ideas, attitudes, beliefs, processes, institutions, norms, or ways of doing things. While it might not serve you to wander through your workday questioning every convention, institution, or practice, there can be neural and psychological value in critically assessing some of the circumstances or processes you experience each day. Further, this questioning helps you exert your own control, choice, and agency over your work and circumstances. When you question some conventions—especially those you don't think are serving you—you sharpen your critical evaluation, thinking, and executive-functioning skills, while also potentially improving your own productivity, efficacy, and situation. It's valuable to have a conscious and objective perspective on the processes, circumstances, routines, or habits you witness or enact each day—like the fish that can suddenly see water. Challenging the inertia of institutions may help you do better and different, and therefore achieve more. No matter how well established something is, if it doesn't hold up to your assessment, or you know it isn't serving you, it doesn't deserve your time, energy, enthusiasm, or resources each day.

Here's an example from my own experience. In my corporate career, it was normal to have my days filled with meetings—daytime meetings were highly normative, expected, and institutionalized. The challenge with this was multiple (expensive, time-consuming, higher-risk for the organization), but for me meant that it left little time for the actual work during the workday—that all got done in the evenings or weekends, which squashed my work-life balance. Meeting requests came from every angle—clients, suppliers, agencies, global business units, colleagues, direct reports. When I finally questioned how well this status quo convention of a meeting culture was working for me, I made some changes. I instituted my own "no-meeting Mondays" because I noticed I was more stressed and less effective in Monday meetings when I didn't have adequate time to prepare for them, and so were my counterparts. Unless the circumstances were extenuating, I didn't agree to meetings in the mornings, either, because that's when I did my best knowledge work, which had to take priority for the business to keep rolling. I stopped taking exploratory meetings or any meeting that lacked a clear objective or formal agenda, because I noticed these were a waste of everyone's time. This policy came about by questioning conventions and experimenting to see what worked best for the business, my colleagues, and myself. To this day, when agreeing to (Tuesday to Friday afternoon-only) meetings, I look for these three things to ensure it will be a valuable use of everyone's time and resources: (1) project; e.g., a knowable, defined project, task, or event to discuss; (2) budget; e.g., allocated resources, including people and dollars; and (3) timeline; e.g., a knowable beginning, duration, and/or end date. Anytime one of these was missing, I noticed the meeting was typically unproductive and multiple people had their time wasted. By simply questioning the ubiquity of the institution of meetings in my business day, I was able to slowly but continuously improve (*kaizen*) how I used, benefited from, and engaged with them, while also protecting and optimizing my own time, balance, energy, and productivity.

Fall in Love with the Process

Another principle that is helpful for improving your mindset toward resilience or antifragility is to fall in love with the process and loosen your grip on the outcomes. When you are overly focused on the outcomes to the exclusion of the process, you are less likely to engage deeply with the process, enjoy your work, have autotelic experiences, pay adequate attention to the details, or make the requisite deliberate and continuous improvements. An overemphasis on the ends to the exclusion of the means (process) leaves you more likely to cut corners, make mistakes, dislike your work, resent the process, and sink into fixed or fragile thinking.

Too rigid a fixation on the outcomes also typically makes you too rigid in the process, which decreases your willingness or ability to learn, experiment, grow, stay curious, tinker, or roll with the inevitable punches. What's more, when you fall in love with the process (or pioneer a process you enjoy), you will almost certainly achieve the intended outcomes sooner and more fully than you would have thought—it may even more readily feel as though the outcomes in fact take care of themselves. As the old saying goes, "When you love what you do, you never work a day in your life." After all, we spend most of our workday and lived existence somewhere in the process, not standing at the finish line or final outcome. Loving the process, loosening your grip on outcomes, and engaging in something for the sake of it helps you with deliberate practice, Flow, and autotelic experiences—working with the intention of personal improvement and performance, with some level of perceived challenge, rather than immediate achievement or reward—which helps you develop your grit and growth-mindset thinking and become more antifragile.

Suppress High Control Needs, Allow Some Randomness and Risk

According to Taleb, high need for control introduces disadvantageous rigidity. Don't seek to control everything in your work or workday. Not only is it exhausting for you, but it results in diminishing marginal returns in your work efforts, and gets in the way of being able to identify potentially serendipitous opportunities. If you get too mired in rules, order, or structure, you fail to be flexible enough to see opportunities or identify new ways of doing things. Some uncertainty, ambiguity, and randomness aren't just inevitable ("the best-laid plans of mice and [wo]men often go awry"), it can also be catalyzing to your creativity, innovative thinking, learning, and problem-solving if you usher them in. Relinquishing some need for control will let you be more growth minded, open, and creative, and less thrown off in general when things don't go exactly to plan. This isn't to say that you should relinquish *all* control—you do need to keep your hands on the steering wheel and remain self-disciplined—but watch for your need for control, order, structure, or rules getting in your way or upholding staid institutions rather than truly serving you. Something to watch for: heightened need for control may originate from self-doubt, personal insecurities, anxiety, high stress, or pre-existing fixed or fragile thought patterns.

Taleb asserts that a system that accommodates smaller, more manageable, consistent risks will experience less shock when faced with larger risks or losses. Allowing yourself to take small, calculated, incremental risks and permit some randomness in your work or workday (e.g., pushing yourself outside your comfort zone just slightly in order to grow; trying a new method that might or might not work; investing in a supposedly more efficient technology at the risk of wasting some time and money) also allows you more antifragility ultimately—your efforts will either work, or you will learn, and either way you'll develop strategies for how to proceed. The idea is you build up confidence and experience by dealing with small risks, so when you are faced with larger risks, volatility, ambiguity, or uncertainty, you will be more prepared to cope, manage, and flourish through them, whatever the outcome.

Forget About Perfect

From a productivity and performance perspective, striving for perfection typically hurts more than it helps. Expecting perfection from yourself or others (expectancy violations abound) can derail an otherwise great working session, working relationship, and your own mental well-being. It is hard to perform and produce something while simultaneously judging yourself doing it. Perfectionism doesn't just ruin a person's progress, satisfaction, happiness, and autotelic experience, it also results in having a harder time identifying when something is good enough to be considered finished—which threatens break times, rest, downtime, work-life balance, and mental wellness.

Perfectionistic tendencies also typically mean projects or tasks take longer to accomplish, as these impulses may have someone mired in the details. When you don't perceive a task or project to be good enough to be finished, you won't get the valuable sense of satisfaction of a job well done and the accompanying surges of feel-good neurohormones like dopamine, norepinephrine, or serotonin. Ultimately, there are diminishing marginal returns on any given task or project as time and effort wear on, which also threatens a sense of hope, efficacy, achievement, optimism, and positive emotions. Forget about perfect and think in terms of productivity, proper ultradian cycling, self-compassion, and overall better mental and cognitive performance. Strive for progress, not perfection.

Follow Your Passion

Joseph Campbell, the creator of the Hero's Journey monomyth, coined the phrase "follow your bliss" to explain the ideal circumstance for your work—that which you enjoy and have endless energy and passion for, a track in life that is meant for you. Positive psychology scholars over the years have echoed this sentiment, encouraging people to pursue activities that they find exciting, energizing, interesting, and a good fit for their natural interests, passions, or skills. Your brain is unique, and what motivates you might be different from what motivates others. When you find what you are passionate about, you are much more likely to feel motivated to work on it, stay engaged, focus, concentrate, persevere, and ignore distractions or obstacles even if the project becomes challenging. By following your path of preferred effort and energy, you can experience less cognitive friction and challenges with concentration or focus and more natural engagement, meaning, achievement, productivity, and intrinsic reward. Take some time to reflect on the type of work you enjoy the most, what you are passionate about, and what you feel intrinsically motivated to do. Author Tony Robbins said it: "Where your focus goes, energy flows."

People also often find that where their energy (or passion) flows, the universe goes—it is as if the world conspires to help you achieve your goals when you genuinely love what you are doing. It's undoubtedly easier to develop a mindset for growth and antifragility when you are passionate about what you do or work on.

Cultivate Inner-World Awareness to Edit Negative Thinking

The only way to know what is happening in your mind—inadvertent or otherwise—is to pay attention to it all. Check-ins with yourself and practicing continuous self-awareness are the keys to success here. Only you can know what is really happening in there.

Take note of your internal narratives, monologues, thoughts, and self-talk. Then, question or edit these, especially during the Fall phase, or other times in your workday when your mind might be most prone to judgmental thinking, HALT sensations, ANTs, or thought distortions. As described in chapter 1, what you repeat to yourself becomes established in neural pathways, which can shape whole neural networks and form the basis for your mindset. Repeated thoughts become reified pathways, and these easy pathways form the basis for your beliefs, attitudes, ideas, and thoughts, spurring your reflexes, responses, and behaviors (read: mindset and resulting outcomes). Talk to yourself as you would a valued friend or colleague and seek to build yourself up instead of tearing yourself down.

Actively managing your internal mental environment and the stories you tell yourself (especially about yourself) can make real differences in your external work and life outcomes—differences that aren't attributable to genetics, inherent talent, luck, or even circumstances. What you tell yourself and let yourself believe (attitudes and beliefs) will dramatically affect what you attend to, how you perceive things, and ultimately what actions you do (or don't) feel empowered to take. Mindset is a predictor of how your reality, environment, and circumstances may ultimately manifest, because it comprises your own internal narratives, proclivities, attitudes, and ingrained beliefs. Because of this, doing the (self) work, spending the time, and taking ownership of your mental space, self-talk, narratives, and perspectives is some of the most critical work you will do toward improving your performance, productivity, well-being, work, and life. When you speak to yourself in a supportive and encouraging way—or edit wayward thoughts that don't—you are more likely to believe in your abilities, improve your confidence and self-efficacy, and achieve your goals. Over time, editing and questioning your own internal narratives will become easier, like second nature, and not something you have to actively or deliberately work on constantly. Here are three ways to manage your self-talk and develop more positive internal narratives:

- **Actively challenge negative thoughts:** When you catch yourself engaging in negative self-talk, challenge those thoughts. Ask yourself if there is any evidence to support those thoughts, as well as what evidence there is to the contrary. Replace negative thoughts with more positive and realistic ones.

- **Focus on your strengths, skills, and abilities:** Everyone has strengths and weaknesses. Focus on your strengths and how you can use them to your advantage in the current situation.

- **Celebrate your own wins:** When you achieve a goal, take the time to celebrate your success, at least with yourself, and even if it is a relatively small one. This will help you build confidence, inhibit ANTs, and develop a more productive headspace.

Managing your internal narratives must start with a willingness to do so, followed by some concerted attention to consciously engage with and edit them.

Conjure Compassion for Yourself

We all make mistakes. When you make a mistake, don't beat yourself up about it—learn from it. A mistake you learn from is not an error; it's a lesson. A mistake you don't learn from is destined to happen again. Berating yourself about things ultimately won't help you, and it can definitely hinder your mental health, motivation, stamina, productivity, and performance. Be at least as kind to yourself as you would be to someone else in that same situation. They say self-care is the new health care. Self-compassion and kindness are great practices for taking better care of yourself. The healthier, happier, and more positive your inner world is, the better your overall outer health, performance, and success.

Research shows that practicing self-kindness also helps you be kinder to others, which can help improve your likability and social standing, especially at work. Self-compassion increases your mental fortitude, resilience, cognitive flexibility, self-efficacy, confidence, and willingness to take on new challenges, learn new things, or embrace change—which are beneficial for career advancement, psychological well-being, and overall health as they represent qualities of a growth or antifragile mindset. Self-compassion also helps you be more in tune with yourself, more mindful, and in the moment, which can improve your emotional stability, mind-body connection, mental health, and happiness. Acknowledging that you are only as fallible as others—and are therefore going to make mistakes sometimes—can be very helpful for right-sizing expectations of yourself, as well as for your mental health and well-being ultimately.

Conclusion
Putting It All Together

*Learn from yesterday,
live for today, look to tomorrow,
rest this afternoon.*

CHARLES M. SCHULZ

IN THE first half of this journey, we looked at the BRAC sequence of your brain's ultradian cycle, which occurs many times a day. Stress flattens this cycle (at least perceptually—less productivity, less recuperation), and technology shortens it (at least perceptually—less attention span, ability to focus, and ability to get in the zone; more distractions). We also discussed how the typically depicted ultradian graph is a hypothetical snapshot of these rhythms, and that there can be great variability for an individual over the day, from day to day, and over the life course.

In the second portion of our journey together, we discussed the five component domains or levers of my MERIT Framework for optimizing overall workday performance. While many factors will affect your workday, work, life, performance, and success—things like culture, peers, policies, regulations, rules, and laws—my MERIT framework presents you with the elements you can typically readily, directly control. How you move, eat, rest, interact, and think are all critical overarching factors for optimizing your health, wellness, and performance—at work and in life.

A Workday Schedule Fit for Your Brain's Rhythms

Looking at your brain's optimum functioning and cycling reveals that multiple factors affect your daily energy, mood, motivation, productivity, and performance fluctuations. No ultradian cycle is necessarily identical to the last or the next, and your day proceeds according to an interaction between many cycles: ultradian, circadian, and infradian, among others. Because of these combinative factors, within any given workday you are more likely to be energetic and productive in the morning, hit a low point in the midafternoon, and gain some momentum again nearing the end of your day, perhaps for different types of tasks. This variability also lends insight into when typical, daily activities might best be scheduled or performed—as it's easier to go with your own flow than against it. While so far we've focused on optimizing the brain during each of the four ultradian phases and through each of the five domains you can control (move, eat, rest, interact, think), as we put it all together, an ideal or typical workday schedule emerges, based on your brain's natural rhythms.

- **Make hay during the magic of mornings:** Starting your day using your freshest brain on your highest-priority tasks is best practice not just because it gives you peace of mind about your day's productivity and progress early on, but also because it sets you up for positive neurochemistry and psychology that can power you through many more tasks and ultradian cycles that day. So eat those frogs for breakfast. Even night owls find they are most rested and best equipped with their daily high of motivation, stamina, willpower, and energy first thing when they wake up. Whatever your natural chronobiology, don't waste your mornings on unimportant or menial tasks—menial starts usually mean menial finishes. The longer you put off the difficult tasks on your list, the less energy, willpower, motivation, and stamina you have for them as the day wears on. In the morning, try not to dwell on others' requests, meetings, or emails. Mornings should be reserved for you to get your highest priorities and heaviest cognitive lifting done. Set and communicate your boundaries early and often, and reclaim the magic of mornings for yourself.

- **Do the four Ms in the afternoon:** During the afternoon, you are more prone to distraction, the Climbs likely feel harder and longer, the Peaks likely feel shorter and shallower, and the Falls may feel more frustrating. The afternoons might be thought of as one longer, deeper Valley. Many chronobiologists think of the afternoon as a bit of a void from a mental and cognitive perspective. Afternoons are often a challenging time for focus, concentration, productivity, or getting in the zone, and your affect, mood, motivation, and morale may dip. Perhaps take longer breaks during the afternoon than you did in the more productive morning. Use the afternoon for the four Ms: meetings, ministrations, moving, and (e)mail. Interface with others, attend a meeting, engage your social brain, have creative discussions, complete some routine administration, go outside, take a walk with a friend, or move your body. Don't berate yourself for what doesn't get done in the afternoon—highest-priority tasks should have been accomplished that morning or scheduled for the following one. Pushing yourself when your brain isn't into it will yield diminishing marginal returns, a greater stress response, and higher levels of dissatisfaction or frustration. The last things to do in the workday are (1) reflect on all the things you did and didn't get done; (2) organize the next workday so that it is ready to go, which will allow your evening and sleeping brain to prepare for what's to come the following day; and (3) transition into your relaxing evening routines that aren't too cognitively taxing so you can sleep properly.

- **Wind down in the evening:** What you do in your 5:00 to 9:00 dictates how you will perform in your following 9:00 to 5:00. Think of your evenings as preparation for your workdays. As a knowledge worker, you were likely up early grinding those mental and cognitive gears. You are probably mentally, physically, and psychologically exhausted come evening—it isn't the time for more work or expectations of yourself if you can avoid it. You need extended breaks sometime during waking hours every day (long breaks that aren't just during sleep or on weekends), and the evening is the perfect time to cease formal work, rest, and do different things. Working throughout the evenings can more readily trigger stress and affect your ability to sleep properly, which means that your productivity tomorrow may suffer. The quality of your evening and nighttime rest directly determines the productivity and quality of your work the following day. Try not to answer emails and messages all evening long, keeping recipients restless and awake as well. Take time to yourself, unwind, read, meditate, walk your dog, spend time with your family. And go to bed early—earlier than you think you must so you'll spend more time in bed than you think you need. Put together a deliberate evening routine you follow consistently that ensures you get rest, relaxation, perhaps some movement, proper nutrition, cuddles, downtime, and self-care. This will help you reclaim evenings as your own, make them as restorative as possible, ensure they don't get trampled by others' priorities, and give your brain the break it needs to be maximally productive tomorrow.

Honor Your Unique Brain, Rhythms, Self, and Process

Each of our brains, bodies, neural systems, perceptions, and ultradian cycling is unique and variable by day, circumstances, and projects. As you (re)conceptualize how you might schedule and organize your workday more effectively to optimize your performance and use your brain better, remember that we each must go with our own flow—different from others and perhaps even different from your flow yesterday. It is both experientially and conceptually true that you are more likely to be productive and perform at your peak—and less likely to experience friction, frustration, and failures—if you work *with* your brain's (and body's) natural rhythms, proclivities, and preferences, rather than against them.

You know the feeling of trying to trudge through a low point in energy, a boring initiative, an interaction your heart isn't into. It feels like pushing water uphill, and with the ever-increasing possibility of real frustration, stress, conflict, or losses. Trying to override your own natural rhythms, inclinations, or instincts typically serves to instigate stress, cause friction with others, and lay the groundwork for demotivation, anxiety, or burnout.

Instead, it pays dividends to respect what your brain and body are telling you about all things, including how and when you might exercise, nourish yourself, sleep, socialize, and think (MERIT). It is important not to ignore your various natural impulses, thresholds, and rigidities. Trust your own obstacles and diversions. Get good at listening to your own system and what it may be trying to tell you about what to do or how hard to push yourself at various times or on various tasks. Your brain and body will find ways to communicate with you, so heed these messages early and often in the interest of avoiding disease, disorder, dysfunction, or disaster. Be a curious student of your own self, mind, and systems—the outcomes you desire will develop from this willingness and developing skill.

Honor your own process, rhythms, mind, needs, obstacles, and limitations—aim for the right direction, not perfection.

As with so many things in life, use the prescriptive ideas in this book as a guide, but not as gospel: only you can decide what's right for you at every stage of your day, life, and career. Everyone wants to move the needle, improve, be better, and enact things differently (we can't expect better or different results by doing the same things perpetually), but it's important to remember that it's all a process, and you should be looking for continual progress, not perfection. "Rome wasn't built in a day," there is no sustainable "get rich quick" scheme, and no two journeys are identical. Giving yourself the proper time, resources, space, consideration, education, and downtime will ultimately increase your performance each workday and through your career. You may have heard this rhyme before: "Aim for the right direction, not for perfection."

May This "Missing Manual" Be Your Map for Further Inquiry

I wrote this book because of an internal, purpose-driven need to help people exactly like you: hard-working, high-achieving professionals who use their brain every day at work and therefore deserve better access to myth-free information and guidelines about how your brain functions and perhaps how to use it better—especially at work or during each workday.

I intended this book to be an overview of things you might like or need to know as an owner, operator, and user of your own wonderfully complex and unknowably powerful human brain. I wanted to provide you with something like the missing manual for how your brain works, or a survey course covering all the fundamental topics that you might benefit from knowing or knowing more about. There's more science to know than could be covered in these pages; there's more research to learn than can be referenced; there's much more to read than can be listed. You likely already knew a bit about some of the topics you read in these pages, though some you likely discovered, rediscovered, or want to investigate further. Either way, my hope is that these frameworks and chapters provide you with a map or overarching framework for how it all fits together and where you might go from here with your curiosities, investigations, self-discovery, and personal and professional development.

Finally, it is my wish for you that you will take whatever lessons you have read and learned through these pages; apply them in your own workday, life, and career; and also pay it forward to others you know, love, and work with. Research shows that when you learn things to teach them (as opposed to simply learning them to know them for yourself), you encode them into neural networks more deeply and broadly, to greater personal and professional avail (not to mention that of others). Teaching others what you learned improves your outcomes as much as or more than theirs: it improves your learning, knowledge, memory, practices, wellness, and professional outcomes, while also potentially benefiting others—a win all around. Here's to your amazing human brain, your optimized workday, and your most successful career.

Nutritional Reference Lists

Essential Amino Acids—Example Sources, Uses

Histidine

Where you get it: Meat, fish, poultry, nuts, seeds, whole grains

What it does: Important for growth and repair of tissues, production of histamine (involved in immune response, digestion, and sleep-wake cycles)

Isoleucine

Where you get it: Meat, fish, poultry, eggs, dairy products, legumes, nuts, seeds

What it does: Helps regulate blood sugar levels, prevents muscle loss, muscle metabolism, energy production, hemoglobin formation

Leucine

Where you get it: Meat, fish, poultry, dairy products, soy products, beans, legumes

What it does: Stimulates muscle protein synthesis, aids in muscle repair, regulates blood sugar levels

Lysine

Where you get it: Meat, fish, poultry, dairy products, legumes, quinoa

What it does: Helps produce carnitine, a molecule involved in energy metabolism; important for protein synthesis, enzyme and hormone production, calcium absorption, immune function

Methionine

Where you get it: Meat, fish, poultry, eggs, dairy products, Brazil nuts, seeds

What it does: Helps produce S-adenosylmethionine, a molecule involved in mood regulation and cognitive function; synthesis of proteins and important molecules, aids in detoxification and metabolism

Phenylalanine

Where you get it: Meat, fish, poultry, eggs, dairy products, soy products, nuts, seeds

What it does: Helps produce tyrosine; is a precursor to dopamine, norepinephrine, and epinephrine; involved in the production of thyroid hormones

Threonine

Where you get it: Meat, fish, poultry, eggs, dairy products, beans, lentils

What it does: Helps produce collagen and elastin (proteins involved in brain structure and function), immune function, fat metabolism

Tryptophan

Where you get it: Turkey, chicken, salmon, tofu, milk, cheese, yogurt, eggs, nuts, seeds

What it does: Helps produce serotonin (a neurotransmitter involved in mood, sleep, and appetite), involved in niacin (vitamin B3) production

Valine

Where you get it: Meat, fish, poultry, dairy products, soy products, beans, legumes

What it does: Helps produce glutamate (a neurotransmitter involved in learning and memory), involved in muscle metabolism, tissue repair, and energy production

Carbohydrates—Example Sources, Uses

Glucose

Where you get it: Fruits, vegetables, grains, dairy products

What it does: Is a primary source of energy for cells

Fructose

Where you get it: Fruits, processed foods

What it does: Sweetens foods

Galactose

Where you get it: Dairy products, avocados, beets

What it does: Is essential for the development of the brain and nervous system

Sucrose
Where you get it: Table sugar, processed foods
What it does: Sweetens food

Lactose
Where you get it: Milk and other dairy products
What it does: Is a primary source of energy for infants and young children

Maltose
Where you get it: Grains, cereals, processed foods
What it does: Sweetens food

Sugar Alcohols
Where you get it: Artificial sweeteners (e.g., aspartame, saccharin, acesulfame)
What it does: Sweetens foods artificially

Sugar Syrups
Where you get it: Corn syrup, high-fructose corn syrup, agave
What it does: Sweetens processed foods and beverages

Dietary Fats—Example Sources, Effects

Monounsaturated Fats
Consumption: Good in moderation
Where you get it: Olive oil, avocados, nuts, seeds
What it does for your health: Helps lower low-density lipoprotein (LDL) cholesterol (bad) and raise high-density lipoprotein (HDL) cholesterol (good)

What it does for your brain: May improve cognitive function and reduce the risk of Alzheimer's disease, dementia

Polyunsaturated Fats

Consumption: Good in moderation

Where you get it: Fatty fish such as salmon, tuna, mackerel; some vegetable oils

What it does for your health: Helps lower triglycerides

What it does for your brain: May improve mood and reduce the risk of depression

Omega-3 Fatty Acids

Consumption: Good in moderation

Where you get it: Fatty fish such as salmon, tuna, mackerel

What it does for your health: May reduce inflammation, lower the risk of heart disease, and improve cognitive function

What it does for your brain: May improve memory, reduce the risk of Alzheimer's disease or dementia

Trans Fats

Consumption: Limit or avoid intake

Where you get it: Fried foods, processed foods, margarine

What it does for your health: Raises LDL cholesterol (bad) and lowers HDL cholesterol (good)

What it does for your brain: May increase the risk of Alzheimer's disease, dementia, depression

Saturated Fats

Consumption: Limit or avoid intake

Where you get it: Beef, lamb, pork, organ meats, processed meats, cream, cheese, ice cream, tropical oils such as palm oil, coconut oil

What it does for your health: Raises LDL (bad) cholesterol

What it does for your brain: May increase the risk of cognitive decline

Essential Micronutrients—Example Sources, Effects

VITAMINS

Vitamin A

Where you get it: Orange and yellow fruits and vegetables, leafy green vegetables, dairy products

Color: Orange, yellow, green

Function in the brain: Essential for vision, cell growth, and immune function

Vitamin B1 (thiamin)

Where you get it: Beef, legumes, nuts, seeds

Color: Reddish-brown

Function in the brain: Involved in energy production and neurotransmitter function

Vitamin B2 (riboflavin)

Where you get it: Milk, eggs, leafy green vegetables, meat, poultry, fish

Color: Yellow, orange

Function in the brain: Involved in energy production and cell growth and repair

Vitamin B3 (niacin)

Where you get it: Meat, poultry, fish, eggs, legumes, nuts, seeds

Color: Pale yellow

Function in the brain: Involved in energy production and cell signaling

Vitamin B5 (pantothenic acid)

Where you get it: Meat, fish, eggs, dairy products, legumes, nuts, seeds

Color: Colorless

Function in the brain: Involved in energy production, hormone synthesis, and neurotransmitter function

Vitamin B6 (pyridoxine)

Where you get it: Meat, fish, eggs, dairy products, legumes, nuts, seeds

Color: Colorless

Function in the brain: Involved in amino acid metabolism, neurotransmitter function, and mood regulation

Vitamin B7 (biotin)

Where you get it: Eggs, liver, leafy green vegetables, legumes, nuts, seeds

Color: Colorless

Function in the brain: Involved in energy production, fatty acid metabolism, and amino acid metabolism

Vitamin B9 (folate)

Where you get it: Leafy green vegetables, legumes, nuts, seeds

Color: Dark green

Function in the brain: Involved in DNA synthesis, cell division

Vitamin B12 (cobalamin)

Where you get it: Meat, fish, eggs, dairy products

Color: Reddish-purple

Function in the brain: Involved in nerve function, DNA synthesis, red blood cell formation

Vitamin C

Where you get it: Citrus fruits, strawberries, bell peppers, broccoli

Color: Orange, yellow, green

Function in the brain: Antioxidant, involved in collagen synthesis, immune function

Vitamin D

Where you get it: Fatty fish such as salmon, egg yolks, fortified milk

Color: Yellowish-white

Function in the brain: Involved in calcium absorption, bone health, immune function

Vitamin E

Where you get it: Nuts, seeds, leafy green vegetables

Color: Orange, yellow, green

Function in the brain: Antioxidant, involved in immune function, cell protection

Vitamin K

Where you get it: Leafy green vegetables, broccoli, brussels sprouts

Color: Dark green

Function in the brain: Involved in blood clotting, bone health

MINERALS

Calcium

Where you get it: Dairy products, leafy green vegetables, fortified foods

Color: White

Function: Involved in bone health, muscle function, and nerve transmission

Chloride

Where you get it: Salt

Color: White

Function: Involved in fluid balance, component of digestive juices, muscle function

Chromium

Where you get it: Meat, whole grains, nuts, seeds

Color: Gray or white

Function: Involved in blood sugar regulation, enhances insulin action, involved in carbohydrate, fat, and protein metabolism

Copper

Where you get it: Meat, seafood, nuts, seeds, legumes

Color: Brown or red

Function: Involved in energy production, connective tissue formation, immune function; role in iron metabolism, formation of red blood cells; helps maintenance of healthy bones, blood vessels, nerves

Fluoride

Where you get it: Treated water, black tea, green tea, poultry, seafood, dental products

Color: Pale yellow or white

Function: Involved in dental health, preventing tooth decay

Iodine

Where you get it: Seafood, dairy products, iodized salt

Color: Purple or brown

Function: Involved in thyroid hormone production, helps regulate metabolism

Iron

Where you get it: Meat, fish, beans, lentils, fortified cereals

Color: Red or brown

Function: Involved in oxygen transport, formation of hemoglobin, energy production

Magnesium

Where you get it: Nuts, seeds, leafy green vegetables, whole grains

Color: Silvery-white

Function: Involved in over 300 biochemical reactions in the body, including muscle and nerve function, enzyme activity, blood sugar control, and blood pressure regulation

Manganese

Where you get it: Nuts, seeds, leafy green vegetables, whole grains

Color: Pale pink

Function: Involved in enzyme activity, bone formation and health, blood sugar control, blood clotting, reduces inflammation

Molybdenum

Where you get it: Legumes, nuts, seeds, whole grains

Color: Grayish-white

Function: Involved in enzyme activity and sulfur metabolism

Phosphorus

Where you get it: Meat, fish, dairy products, whole grains

Color: Yellowish-white

Function: Involved in energy production, builds bone and teeth, bone health, cell signaling, involved in energy production

Potassium

Where you get it: Bananas, potatoes, leafy green vegetables, dairy products

Color: White

Function: Involved in fluid balance, muscle function, muscle contractions, nerve transmission

Selenium

Where you get it: Seafood, meat, nuts, seeds

Color: Grayish-black

Function: Antioxidant involved in immune function and thyroid hormone metabolism, DNA synthesis, protection from oxidative damage, protection from infection

Sodium

Where you get it: Salt

Color: White

Function: Involved in fluid balance, muscle function, nerve transmission, regulating blood pressure, blood volume

Sulfur

Where you get it: Meat, eggs, fish, dairy, cruciferous vegetables, asparagus, kale, beans, nuts, seeds

Color: Pale yellow

Function: Involved in cellular function and structure

Zinc

Where you get it: Meat, poultry, seafood, beans, lentils, nuts, seeds

Color: Silvery-white

Function: Involved in enzyme activity, wound healing, immune function, DNA synthesis, and cell division

Major Neurochemicals—Typical Functions and Agonists

Serotonin: The Happy Hormone

What it does: Mood, sense of well-being, contentedness, happiness, digestion, sleep cycles

Activities that increase it: Light exposure, exercise, meditation, healthy microbiota

Foods that increase it: Tryptophan agonists like salmon, turkey, tofu

Dopamine: The Get-it-Done, Reward Hormone

What it does: Movement, motivation, emotions, pleasure, addiction regulation, behavioral repetition

Activities that increase it: Physical activity, repeating behaviors, movement, addictive behavior

Foods that increase it: Tyrosine agonists like turkey, beef, eggs, dairy, soy, green tea

Noradrenaline: The Concentration Hormone

What it does: Focus, alertness, response to environmental stimuli, vasoconstriction, blood pressure, Flow, fight-or-flight reaction

Activities that increase it: High stimuli environments, physical activity, engaging in Flow activities

Foods that increase it: Phenylalanine, tyrosine agonists like bananas, beans, legumes, chicken, cheese, fish, oatmeal

Adrenaline: The Fight-or-Flight Hormone

What it does: Response to stressful situations, heart rate and blood pressure, sweating, alertness, situational awareness, readiness for physical action

Activities that increase it: Any situation you find stressful

Foods that increase it: Adrenaline agonists include white flour, sugar, refined carbs, refined foods, alcohol, caffeine if consumed in excess; antagonists include beta-blockers like magnesium, potassium, garlic, red yeast rice, fish, berries

GABA: The Stay-Calm-and-Focus Neurotransmitter

What it does: Firing nerves, feelings of calmness, attention and focus, motor control and coordination, vision

Activities that increase it: Meditation, yoga, deep breathing

Foods that increase it: Agonists of glutamic acid; 5-HTP; theanine like tea, berries, beans, bananas, potatoes, tomatoes, vitamin B6, lentils, wild fish, broccoli, brussels sprouts, spinach, nuts, beef, fermented foods

Acetylcholine: The Thinking-Learning-Knowledge Hormone

What it does: Thinking, learning, knowledge, memory; attention, awakening, alertness; muscular activity, and readiness for action

Activities that increase it: Meditation, yoga, deep breathing, learning

Foods that increase it: Cholinergic foods; acetyl coenzyme agonists like eggs, soy, chicken breast, cod, shiitake mushrooms, quinoa, milk, broccoli, brussels sprouts, caffeine

Glutamate: The Learning and Memory Neurotransmitter

What it does: Learning, knowledge, memory; synaptic interaction and nerve contacts

Activities that increase it: Exercise, meditation, yoga, learning

Foods that increase it: GABA agonists; 5-HTP; theanine sources like cheese, beets, asparagus, seaweed, eggs, mushrooms, soy, fermented foods, bone broth

Endorphins: The Feel-Good Hormone

What it does: Sense of well-being, euphoria, excitement, positive emotions, down regulates pain

Activities that increase it: Exercise, sex and orgasm, exciting events, laughing, acupuncture, yoga

Foods that increase it: Agonists of all 20 amino acids like peppers, spicy foods, strawberries, meat, seafood, dairy products, eggs, soy, cocoa, vanilla bean, probiotics

Enkephalins: The Painkiller Hormone

What it does: Pain mediation, perception, cessation, mood enhancer

Activities that increase it: Exercise, orgasm, acupuncture

Foods that increase it: Peptide agonists like protein, meat, seafood, dairy, soy, probiotics

Oxytocin: The Love Hormone

What it does: Feelings of trust; sexual arousal; relationship building; feelings of liking, love, kinship; relaxation; uterine contractions during menstrual cycle; childbirth; breastfeeding; stress; cortisol; blood pressure; heart rate

Activities that increase it: Exercise, orgasm, childbirth, menstruation, cuddling, hugging, making new friends, engaging with someone you find attractive

Foods that increase it: Eggs, bananas, salmon, nuts, beans, legumes

Acknowledgements

'M DEDICATING this book to my husband. His patience with the long (and sometimes expensive!) book-writing process has been nothing short of magnificent—as he is in all domains of his work and life. Thank you, Adam, you're the greatest.

I dedicate this book also to—and would like to thank sincerely—my parents, Bill and Sandy, for putting me in the world to begin with, and being such kind, caring, loving individuals. Additional sincerest and enormous thanks also to my mother for her editing, advising, and help with this book—she's read every iteration of the manuscript over the course of a couple of years and seen these words almost as many times as I have. Thank you, Mum, I couldn't have written this book without you (for many reasons). Thanks also to my late grandmother Mary, a lifelong learner and educator herself, an encouragement for me in my work and studies, and who always felt like my greatest champion growing up. To my Grandpa Winegard, an inspirational man, educator, and mentor to me and others—thank you for all you did in your life, for me, and what you represent. You are missed. Thanks to my extended family, my husband's family, and the many friends who bought this book on pre-order, encouraged me as I wrote, and were helpful sounding boards along the way—you know who you are, and I thank you sincerely.

The book-writing process is both lengthy and plural: authors always have help, and so did I. To thank everyone involved directly or indirectly is perhaps impossible, so if I've left anyone out, my apologies—any omissions were inadvertent.

Thank you to the Page Two publishing team of Trena, Adrineh, James, Peter, Fiona, Meghan, Melissa, Carmen, and Rony, among many others. I'd been through many possible publication homes for this book—thank you for being the ultimate champions, helpers, ushers, and safe landing spot for this project. You were all critical in getting this book into the hands of working professionals who can benefit most from it.

Thank you to a special group of people, composed of colleagues, mentors, and friends who I think of in my head as "champions"—in their own right for sure, as well as of me. Everyone needs a champion from time or time, and you've all served as mine. To Dr. Ashwin Joshi for your championship, aid, guidance, kindness, and generosity of spirit—you're a venerable professional and human, and an inspiration to me. To Dr. Tracy Vaillancourt, a guiding light in my mind and studies, even from an early age—a true champion in her own right, of me, and of many others without a voice. To Theresa Beenken, a wonderful colleague, friend, and mentor whose even-keel and thoughtful insights have often been a soothing balm in this business and who readers can thank for this book ("You definitely have a book in you, Brynn!"). To Jennifer Clarkson, may she rest in peace, my original champion and usher into the world of professional speaking—"my first agent" (though that doesn't nearly cover it). She was an angel for me on earth as she is now in heaven. To Cathy

Hayes, Brandon Lamb, Hal Eckensweiler, Sawa D'Souza, Jeanne-Marie Robillard, Emilie Morvan, Hayley Citron, Natasha Daneman, Jeff Lohnes, and Christy de Couto for being my "home in this business." I can't thank each of you enough for all of your individual and collective collegiality, insights, and collaborations over the years. To Effi Lipsman, you're a wonderful friend and colleague, and, unbeknownst to you, the avatar for this book—in a sense, I wrote this book for you (and the other insightful, front-row high-achievers just like you). Some people do heavy lifting in the background, give support freely, raise spirits without trying, help for the sake of it, and never ask for acknowledgement or thanks. To Sanjay Dhebar, Lynn Petruzzella, Christopher Psutka, Crystal Soojeong Lim, Sara Nancoo, Elana Kentner, Dr. Kathleen Rodenburg, Catherine Statton, Dr. Andrea Merrill—thank you for being colleagues, champions, and friends along the way.

Finally, to the audience members, students, clients, and readers who give my work and life continual purpose and joy: thank you sincerely for showing up, reading, learning, asking good questions, staying curious, and paying it forward—we are all better when you are.

Notes

GIVEN THE breadth of topic matter and space constraints, it wasn't possible to include every potentially relevant citation for this work. The selected notes are intended to give necessary credit and be of interest to you (the non-academic, non-neuroscientist working professional) for further investigation or reading. Should you have questions about citations or are interested in a particular topic for further reading, please see the following section or feel free to reach out to us (DrBrynn.com/contact).

Preface

"... the most impressive, complex technology." Pang, D. K. F. (2023, September 2). The staggering complexity of the human brain. *Psychology Today*. psychologytoday.com/us/blog/consciousness-and-beyond/202309/the-staggering-complexity-of-the-human-brain

"... 'black box' concept of the brain." Gerner, M. (1981). The brain and behavior: Casting light into the "black-box." *Psychological Reports*, 49(2), 511–518. doi.org/10.2466/pr0.1981.49.2.511

Chapter 1: Marvel, Masterpiece, Misfit

"... HP monstrosity named Frontier." Rajaraman, V. (2023). Frontier—World's first ExaFLOPS supercomputer. *Resonance*, 28(4), 567–576. doi.org/10.1007/s12045-023-1583-7

"... your brain's phenomenal capacity." Gardner, H. E. (2011). *Frames of mind: The theory of multiple intelligences*. Basic Books.

291

"... has relatively limited bandwidth." Marois, R., & Ivanoff, J. (2005). Capacity limits of information processing in the brain. *Trends in Cognitive Sciences*, *9*(6), 296–305. doi.org/10.1016/j.tics.2005.04.010

"... experts estimate that as much as one percent." Pradeep, A. K. (Ed.). (2012). *The buying brain: Secrets for selling to the subconscious mind.* Wiley. doi.org/10.1002/9781119200079

"... 128 billion neurons." Barrett, L. F. (2021). *Seven and a half lessons about the brain.* Mariner Books.

"... by approximately age 25 your brain is thought to be." Arain, M., Haque, M., Johal, L., Mathur, P., Nel, W., Rais, A., Sandhu, R., & Sharma, S. (2013). Maturation of the adolescent brain. *Neuropsychiatric Disease and Treatment*, 449–461. doi.org/10.2147/ndt.s39776

"... sometimes these networks are highly diversified and spread out." Duffau, H. (2018). The error of Broca: From the traditional localizationist concept to a connectomal anatomy of human brain. *Journal of Chemical Neuroanatomy*, *89*, 73–81. doi.org/10.1016/j.jchemneu.2017.04.003

"... scaffold up whole networks because it is plastic." Costandi, M. (2016). *Neuroplasticity.* MIT Press. doi.org/10.7551/mitpress/10499.001.0001

"... For a neuron to survive." Pfisterer, U., & Khodosevich, K. (2017). Neuronal survival in the brain: Neuron type-specific mechanisms. *Cell Death and Disease*, *8*(3), e2643. doi.org/10.1038/cddis.2017.64

"... your plastic brain is constantly learning." Sur, M., & Rubenstein, J. L. R. (2005). Patterning and plasticity of the cerebral cortex. *Science*, *310*(5749), 805–810. doi.org/10.1126/science.1112070

"... your brain is a survival tool." Barkow, J. H., Cosmides, L., & Tooby, J. (1992). *The adapted mind: Evolutionary psychology and the emergence of culture.* Oxford University Press.

"... like mental shortcuts." Rumelhart, D. E. (2017). Schemata: The building blocks of cognition. In R. J. Spiro, B. C. Bruce, & W. F. Brewer (Eds.), *Theoretical issues in reading comprehension* (pp. 33–58). Routledge. doi.org/10.4324/9781315107493-4

"... allow us to operate largely on autopilot." Kahneman, D. (2011). *Thinking, fast and slow.* Farrar, Straus and Giroux.

"... and default mode network." Raichle, M. E. (2015). The brain's default mode network. *Annual Review of Neuroscience*, *38*(1), 433–447. doi.org/10.1146/annurev-neuro-071013-014030

"... one factory owner named Sir John Lubbock." Pang, A. S. K. (2016). *Rest: Why you get more done when you work less.* Basic Books.

"... twenty-first-century knowledge work is not nineteenth-century factory work." Pink, D. H. (2011). *Drive: The surprising truth about what motivates us.* Riverhead Books.

"... in an extended block of time in the middle of the day." Pang, A. S. K. (2016). *Rest: Why you get more done when you work less.* Basic Books.

"... its schedule for work should be, too." Roenneberg, T. (2012). *Internal time: Chronotypes, social jet lag, and why you're so tired.* Harvard University Press.

Chapter 2: The Rhythm of Your Brain

"... You have probably heard of the circadian rhythm." Kleitman, N. (1949). Biological rhythms and cycles. *Physiological Reviews*, 29(1), 1–30. doi.org/10.1152/physrev.1949.29.1.1

"... Kleitman's sleep research revealed." Kleitman, N. (1982). Basic rest-activity cycle—22 years later. *Sleep*, 5(4), 311–317. doi.org/10.1093/sleep/5.4.311

"... followed a shorter cycling in the brain." Kleitman, N. (1987). *Sleep and wakefulness.* University of Chicago Press.

"... This basic rest-activity cycle." Loehr, J., & Schwartz, T. (2003). *The power of full engagement: Managing energy, not time, is the key to high performance and personal renewal.* Free Press.

"... variable levels of attention, energy, and alertness." Spiga, F., Pooley, J., Russell, G., & Lightman, S. L. (2017). Ultradian rhythms. In G. Fink (Ed.), *Handbook of stress series: Vol. 2. Stress: Neuroendocrinology and neurobiology* (pp. 429–437). Academic Press. doi.org/10.1016/b978-0-12-802175-0.00043-7

"... constantly being adjusted according to variable system resources." Barrett, L. F. (2021). *Seven and a half lessons about the brain.* Mariner Books.

"... creates rhythmic patterns of electrical activity." Da Silva, F. L. (1991). Neural mechanisms underlying brain waves: From neural membranes to networks. *Electroencephalography and Clinical Neurophysiology*, 79(2), 81–93. doi.org/10.1016/0013-4694(91)90044-5

"... basics about your own neural activity." Bear, M. F., Connors, B. W., & Paradiso, M. A. (2016). *Neuroscience: Exploring the brain* (4th ed.). Wolters Kluwer.

"... constantly bombarded with distractions." Becker, L., Kaltenegger, H. C., Nowak, D., Weigl, M., & Rohleder, N. (2022). Physiological stress in response to multitasking and work interruptions: Study protocol. *PLOS ONE*, *17*(2), e0263785. doi.org/10.1371/journal.pone.0263785

"... which ultradian phase we are in." Harper, D. G., Tornatzky, W., & Miczek, K. A. (1996). Stress induced disorganization of circadian and ultradian rhythms: Comparisons of effects of surgery and social stress. *Physiology & Behavior*, *59*(3), 409–419. doi.org/10.1016/0031-9384(95)02012-8

"... technology can also disrupt the natural rhythm." Cajochen, C., Frey, S., Anders, D., Späti, J., Bues, M., Pross, A., Mager, R., Wirz-Justice, A., & Stefani, O. (2011). Evening exposure to a light-emitting diodes (LED)-backlit computer screen affects circadian physiology and cognitive performance. *Journal of Applied Physiology: Respiratory, Environmental, and Exercise Physiology*, *110*(5), 1432–1438. doi.org/10.1152/japplphysiol.00165.2011

"... people's attention spans decrease." Greenfield, S. (2015). *Mind change: How digital technologies are transforming our mental lives.* Random House.

"... technology can overwhelm and disrupt." Gazzaley, A., & Rosen, L. D. (2017). Are you a self-interrupter? *Nautilus*, 16–18. nautil.us/are-you-a-self_interrupter-236623

"... resulting functioning of the brain." Golkar, A., Johansson, E., Kasahara, M., Osika, W., Perski, A., & Savic, I. (2014). The influence of work-related chronic stress on the regulation of emotion and on functional connectivity in the brain. *PLOS ONE*, *9*(9), e104550. doi.org/10.1371/journal.pone.0104550

"... productivity purgatory or limbo." Lightman, S. L. (2008). The neuroendocrinology of stress: A never ending story. *Journal of Neuroendocrinology*, *20*(6), 880–884. doi.org/10.1111/j.1365-2826.2008.01711.x

"... affecting cognitive function, emotional regulation, and overall health." Siegrist, J. (2008). Chronic psychosocial stress at work and risk of depression: Evidence from prospective studies. *European Archives of Psychiatry and Clinical Neuroscience*, *258*(S5), 115–119. doi.org/10.1007/s00406-008-5024-0

"... It has been linked to the development of anxiety." McGonagle, K. A., & Kessler, R. C. (1990). Chronic stress, acute stress, and depressive symptoms. *American Journal of Community Psychology*, *18*(5), 681–706. doi.org/10.1007/bf00931237

"... Actually, some stress is highly functional." Mattson, M. P., & Calabrese, E. J. (2009). Hormesis: What it is and why it matters. In M. Mattson & E. J. Calabrese (Eds.), *Hormesis: A revolution in biology, toxicology, and medicine* (pp. 1–13). Humana Press. doi.org/10.1007/978-1-60761-495-1_1

"... Yerkes-Dodson law." Teigen, K. H. (1994). Yerkes-Dodson: A law for all seasons. *Theory & Psychology*, *4*(4), 525–547. doi.org/10.1177/0959354394044004

"... some stress is useful." Zimmermann, A., Bauer, M. A., Kroemer, G., Madeo, F., & Carmona-Gutierrez, D. (2014). When less is more: Hormesis against stress and disease. *Microbial Cell*, *1*(5), 150–153. doi.org/10.15698/mic2014.05.148

"... can be converted into functional stress." Fabritius, F., & Hagemann, H. W. (2017). *The leading brain: Powerful science-based strategies for achieving peak performance*. Penguin Random House.

"... downtime will ultimately *increase* your output." Pang, A. S. K. (2016). *Rest: Why you get more done when you work less*. Basic Books.

"... Pomodoro Technique." Cirillo, F. (2018). *The Pomodoro technique: The acclaimed time-management system that has transformed how we work*. Currency.

"... Focusing on the here and now." Di Nocera, F., De Piano, R., Rullo, M., & Tempestini, G. (2023). A lack of focus, not task avoidance, makes the difference: Work routines in procrastinators and non-procrastinators. *Behavioral Sciences*, *13*(4), 333. doi.org/10.3390/bs13040333

"... Avoiding distractions and facilitating focus." Moran, A. P. (2016). *The psychology of concentration in sport performers: A cognitive analysis*. Psychology Press. doi.org/10.4324/9781315784946

"... technology is a wonderful tool for workday productivity." Steinhorst, C. (2017). *Can I have your attention? Inspiring better work habits, focusing your team, and getting stuff done in the constantly connected workplace*. Wiley.

"... Similar to the concept of deliberate practice." Duckworth, A. L., Peterson, C., Matthews, M. D., & Kelly, D. R. (2007). Grit: Perseverance and passion for long-term goals. *Journal of Personality and Social Psychology*, *92*(6), 1087–1101. doi.org/10.1037/0022-3514.92.6.1087

"... Being more deliberate and present." Coo, C., & Salanova, M. (2017). Mindfulness can make you happy-and-productive: A mindfulness controlled trial and its effects on happiness, work engagement, and performance. *Journal of Happiness Studies*, *19*(6), 1691–1711. doi.org/10.1007/s10902-017-9892-8

"... Short periods spent being more deliberate." Kersemaekers, W., Rupprecht, S., Wittmann, M., Tamdjidi, C., Falke, P., Donders, R., Speckens, A., & Kohls, N. (2018). A workplace mindfulness intervention may be associated with improved psychological well-being and productivity: A preliminary field study in a company setting. *Frontiers in Psychology*, *9*, 195. doi.org/10.3389/fpsyg.2018.00195

"... Some people will engage in attempts to multitask." Peifer, C., & Zipp, G. (2019). All at once? The effects of multitasking behavior on flow and subjective performance. *European Journal of Work and Organizational Psychology*, *28*(5), 682–690. doi.org/10.1080/1359 432x.2019.1647168

"... Prioritization can be tricky." Covey, S. R. (2022). *The 7 habits of highly effective people: The infographics edition*. Mango Media.

"... list everything you want to accomplish." Tien, S. (2023, November 14). *5 benefits of checklists: Why checklists are more important than you think*. PixieBrix. pixiebrix.com/blog/5-benefits-of-checklists-why-checklists-are-more-important-than-you-think

"... having something to look forward to." Luo, Y., Chen, X., Qi, S., You, X., & Huang, X. (2018). Well-being and anticipation for future positive events: Evidences from an fMRI study. *Frontiers in Psychology*, *8*, 2199. doi.org/10.3389/fpsyg.2017.02199

"... The psychology of positive anticipation." D'Argembeau, A., Stawarczyk, D., Majerus, S., Collette, F., Van der Linden, M., Feyers, D., Maquet, P., & Salmon, E. (2010). The neural basis of personal goal processing when envisioning future events. *Journal of Cognitive Neuroscience*, *22*(8), 1701–1713. doi.org/10.1162/jocn.2009.21314

"... merits and methods of goal setting for achievement." Locke, E. A., & Latham, G. P. (2006). New directions in goal-setting theory. *Current Directions in Psychological Science*, *15*(5), 265–268. doi.org/10.1111/j.1467-8721.2006.00449.x

"... Being aware of yourself physically and mentally." Yan, Z., Chiu, M. M., & Ko, P. Y. (2020). Effects of self-assessment diaries on academic achievement, self-regulation, and motivation. *Assessment in Education*, *27*(5), 562–583. doi.org/10.1080/0969 594x.2020.1827221

Chapter 3: The Climb

"... During this phase, the brain activates the various systems." Shannahoff-Khalsa, D. (2007). Psychophysiological states: The ultradian dynamics of mind–body interactions. *International Review of Neurobiology*, *80*, 1–220. doi.org/10.1016/s0074-7742(07)80001-8

"... The Climb features increased heart rate, blood pressure." Peters, A., Schweiger, U., Pellerin, L., Hubold, C., Oltmanns, K., Conrad, M., Schultes, B., Born, J., & Fehm, H. (2004). The selfish brain: Competition for energy resources. *Neuroscience and Biobehavioral Reviews*, *28*(2), 143–180. doi.org/10.1016/j.neubiorev.2004.03.002

"... neurochemical cocktail that helps us build alertness." Baghdoyan, H. A., & Lydic, R. (2012). The neurochemistry of sleep and wakefulness. In S. T. Brady, G. J. Siegel, R. W. Albers, & D. L. Price (Eds.), *Basic neurochemistry* (8th ed., pp. 982–999). Academic Press. doi.org/10.1016/b978-0-12-374947-5.00057-2

"... neurotransmitters that are typically active." Merica, H., & Fortune, R. D. (2004). State transitions between wake and sleep, and within the ultradian cycle, with focus on the link to neuronal activity. *Sleep Medicine Reviews*, *8*(6), 473–485. doi.org/10.1016/j.smrv.2004.06.006

"... and some of their effects." Bear, M. F., Connors, B. W., & Paradiso, M. A. (2016). *Neuroscience: Exploring the brain* (4th ed.). Wolters Kluwer.

"... to more alert and excited beta waves." Chapotot, F., Jouny, C., Muzet, A., Buguet, A., & Brandenberger, G. (2000). High frequency waking EEG. *NeuroReport*, *11*(10), 2223–2227. doi.org/10.1097/00001756-200007140-00032

"... difficulty concentrating." Moran, A. (2012). Concentration: Attention and performance. In S. M. Murphy (Ed.), *The Oxford handbook of sport and performance psychology* (pp. 117–130). Oxford Academic. doi.org/10.1093/oxfordhb/9780199731763.013.0006

"... associated with increased energy expenditures." Schölvinck, M. L., Howarth, C., & Attwell, D. (2008). The cortical energy needed for conscious perception. *NeuroImage*, *40*(4), 1460–1468. doi.org/10.1016/j.neuroimage.2008.01.032

"... Identify your own task-avoidance behaviors." Tracy, B. (2017). *Eat that frog! 21 great ways to stop procrastinating and get more done in less time.* Berrett-Koehler Publishers.

"... everyone has their own ways of procrastinating." Ng, J. C. Y., Shao, I. Y. T., & Liu, Y. (2016). This is not what I wanted. *Employee Relations*, *38*(4), 466–486. doi.org/10.1108/er-12-2015-0216

"... recognizing these task-avoidance behaviors." Covey, S. R. (2022). *The 7 habits of highly effective people: The infographics edition*. Mango Media.

"... monitor yourself when you are procrastinating." Weiss, M. R. (1987). Applied sport psychology: Personal growth to peak performance. *Sport Psychologist*, *1*(1), 83-87. doi.org/10.1123/tsp.1.1.83

"... into many smaller, more manageable pieces." Cheng, J., Teevan, J., Iqbal, S. T., & Bernstein, M. S. (2015, April). Break it down: A comparison of macro-and microtasks. In *Proceedings of the 33rd annual ACM conference on human factors in computing systems* (pp. 4061-4064). Association for Computing Machinery. doi.org/10.1145/2702123.2702146

"... because leaving something unfinished." Markman, K. D., & Guenther, C. L. (2007). Psychological momentum: Intuitive physics and naive beliefs. *Personality and Social Psychology Bulletin*, *33*(6), 800-812. doi.org/10.1177/0146167207301026

"... Bluma Zeigarnik investigated." Zeigarnik, B. (1938). On finished and unfinished tasks. In W. D. Ellis (Ed.), *A source book of Gestalt psychology* (pp. 300-314). Kegan Paul, Trench, Trubner & Company. doi.org/10.1037/11496-025

"... discovered that interrupted tasks." Denmark, F. L. (2010). Zeigarnik effect. In I. B. Weiner and W. E. Craighead (Eds.), *The Corsini encyclopedia of psychology*. Wiley. doi.org/10.1002/9780470479216.corpsy0924

"... Committing to just 15 minutes." Stulberg, B., & Magness, S. (2017). *Peak performance: Elevate your game, avoid burnout, and thrive with the new science of success*. Rodale.

"... Switch Up Overwhelming Tasks." Monsell, S. (2003). Task switching. *Trends in Cognitive Sciences*, *7*(3), 134-140. doi.org/10.1016/s1364-6613(03)00028-7

"... Switching tasks spontaneously." Schmid, P. C., Mast, M. S., & Mast, F. W. (2015). Prioritizing: The task strategy of the powerful? *Quarterly Journal of Experimental Psychology*, *68*(10), 2097-2105. doi.org/10.1080/17470218.2015.1008525

"... Play can be both a physical activity and a state of mind." Bateson, P. P. G., & Martin, P. (2013). *Play, playfulness, creativity, and innovation*. Cambridge University Press.

"... Turning your tasks into games." Oprescu, F., Jones, C., & Katsikitis, M. (2014). I play at work: Ten principles for transforming work processes through gamification. *Frontiers in Psychology*, *5*, 14. doi.org/10.3389/fpsyg.2014.00014

"... Competition is an excellent way." Ferreira, A. T., Araújo, A. M., Fernandes, S., & Miguel, I. C. (2017). Gamification in the workplace: A systematic literature review. In Á. Rocha, A. Correia, H. Adeli, L. Reis, & S. Costanzo (Eds.), *Recent advances in information systems and technologies* (Vol. 3, pp. 283–292). Springer. doi.org/10.1007/978-3-319-56541-5_29

"... great way to motivate a group." van Gaalen, A. E. J., Brouwer, J., Schönrock-Adema, J., Bouwkamp-Timmer, T., Jaarsma, A. D. C., & Georgiadis, J. R. (2021). Gamification of health professions education: A systematic review. *Advances in Health Sciences Education: Theory and Practice, 26*(2), 683–711. doi.org/10.1007/s10459-020-10000-3

"... Reframe Immense Challenges." Orson, C. N., & Larson, R. W. (2020). Helping teens overcome anxiety episodes in project work: The power of reframing. *Journal of Adolescent Research, 36*(2), 127–153. doi.org/10.1177/0743558420913480

"... Sometimes saying no to tasks." Brooke, J. (2013). *The need to say no: The importance of setting boundaries in love, life, and your world.* Hatherleigh Press.

"... of healthy self-awareness and self-respect." Cloud, H., & Townsend, J. (2017). *Boundaries: When to say yes, how to say no to take control of your life.* Zondervan.

Chapter 4: The Peak

"... the Peak might be considered 'the main event.'" Hartley, S. (2012). *Peak performance every time.* Routledge.

"... neural and physiological systems should be working optimally." Lardon, M. (2008). *Finding your zone: Ten core lessons for achieving peak performance in sports and life.* Perigee Book.

"... A Peek Inside." Lehnertz, K., Rings, T., & Bröhl, T. (2021). Time in brain: How biological rhythms impact on EEG signals and on EEG-derived brain networks. *Frontiers in Network Physiology, 1,* 755016. doi.org/10.3389/fnetp.2021.755016

"... some expected neurochemical and hormonal processes also occur." Bear, M. F., Connors, B. W., & Paradiso, M. A. (2016). *Neuroscience: Exploring the brain* (4th ed.). Wolters Kluwer.

"... Pressure to perform." Rice, K. G., Richardson, C. M. E., & Clark, D. (2012). Perfectionism, procrastination, and psychological distress. *Journal of Counseling Psychology, 59*(2), 288–302. doi.org/10.1037/a0026643

"... facilitate habits for productivity." Clear, J. (2018). *Atomic habits: An easy and proven way to build good habits and break bad ones*. Avery.

"... Seek Challenge to Stimulate a Flow State." Jackson, S. A. (1995). Factors influencing the occurrence of flow state in elite athletes. *Journal of Applied Sport Psychology, 7*(2), 138–166. doi.org/10.1080/10413209508406962

"... coined the term 'Flow.'" Csikszentmihalyi, M. (1990). Flow and the psychology of optimal experience. *American Psychologist, 45*(8), 930–936. researchgate.net/publication/224927532_Flow_The_Psychology_of_Optimal_Experience

"... intrinsically motivated and fully absorbed." Csikszentmihalyi, M. (1990). *Flow: The psychology of optimal experience*. Harper & Row.

"... you find rewarding in and of themselves." Csikszentmihalyi, M., & Larson, R. (2014). *Flow and the foundations of positive psychology* (Vol. 10, pp. 978–994). Springer.

"... known as autotelic experience." Nakamura, J., & Csikszentmihalyi, M. (2001). *The concept of flow* (pp. 89–105). doi.org/10.1093/oso/9780195135336.003.0007

"... when you enjoy what you are doing." Rogatko, T. P. (2007). The influence of flow on positive affect in college students. *Journal of Happiness Studies, 10*(2), 133–148. doi.org/10.1007/s10902-007-9069-y

"... but there can be too much of a good thing." Mardlin, E. (2019). *Out of your comfort zone: Breaking boundaries for a life beyond limits*. Simon & Schuster.

"... Reclaim Your Sense of Task Autonomy." Lee, F. K., Sheldon, K. M., & Turban, D. B. (2003). Personality and the goal-striving process: The influence of achievement goal patterns, goal level, and mental focus on performance and enjoyment. *Journal of Applied Psychology, 88*(2), 256–265. doi.org/10.1037/0021-9010.88.2.256

"... autonomy, control, or choice in your work." Chaudhry, S. J., & Klinowski, D. (2016). Enhancing autonomy to motivate effort: An experiment on the delegation of contract choice. In S. J. Goerg & J. R. Hamman (Eds.), *Research in experimental economics: Vol. 19. Experiments in organizational economics* (pp. 141–157). doi.org/10.1108/s0193-230620160000019005

"... try to choose the tasks you work on." Khoshnaw, S., & Alavi, H. (2020). Examining the interrelation between job autonomy and job performance: A critical literature review. *Multidisciplinary*

Aspects of Production Engineering, *3*(1), 606–616. doi.org/10.2478/mape-2020-0051

"... music helps them focus." Das, P., Gupta, S., & Neogi, B. (2020). Measurement of effect of music on human brain and consequent impact on attentiveness and concentration during reading. *Procedia Computer Science*, *172*, 1033–1038. doi.org/10.1016/j.procs.2020.05.151

"... When selecting music for concentration." Huang, R. H., & Shih, Y. N. (2011). Effects of background music on concentration of workers. *Work*, *38*(4), 383–387. doi.org/10.3233/wor-2011-1141

"... music without lyrics can help you study." Shih, Y. N., Huang, R. H., & Chiang, H. Y. (2012). Background music: Effects on attention performance. *Work*, *42*(4), 573–578. doi.org/10.3233/wor-2012-1410

"... Musical preferences vary." Park, S., Kwak, C., & Han, W. (2020). Effect of background music for attentive concentration in working. *Audiology and Speech Research*, *16*(3), 188–195. doi.org/10.21848/asr.200044

"... direct your attention so you can engage more deeply." Shih, Y. N., Huang, R. H., & Chiang, H. S. (2009). Correlation between work concentration level and background music: A pilot study. *Work*, *33*(3), 329–333. doi.org/10.3233/wor-2009-0880

Chapter 5: The Fall

"... ultradian stress response." Russell, G., & Lightman, S. (2019). The human stress response. *Nature Reviews Endocrinology*, *15*(9), 525–534. doi.org/10.1038/s41574-019-0228-0

"... stress response gaining momentum." Arpin-Cribbie, C. A., & Cribbie, R. A. (2007). Psychological correlates of fatigue: Examining depression, perfectionism, and automatic negative thoughts. *Personality and Individual Differences*, *43*(6), 1310–1320. doi.org/10.1016/j.paid.2007.03.020

"... negative thoughts, arguments with others." Harper, D. G., Tornatzky, W., & Miczek, K. A. (1996). Stress induced disorganization of circadian and ultradian rhythms: Comparisons of effects of surgery and social stress. *Physiology & Behavior*, *59*(3), 409–419. doi.org/10.1016/0031-9384(95)02012-8

"... You shouldn't try to push through a Fall." Sarabdjitsingh, R. A., Conway-Campbell, B. L., Leggett, J. D., Waite, E. J., Meijer, O. C.,

De Kloet, E. R., & Lightman, S. L. (2010). Stress responsiveness varies over the ultradian glucocorticoid cycle in a brain-region-specific manner. *Endocrinology, 151*(11), 5369–5379. doi.org/10.1210/en.2010-0832

"... The body's ultradian stress response." Spiga, F., Pooley, J., Russell, G., & Lightman, S. (2017). Ultradian rhythms. In G. Fink (Ed.), *Handbook of stress series: Vol. 2. Stress: Neuroendocrinology and neurobiology* (pp. 429–437). Academic Press. doi.org/10.1016/b978-0-12-802175-0.00043-7

"... ANTs may creep in." Eichinger, R. W. (2018). Should we get aboard the brain train? *Consulting Psychology Journal, 70*(1), 89–94. doi.org/10.1037/cpb0000107

"... Negative Emotions as Informative." Barrett, L. F., & Bliss-Moreau, E. (2009). Affect as a psychological primitive. In M. P. Zanna (Ed.), *Advances in experimental social psychology* (Vol. 41, pp. 167–218). Academic Press. doi.org/10.1016/s0065-2601(08)00404-8

"... Negative emotions such as." Barrett, L. F., Mesquita, B., Ochsner, K. N., & Gross, J. J. (2007). The experience of emotion. *Annual Review of Psychology, 58*(1), 373–403. doi.org/10.1146/annurev.psych.58.110405.085709

"... Give Yourself a Smile." Lupu-Merca, V., & Vaida, S. (2024). Benefits of the Duchenne smile and positive emotions: A systematic review. *Educatia, 21*(27), 93–102. doi.org/10.24193/ed21.2024.27.09

"... Laughing works in much the same way." Yim, J. (2016). Therapeutic benefits of laughter in mental health: A theoretical review. *Tohoku Journal of Experimental Medicine, 239*(3), 243–249. doi.org/10.1620/tjem.239.243

"... smiling and laughing improve neurochemistry." Cross, M. P., Acevedo, A. M., Leger, K. A., & Pressman, S. D. (2022). How and why could smiling influence physical health? A conceptual review. *Health Psychology Review, 17*(2), 321–343. doi.org/10.1080/17437199.2022.2052740

"... real smiles are better than forced." Mora-Ripoll, R. (2011). Potential health benefits of simulated laughter: A narrative review of the literature and recommendations for future research. *Complementary Therapies in Medicine, 19*(3), 170–177. doi.org/10.1016/j.ctim.2011.05.003

"... Do what you can to infuse joy, humor." Burgdorf, J., & Panksepp, J. (2006). The neurobiology of positive emotions. *Neuroscience and*

Biobehavioral Reviews, 30(2), 173-187. doi.org/10.1016/j.neubiorev .2005.06.001

"... 'Right-Size' Expectations of Yourself." Carter, T. J., & Dunning, D. (2007). Faulty self-assessment: Why evaluating one's own competence is an intrinsically difficult task. *Social and Personality Psychology Compass, 2*(1), 346-360. doi.org/10.1111/j.1751-90 04.2007.00031.x

"... the resulting disappointment." Burgoon, J. K., & Walther, J. B. (1990). Nonverbal expectancies and the evaluative consequences of violations. *Human Communication Research, 17*(2), 232-265. doi.org/10.1111/j.1468-2958.1990.tb00232.x

"... momentum, and work-related enjoyment." Barczak, N., & Eklund, R. C. (2018). The moderating effect of self-compassion on relationships between performance and subsequent coping and motivation. *International Journal of Sport and Exercise Psychology, 18*(2), 256-268. doi.org/10.1080/1612197x.2018.1511620

"... Take a Perceived Stress Test." Cohen, S., Kamarck, T., & Mermelstein, R. (1983). *Perceived stress scale*. PsycTESTS Dataset. doi.org/10.1037/t02889-000

"... The way you experience stress." Cohen, S., Kamarck, T., & Mermelstein, R. (1983). A global measure of perceived stress. *Journal of Health and Social Behavior, 24*(4), 385. doi.org/ 10.2307/2136404

Chapter 6: The Valley

"... as the ultradian healing response." Lyubykh, Z., Gulseren, D., Premji, Z., Wingate, T. G., Deng, C., Bélanger, L. J., & Turner, N. (2022). Role of work breaks in well-being and performance: A systematic review and future research agenda. *Journal of Occupational Health Psychology, 27*(5), 470-487. doi.org/10.1037/ ocp0000337

"... without taking some time to rest and heal." Trougakos, J. P., & Hideg, I. (2009). Momentary work recovery: The role of within-day work breaks. In S. Sonnetag, P. L. Perrewé, & D. C. Ganster (Eds.), *Research in occupational stress and well being: Vol. 7. Current perspectives on job-stress recovery* (pp. 37-84). doi.org/10.1108/ s1479-3555(2009)0000007005

"... lasts from 12 to 20 minutes." Dababneh, A. J., Swanson, N., & Shell, R. L. (2001). Impact of added rest breaks on the productivity and well-being of workers. *Ergonomics, 44*(2), 164-174. doi.org/10.1080/00140130121538

"... important things to accomplish during the ultradian healing response." Loehr, J. E., & Schwartz, T. (2005). *The power of full engagement: Managing energy, not time, is the key to high performance and personal renewal.* Free Press.

"... our brain and body collaborate to assist with recovery and healing." Bear, M. F., Connors, B. W., & Paradiso, M. A. (2016). *Neuroscience: Exploring the brain* (4th ed.). Wolters Kluwer.

"... Lean In to Break Time." Fritz, C., Ellis, A. M., Demsky, C. A., Lin, B. C., & Guros, F. (2013). Embracing work breaks. *Organizational Dynamics, 42*(4), 274-280. doi.org/10.1016/j.orgdyn.2013.07.005

"... Take breaks as many times as you feel you need to." Kühnel, J., Zacher, H., De Bloom, J., & Bledow, R. (2016). Take a break! Benefits of sleep and short breaks for daily work engagement. *European Journal of Work and Organizational Psychology, 26*(4), 481-491. doi.org/10.1080/1359432x.2016.1269750

"... Try not to engage with more tech." Henning, R. A., Jacques, P., Kissel, G. V., Sullivan, A. B., & Alteras-Webb, S. M. (1997). Frequent short rest breaks from computer work: Effects on productivity and well-being at two field sites. *Ergonomics, 40*(1), 78-91. doi.org/10.1080/001401397188396

"... Use Breaks to Declutter." Palmer, B. (2012). *Clutter busting your life: Clearing physical and emotional clutter to reconnect with yourself and others.* New World Library.

"... and reset your physical space." Roster, C. A., & Ferrari, J. R. (2019). Does work stress lead to office clutter, and how? Mediating influences of emotional exhaustion and indecision. *Environment and Behavior, 52*(9), 923-944. doi.org/10.1177/0013916518823041

"... Do Something Physical." Peterson, D., & Lee, J. (2023, May 18). *Boost your energy with "movement snacks": 14 quick exercises for a busy day.* Hinge Health. hingehealth.com/resources/articles/movement-snacks

"... Physical activity is a key component." Wells, G. (2023). *Powerhouse: Protect your energy, optimize your health, and supercharge your performance.* HarperCollins.

"... Find a Way to Greet Mother Nature." An, M., Colarelli, S. M., O'Brien, K., & Boyajian, M. E. (2016). Why we need more nature at work: Effects of natural elements and sunlight on employee mental health and work attitudes. *PLOS ONE*, *11*(5), e0155614. doi.org/10.1371/journal.pone.0155614

"... Whenever possible on a break." Meyer, S., & Pagel, M. (2024). Fresh air eases work: The effect of air quality on individual investor activity. *Review of Finance*, *28*(3), 1105-1149. doi.org/10.1093/rof/rfae005

"... Studies show that movement and exercise in nature." Sianoja, M., Syrek, C. J., De Bloom, J., Korpela, K., & Kinnunen, U. (2018). Enhancing daily well-being at work through lunchtime park walks and relaxation exercises: Recovery experiences as mediators. *Journal of Occupational Health Psychology*, *23*(3), 428-442. doi.org/10.1037/ocp0000083

"... work near a window whenever possible." Leather, P., Pyrgas, M., Beale, D., & Lawrence, C. (1998). Windows in the workplace. *Environment and Behavior*, *30*(6), 739-762. doi.org/10.1177/001391659803000601

"... Spend Some 'Time In' Your Mind." Rock, D., Siegel, D. J., & Poelmans, S. (2010). The healthy mind platter: A framework for nurturing the brain and optimizing well-being. *NeuroLeadership Journal*, *1*(1), 1-10. davidrock.net/files/02_The_Healthy_Mind_Platter_US.pdf

"... take some time for ourselves to relax, reflect, and recharge." Schwartz, T., Gomes, J., & McCarthy, C. (2010). *The way we're working isn't working: The four forgotten needs that energize great performance.* Simon & Schuster.

"... Daydreaming is not so much." Baer, M., Dane, E., & Madrid, H. P. (2021). Zoning out or breaking through? Linking daydreaming to creativity in the workplace. *Academy of Management Journal*, *64*(5), 1553-1577. doi.org/10.5465/amj.2017.1283

"... During this time, your brain." McMillan, R. L., Kaufman, S. B., & Singer, J. L. (2013). Ode to positive constructive daydreaming. *Frontiers in Psychology*, *4*, 626. doi.org/10.3389/fpsyg.2013.00626

Chapter 7: Move

"... we must also consider the bigger-picture factors." Lianov, L. S., Barron, G. C., Fredrickson, B. L., Hashmi, S., Klemes, A., Krishnaswami, J., Lee, J., Le Pertel, N., Matthews, J. A., Millstein, R. A., Phillips, E. M., Sannidhi, D., Purpur de Vries, P., Wallace, A., & Winter, S. J. (2020). Positive psychology in health care: Defining key stakeholders and their roles. *Translational Behavioral Medicine*, *10*(3), 637-647. doi.org/10.1093/tbm/ibz150

"... the good news is that there are other universal factors." American College of Lifestyle Medicine. (2023). *6 ways to take control of your health*. lifestylemedicine.org/wp-content/uploads/2023/06/Pillar-Booklet.pdf

"... an unrelenting ache for hours." Ruby, M. B., Dunn, E. W., Perrino, A., Gillis, R., & Viel, S. (2011). The invisible benefits of exercise. *Health Psychology*, *30*(1), 67-74. doi.org/10.1037/a0021859

"... inspired by yoga and Pilates." Lange, C., Unnithan, V. B., Larkam, E., & Latta, P. M. (2000). Maximizing the benefits of Pilates-inspired exercise for learning functional motor skills. *Journal of Bodywork and Movement Therapies*, *4*(2), 99-108. doi.org/10.1054/jbmt.1999.0161

"... I also exercised more than the ankle itself." Lieberman, D. E. (2015). Is exercise really medicine? An evolutionary perspective. *Current Sports Medicine Reports*, *14*(4), 313-319. doi.org/10.1249/jsr.0000000000000168

"... Movement, as it turned out, did what painkillers." Vina, J., Sanchis-Gomar, F., Martinez-Bello, V., & Gomez-Cabrera, M. (2012). Exercise acts as a drug: The pharmacological benefits of exercise. *British Journal of Pharmacology*, *167*(1), 1-12. doi.org/10.1111/j.1476-5381.2012.01970.x

"... My methods weren't novel." Berryman, J. W. (2010). Exercise is medicine. *Current Sports Medicine Reports*, *9*(4), 195-201. doi.org/10.1249/jsr.0b013e3181e7d86d

"... documented in the relevant physiotherapy." Phillips, E. M., Frates, E. P., & Park, D. J. (2020). Lifestyle medicine. *Physical Medicine and Rehabilitation Clinics of North America*, *31*(4), 515-526. doi.org/10.1016/j.pmr.2020.07.006

"... preventative and rehabilitative treatment." Phillips, E. M., Frates, E. P., & Park, D. J. (2020). Lifestyle medicine. *Physical Medicine and Rehabilitation Clinics of North America*, *31*(4), 515-526. doi.org/10.1016/j.pmr.2020.07.006

"... And here's the thing." Wayne, P. M., Yeh, G., & Mehta, D. H. (2018). Minding the mind-body literature: Aging and cognitive decline. *Journal of Alternative and Complementary Medicine*, *24*(3), 196-199. doi.org/10.1089/acm.2018.29044.pjw

"... It also works amazingly for." Ploughman, M. (2008). Exercise is brain food: The effects of physical activity on cognitive function.

Developmental Neurorehabilitation, 11(3), 236-240. doi.org/10.1080/17518420801997007

"... Movement has been documented to improve." Heyman, E., Gamelin, F. X., Goekint, M., Piscitelli, F., Roelands, B., Leclair, E., Di Marzo, V., & Meeusen, R. (2012). Intense exercise increases circulating endocannabinoid and BDNF levels in humans: Possible implications for reward and depression. *Psychoneuroendocrinology, 37*(6), 844-851. doi.org/10.1016/j.psyneuen.2011.09.017

"... if you want your brain to function optimally." Palmer, C. M. (2022). *Brain energy: A revolutionary breakthrough in understanding mental health—and improving treatment for anxiety, depression, OCD, PTSD, and more.* BenBella Books.

"... Movement is critical for health of every kind." Pedersen, B. K., & Saltin, B. (2015). Exercise as medicine: Evidence for prescribing exercise as therapy in 26 different chronic diseases. *Scandinavian Journal of Medicine & Science in Sports, 25*(S3), 1-72. doi.org/10.1111/sms.12581

"... also for peak cognitive performance." Febbraio, M. A. (2017). Health benefits of exercise: More than meets the eye! *Nature Reviews Endocrinology, 13*(2), 72-74. doi.org/10.1038/nrendo.2016.218

"... *must* be highly tied to our physical." Ruegsegger, G. N., & Booth, F. W. (2017). Health benefits of exercise. *Cold Spring Harbor Perspectives in Medicine, 8*(7), a029694. doi.org/10.1101/cshperspect.a029694

"... it will add to it." Sallis, R. E. (2008). Exercise is medicine and physicians need to prescribe it! *British Journal of Sports Medicine, 43*(1), 3-4. doi.org/10.1136/bjsm.2008.054825

"... Physical activity doesn't have to." Phillips, E. M., & Kennedy, M. A. (2012). The exercise prescription: A tool to improve physical activity. *PM&R: The journal of injury, function, and rehabilitation, 4*(11), 818-825. doi.org/10.1016/j.pmrj.2012.09.582

"... Feeling stressed?" Edenfield, T. M., & Blumenthal, J. A. (2011). Exercise and stress reduction. In R. J. Contrada and A. Baum (Eds.), *The handbook of stress science: Biology, psychology, and health* (pp. 301-319). Springer.

"... Feeling overwhelmed?" Esch, T., & Stefano, G. B. (2010). Endogenous reward mechanisms and their importance in stress reduction, exercise, and the brain. *Archives of Medical Science, 6*(3), 447-455. doi.org/10.5114/aoms.2010.14269

"... Movement can decrease your pain perception." Lima, L. V., Abner, T. S. S., & Sluka, K. A. (2017). Does exercise increase or decrease pain? Central mechanisms underlying these two phenomena. *Journal of Physiology*, *595*(13), 4141-4150. doi.org/10.1113/jp273355

"... sedentary lifestyle increases risks of disease, disorder." Pedersen, B. K. (2019). The physiology of optimizing health with a focus on exercise as medicine. *Annual Review of Physiology*, *81*(1), 607-627. doi.org/10.1146/annurev-physiol-020518-114339

"... lessen physical and mental issues." Iso-Ahola, S. E. (2013). Exercise: Why it is a challenge for both the nonconscious and conscious mind. *Review of General Psychology*, *17*(1), 93-110. doi.org/10.1037/a0030657

"... While your brain does most of the 'budgeting.'" Barrett, L. F. (2021). *Seven and a half lessons about the brain*. Mariner Books.

"... exercise excites the mitochondria." Wells, G. (2023). *Powerhouse: Protect your energy, optimize your health, and supercharge your performance*. HarperCollins.

"... Second, exercise increases the rate of blood volume." Nystoriak, M. A., & Bhatnagar, A. (2018). Cardiovascular effects and benefits of exercise. *Frontiers in Cardiovascular Medicine*, *5*, 135. doi.org/10.3389/fcvm.2018.00135

"... benefits for every part of your body, especially the brain." Querido, J. S., & Sheel, A. W. (2007). Regulation of cerebral blood flow during exercise. *Sports Medicine*, *37*(9), 765-782. doi.org/10.2165/00007256-200737090-00002

"... Physical activity and its metabolic outcomes." Zhang, X., Zong, B., Zhao, W., & Li, L. (2021). Effects of mind-body exercise on brain structure and function: A systematic review on MRI studies. *Brain Sciences*, *11*(2), 205. doi.org/10.3390/brainsci11020205

"... when you exercise, you jump-start." Basso, J. C., & Suzuki, W. A. (2017). The effects of acute exercise on mood, cognition, neurophysiology, and neurochemical pathways: A review. *Brain Plasticity*, *2*(2), 127-152. doi.org/10.3233/bpl-160040

"... You would be hard pressed to find any health, wellness." Herrera, J. J., Fedynska, S., Ghasem, P. R., Wieman, T., Clark, P. J., Gray, N., Loetz, E., Campeau, S., Fleshner, M., & Greenwood, B. N. (2016). Neurochemical and behavioural indices of exercise reward are independent of exercise controllability. *European Journal of Neuroscience*, *43*(9), 1190-1202. doi.org/10.1111/ejn.13193

"... exercise has been shown to improve." Ruegsegger, G. N., & Booth, F. W. (2017). Health benefits of exercise. *Cold Spring Harbor Perspectives in Medicine*, *8*(7), a029694. doi.org/10.1101/cshperspect.a029694

"... experts agree that fitness has three main components." Miller, K. R., McClave, S. A., Jampolis, M. B., Hurt, R. T., Krueger, K., Landes, S., & Collier, B. (2016). The health benefits of exercise and physical activity. *Current Nutrition Reports*, 5(3), 204–212. doi.org/10.1007/s13668-016-0175-5

"... you'll want to vary your exercises each week." Duncan, L. R., Hall, C. R., Wilson, P. M., & O, J. (2010). Exercise motivation: A cross-sectional analysis examining its relationships with frequency, intensity, and duration of exercise. *International Journal of Behavioural Nutrition and Physical Activity*, 7(1), 7. doi.org/10.1186/1479-5868-7-7

"... The American Council on Exercise." US Department of Health & Human Services. (2018). *Physical activity guidelines for Americans* (2nd ed.). health.gov/sites/default/files/2019-09/Physical_Activity_Guidelines_2nd_edition.pdf

"... More recent research has spurred." American Council on Exercise. (2002, September 16). *American Council on Exercise recommends 60 minutes of physical activity a day*. acefitness.org/about-ace/press-room/press-releases/300/american-council-on-exercise-recommends-60-minutes-of-physical-activity-a-day

"... By cycling between different types of activities." National Institute on Aging. (2021, January 29). *Four types of exercise can improve your health and physical ability.* nia.nih.gov/health/exercise-and-physical-activity/four-types-exercise-can-improve-your-health-and-physical

"... Novel movements increase heart rate." Glaros, N. M., & Janelle, C. M. (2001). Varying the mode of cardiovascular exercise to increase adherence. *Journal of Sport Behavior*, 24(1), 42–62. psycnet.apa.org/record/2001-14557-005

"... The oxygen you breathe." Zhang, X., Zhang, X., & Chen, X. (2017). Happiness in the air: How does a dirty sky affect mental health and subjective well-being? *Journal of Environmental Economics and Management*, 85, 81–94. doi.org/10.1016/j.jeem.2017.04.001

"... Go ahead, try it right now." Jerath, R., Crawford, M. W., Barnes, V. A., & Harden, K. (2015). Self-regulation of breathing as a primary treatment for anxiety. *Applied Psychophysiology and Biofeedback*, 40(2), 107–115. doi.org/10.1007/s10484-015-9279-8

"... Deliberately resting the body." Bishop, P. A., Jones, E., & Woods, A. K. (2008). Recovery from training: A brief review. *Journal of Strength and Conditioning Research*, 22(3), 1015–1024. doi.org/10.1519/jsc.0b013e31816eb518

"... Therefore, deliberate, purposeful, restorative rest." Peake, J. M., & Gandevia, S. C. (2017). Replace, restore, revive: The keys to recovery after exercise. *Journal of Applied Physiology*, 122(3), 531-532. doi.org/10.1152/japplphysiol.00086.2017

"... are key for ensuring an injury-free progression toward your goal." Yang, Y. J. (2019). An overview of current physical activity recommendations in primary care. *Korean Journal of Family Medicine*, 40(3), 135-142. doi.org/10.4082/kjfm.19.0038

"... Variation Is Key." Phillips, E. M., & Roy, B. A. (2009). Exercise is medicine: Partnering with physicians. *ACSM's Health and Fitness Journal*, 13(6). doi.org/10.1249/fit.0b013e3181bcd74f

"... No matter what type of exercise or component of fitness." Weerapong, P., Hume, P. A., & Kolt, G. S. (2004). Stretching: Mechanisms and benefits for sport performance and injury prevention. *Physical Therapy Reviews*, 9(4), 189-206. doi.org/10.1179/108331904225007078

"... Exercise When Your Brain Needs a Break." Chtourou, H., & Souissi, N. (2012). The effect of training at a specific time of day. *Journal of Strength and Conditioning Research*, 26(7), 1984-2005. doi.org/10.1519/jsc.0b013e3182577oa7

"... Move to Improve Sleep." Youngstedt, S. D. (2005). Effects of exercise on sleep. *Clinics in Sports Medicine*, 24(2), 355-365. doi.org/10.1016/j.csm.2004.12.003

"... Special Benefits of Exercising Socially." Davis, A. J., MacCarron, P., & Cohen, E. (2021). Social reward and support effects on exercise experiences and performance: Evidence from parkrun. *PLOS ONE*, 16(9), e0256546. doi.org/10.1371/journal.pone.0256546

"... green exercise is also a best practice." Lahart, I., Darcy, P., Gidlow, C., & Calogiuri, G. (2019). The effects of green exercise on physical and mental wellbeing: A systematic review. *International Journal of Environmental Research and Public Health*, 16(8), 1352. doi.org/10.3390/ijerph16081352

"... Breathing Techniques Can Help Regulate." Brown, R. P., & Gerbarg, P. L. (2009). Yoga breathing, meditation, and longevity. *Annals of the New York Academy of Sciences*, 1172(1), 54-62. doi.org/10.1111/j.1749-6632.2009.04394.x

"... Alternate nostril breathing." Raghuraj, P., & Telles, S. (2003). Effect of yoga-based and forced uninostril breathing on the autonomic nervous system. *Perceptual and Motor Skills*, 96(1), 79-80. doi.org/10.2466/pms.2003.96.1.79

"... Purposeful breathing techniques." Kanchibhotla, D., Saisudha, B., Ramrakhyani, S., & Mehta, D. H. (2021). Impact of a Yogic breathing technique on the well-being of healthcare professionals during the COVID-19 pandemic. *Global Advances in Integrative Medicine and Health*. doi.org/10.1177/21649561209829 56

Chapter 8: Eat

"... misinterpreting their thirst signals for hunger." McKinley, M. J., Denton, D. A., Oldfield, B. J., De Oliveira, L. B., & Mathai, M. L. (2006). Water intake and the neural correlates of the consciousness of thirst. *Seminars in Nephrology*, 26(3), 249-257. doi.org/10.1016/j.semnephrol.2006.02.001

"... they were a slow metabolizer of caffeine." Nehlig, A. (2018). Interindividual differences in caffeine metabolism and factors driving caffeine consumption. *Pharmacological Reviews*, 70(2), 384-411. doi.org/10.1124/pr.117.014407

"... Food choices have a huge effect." Fernstrom, J. D., & Fernstrom, M. H. (2010). Nutrition and the brain. In S. A. Lanham-New, I. A. Macdonald, & H. M. Roche (Eds.), *Nutrition and metabolism* (2nd ed., pp. 155-183). Wiley. doi.org/10.1002/9781444327779.ch8

"... Because your diet and nutrition relate." Galland, L. (2014). The gut microbiome and the brain. *Journal of Medicinal Food*, 17(12), 1261-1272. doi.org/10.1089/jmf.2014.7000

"... What our brains need is partly determined." Biesalski, H. K. (2023). Micronutrients and the evolution of the human brain. *NFS Journal*, 33, 100150. doi.org/10.1016/j.nfs.2023.100150

"... The most significant challenges during the EEA." Leonard, W. R., Snodgrass, J. J., & Robertson, M. L. (2007). Effects of brain evolution on human nutrition and metabolism. *Annual Review of Nutrition*, 27(1), 311-327. doi.org/10.1146/annurev.nutr.27.061406.093659

"... This also means that our preference." Leonard, W. R., & Robertson, M. L. (1994). Evolutionary perspectives on human nutrition: The influence of brain and body size on diet and metabolism. *American Journal of Human Biology*, 6(1), 77-88. doi.org/10.1002/ajhb.1310060111

"... dietary preferences often lead us astray." Kopp, W. (2019). How Western diet and lifestyle drive the pandemic of obesity and civilization diseases. *Diabetes, Metabolic Syndrome, and Obesity*, 12, 2221-2236. doi.org/10.2147/dmso.s216791

"... in which most of it is grown." Mejía, N. V., Reyes, R. P., Martinez, Y., Carrasco, O., & Cerritos, R. (2018). Implications of the Western diet for agricultural production, health and climate change. *Frontiers in Sustainable Food Systems, 2*, 88. doi.org/10.3389/fsufs.2018.00088

"... Westernized food cultures." López-Taboada, I., González-Pardo, H., & Conejo, N. M. (2020). Western diet: Implications for brain function and behavior. *Frontiers in Psychology, 11*, 564413. doi.org/10.3389/fpsyg.2020.564413

"... uptick in all the 'diseases of affluence.'" Campbell, T. C., & Campbell, T. M. (2016). *The China study: The most comprehensive study of nutrition ever conducted and the startling implications for diet, weight loss, and long-term health.* BenBella Books.

"... in our era of IFC abundance." Cordain, L., Eaton, S. B., Sebastian, A., Mann, N., Lindeberg, S., Watkins, B. A., O'Keefe, J. H., & Brand-Miller, J. (2005). Origins and evolution of the Western diet: Health implications for the 21st century. *American Journal of Clinical Nutrition, 81*(2), 341–354. doi.org/10.1093/ajcn.81.2.341

"... You (and Your Brain) Are What You Eat." Gómez-Pinilla, F. (2008). Brain foods: The effects of nutrients on brain function. *Nature Reviews Neuroscience, 9*(7), 568–578. doi.org/10.1038/nrn2421

"... Water is critical in the human brain." Armstrong, L. E., & Johnson, E. C. (2018). Water intake, water balance, and the elusive daily water requirement. *Nutrients, 10*(12), 1928. doi.org/10.3390/nu10121928

"... proteins and amino acids as critical building blocks." Gietzen, D. W., & Aja, S. M. (2012). The brain's response to an essential amino acid-deficient diet and the circuitous route to a better meal. *Molecular Neurobiology, 46*(2), 332–348. doi.org/10.1007/s12035-012-8283-8

"... 'essential' meaning they must be eaten." He, W., & Wu, G. (2020). Metabolism of amino acids in the brain and their roles in regulating food intake. In G. Wu (Ed.), *Advances in experimental medicine and biology: Vol. 1265. Amino acids in nutrition and health* (pp. 167–185). Springer. doi.org/10.1007/978-3-030-45328-2_10

"... getting enough healthy, unaltered dietary protein." Francis, H., & Stevenson, R. (2013). The longer-term impacts of Western diet on human cognition and the brain. *Appetite, 63*, 119–128. doi.org/10.1016/j.appet.2012.12.018

"... typically have lower nutrient density." Song, Z., Song, R., Liu, Y., Wu, Z., & Zhang, X. (2023). Effects of ultra-processed foods on the microbiota-gut-brain axis: The bread-and-butter issue. *Food Research International*, *167*, 112730. doi.org/10.1016/j.foodres.2023.112730

"... protein helps you feel full more quickly and for longer." Veldhorst, M., Smeets, A., Soenen, S., Hochstenbach-Waelen, A., Hursel, R., Diepvens, K., Lejeune, M., Luscombe-Marsh, N., & Westerterp-Plantenga, M. (2008). Protein-induced satiety: Effects and mechanisms of different proteins. *Physiology & Behavior*, *94*(2), 300–307. doi.org/10.1016/j.physbeh.2008.01.003

"... very significant amount of fat." Chang, C. Y., Ke, D. S., & Chen, J. Y. (2009). Essential fatty acids and human brain. *Acta Neurologica Taiwanica*, *18*(4), 231–241. pubmed.ncbi.nlm.nih.gov/20329590

"... Consuming fat is critical for brain functioning." Bourre, J. M. (2009). Diet, brain lipids, and brain functions: Polyunsaturated fatty acids, mainly omega-3 fatty acids. In A. Lajtha, G. Tettamanti, & G. Goracci (Eds.), *Handbook of neurochemistry and molecular neurobiology* (3rd ed., pp. 409–441). Springer. doi.org/10.1007/978-0-387-30378-9_17

"... Healthy fats are nutritionally critical." Youdim, K. A., Martin, A., & Joseph, J. A. (2000). Essential fatty acids and the brain: Possible health implications. *International Journal of Developmental Neuroscience*, *18*(4–5), 383–399. doi.org/10.1016/s0736-5748(00)00013-7

"... In moderation, good fats are used as energy." Panov, A., Orynbayeva, Z., Vavilin, V., & Lyakhovich, V. (2014). Fatty acids in energy metabolism of the central nervous system. *BioMed Research International*, *2014*, 1–22. doi.org/10.1155/2014/472459

"... which levels out glucose." Magistretti, P. J., & Allaman, I. (2022). Brain energy and metabolism. In D. W. Pfaff, N. D. Volkow, & J. L. Rubenstein (Eds.), *Neuroscience in the 21st Century* (3rd ed., pp. 2197–2227). Springer. doi.org/10.1007/978-3-030-88832-9_56

"... indispensable for brain metabolism." Evans, M., & Amiel, S. A. (1998). Carbohydrates as a cerebral metabolic fuel. *Journal of Pediatric Endocrinology and Metabolism*, *11*(Supplement). doi.org/10.1515/jpem.1998.11.s1.99

"... energy requirements comes from glycogen." Gibson, E. L. (2007). Carbohydrates and mental function: Feeding or impeding the brain? *Nutrition Bulletin*, *32*(s1), 71–83. doi.org/10.1111/j.1467-3010.2007.00606.x

"... metabolic balances, and even damage brain tissues." Hawkins, M. A., Keirns, N. G., & Helms, Z. (2018). Carbohydrates and cognitive function. *Current Opinion in Clinical Nutrition and Metabolic Care, 21*(4), 302-307. doi.org/10.1097/mco.0000000000000471

"... Micronutrients are needed in only small amounts." Swaminathan, S., Edward, B. S., & Kurpad, A. V. (2013). Micronutrient deficiency and cognitive and physical performance in Indian children. *European Journal of Clinical Nutrition, 67*(5), 467-474. doi.org/10.1038/ejcn.2013.14

"... less common than deficiency." Ferry, M., & Roussel, A. M. (2011). Micronutrient status and cognitive decline in ageing. *European Geriatric Medicine, 2*(1), 15-21. doi.org/10.1016/j.eurger.2010.11.014

"... help every cell, including neurons." Prado, E. L., & Dewey, K. G. (2014). Nutrition and brain development in early life. *Nutrition Reviews, 72*(4), 267-284. doi.org/10.1111/nure.12102

"... Eating micronutrient-dense foods." Gómez-Pinilla, F. (2008). Brain foods: The effects of nutrients on brain function. *Nature Reviews Neuroscience, 9*(7), 568-578. doi.org/10.1038/nrn2421

"... water is critical for your brain." Masento, N. A., Golightly, M., Field, D. T., Butler, L. T., & Van Reekum, C. M. (2014). Effects of hydration status on cognitive performance and mood. *British Journal of Nutrition, 111*(10), 1841-1852. doi.org/10.1017/s0007114513004455

"... by the time you feel thirsty." Stachenfeld, N. S., Leone, C. A., Mitchell, E. S., Freese, E., & Harkness, L. (2018). Water intake reverses dehydration associated impaired executive function in healthy young women. *Physiology & Behavior, 185*, 103-111. doi.org/10.1016/j.physbeh.2017.12.028

"... before you reach for a snack." Zizza, C. A. (2014). Healthy snacking recommendations: One size does not fit all. *Physiology & Behavior, 134*, 32-37. doi.org/10.1016/j.physbeh.2014.01.034

"... A Critical Link Between Dietary Choices and Brain Functioning." Martin, C. R., Osadchiy, V., Kalani, A., & Mayer, E. A. (2018). The brain-gut-microbiome axis. *Cellular and Molecular Gastroenterology and Hepatology, 6*(2), 133-148. doi.org/10.1016/j.jcmgh.2018.04.003

"... The microbiome is a collective." Enders, G. (2015). *Gut: The inside story of our body's most underrated organ.* Greystone Books.

"... they're inextricably linked." Perlmutter, D., & Loberg, K. (2015). *Brain maker: The power of gut microbes to heal and protect your brain— for life.* Little, Brown and Company.

"... The microbiome has more recently." Kennedy, P. J., Murphy, A. B., Cryan, J. F., Ross, P. R., Dinan, T. G., & Stanton, C. (2016). Microbiome in brain function and mental health. *Trends in Food Science & Technology*, 57, 289–301. doi.org/10.1016/j.tifs.2016.05.001

"... bidirectional, complex communication network." Sampson, T. R., & Mazmanian, S. K. (2015). Control of brain development, function, and behavior by the microbiome. *Cell Host & Microbe*, 17(5), 565–576. doi.org/10.1016/j.chom.2015.04.011

"... What you fuel yourself with affects." Rogers, G. B., Keating, D. J., Young, R. L., Wong, M. L., Licinio, J., & Wesselingh, S. (2016). From gut dysbiosis to altered brain function and mental illness: Mechanisms and pathways. *Molecular Psychiatry*, 21(6), 738–748. doi.org/10.1038/mp.2016.50

"... cognitive performance and well-being." Noble, E. E., Hsu, T. M., & Kanoski, S. E. (2017). Gut to brain dysbiosis: Mechanisms linking Western diet consumption, the microbiome, and cognitive impairment. *Frontiers in Behavioral Neuroscience*, 11, 9. doi.org/10.3389/fnbeh.2017.00009

"... in direct proportion to how it builds." Mohajeri, M. H., La Fata, G., Steinert, R. E., & Weber, P. (2018). Relationship between the gut microbiome and brain function. *Nutrition Reviews*, 76(7), 481–496. doi.org/10.1093/nutrit/nuy009

"... to your brain's health, functioning, and performance." Gareau, M. (2016). Cognitive function and the microbiome. In J. F. Cryan & G. Clarke (Eds.), *International review of neurobiology: Vol. 131. Gut microbiome and behavior* (pp. 227–246). Academic Press. doi.org/10.1016/bs.irn.2016.08.001

"... Where Neurotoxins Hide." Costa, L. G., Guizzetti, M., Costa-Mallen, P., Vitalone, A., & Tita, B. (2002). Dietary neurotoxins. In M. P. Mattson (Ed.), *Diet–brain connections: Impact on memory, mood, aging, and disease* (pp. 197–213). Springer. doi.org/10.1007/978-1-4615-1067-3_12

"... toxins can hide anywhere." Dolan, L. C., Matulka, R. A., & Burdock, G. A. (2010). Naturally occurring food toxins. *Toxins*, 2(9), 2289–2332. doi.org/10.3390/toxins2092289

"... alcohol has no health benefits." Thakker, K. D. (1998). An overview of health risks and benefits of alcohol consumption. *Alcoholism, Clinical, and Experimental Research*, 22(Supplement 1), 285. doi.org/10.1097/00000374-199807001-00003

"... wine producers can legally include." Pozo-Bayón, M. N., Monagas, M., Bartolomé, B., & Moreno-Arribas, M. V. (2012). Wine features related to safety and consumer health: An integrated perspective. *Critical Reviews in Food Science and Nutrition, 52*(1), 31–54. doi.org/10.1080/10408398.2010.489398

"... If you are what you eat." Carreiro, A. L., Dhillon, J., Gordon, S., Higgins, K. A., Jacobs, A. G., McArthur, B. M., Redan, B. W., Rivera, R. L., Schmidt, L. R., & Mattes, R. D. (2016). The macronutrients, appetite, and energy intake. *Annual Review of Nutrition, 36*(1), 73–103. doi.org/10.1146/annurev-nutr-121415-112624

"... because of how macronutrients are metabolized." Williams, C. (1995). Macronutrients and performance. *Journal of Sports Sciences, 13*(Supplement 1), S1–S10. doi.org/10.1080/02640419508732271

"... proteins and fats are slower to absorb." Prentice, A. M. (2005). Macronutrients as sources of food energy. *Public Health Nutrition, 8*(7a), 932–939. doi.org/10.1079/phn2005779

"... Strive to Eat the Rainbow." Minich, D. M. (2019). A review of the science of colorful, plant-based food and practical strategies for "eating the rainbow." *Journal of Nutrition and Metabolism, 2019*, 1–19. doi.org/10.1155/2019/2125070

"... Consuming these colorful vegetables." Blumfield, M., Mayr, H., De Vlieger, N., Abbott, K., Starck, C., Fayet-Moore, F., & Marshall, S. (2022). Should we "eat a rainbow"? An umbrella review of the health effects of colorful bioactive pigments in fruits and vegetables. *Molecules, 27*(13), 4061. doi.org/10.3390/molecules27134061

"... Eating the rainbow helps ensure." Wärnberg, J., Gomez-Martinez, S., Romeo, J., Díaz, L., & Marcos, A. (2009). Nutrition, inflammation, and cognitive function. *Annals of the New York Academy of Sciences, 1153*(1), 164–175. doi.org/10.1111/j.1749-6632.2008.03985.x

"... your microbiome loves fiber and variation." Enders, G. (2015). *Gut: The inside story of our body's most underrated organ.* Greystone Books.

"... Avoid Processed Foods." Fuhrman, J. (2018). The hidden dangers of fast and processed food. *American Journal of Lifestyle Medicine, 12*(5), 375–381. doi.org/10.1177/1559827618766483

"... work against microbiota health." Leo, E. E. M., & Campos, M. R. S. (2020). Effect of ultra-processed diet on gut microbiota and thus its role in neurodegenerative diseases. *Nutrition, 71*, 110609. doi.org/10.1016/j.nut.2019.110609

"... people cook for themselves." Reicks, M., Kocher, M., & Reeder, J. (2018). Impact of cooking and home food preparation interventions among adults: A systematic review (2011-2016). *Journal of Nutrition Education and Behavior*, *50*(2), 148-172.e1. doi.org/10.1016/j.jneb.2017.08.004

"... is to prepare it yourself." Reicks, M., Trofholz, A. C., Stang, J. S., & Laska, M. N. (2014). Impact of cooking and home food preparation interventions among adults: Outcomes and implications for future programs. *Journal of Nutrition Education and Behavior*, *46*(4), 259-276. doi.org/10.1016/j.jneb.2014.02.001

"... Try to eat with people." Mills, S., White, M., Brown, H., Wrieden, W., Kwasnicka, D., Halligan, J., Robalino, S., & Adams, J. (2017). Health and social determinants and outcomes of home cooking: A systematic review of observational studies. *Appetite*, *111*, 116-134. doi.org/10.1016/j.appet.2016.12.022

"... Fuel for Desired Cognitive Outcomes." Meeusen, R. (2014). Exercise, nutrition, and the brain. *Sports Medicine*, *44*(S1), 47-56. doi.org/10.1007/s40279-014-0150-5

"... Water Your Brain." Jéquier, E., & Constant, F. (2009). Water as an essential nutrient: The physiological basis of hydration. *European Journal of Clinical Nutrition*, *64*(2), 115-123. doi.org/10.1038/ejcn.2009.111

"... Water gets to the brain through the bloodstream." Benelam, B., & Wyness, L. (2010). Hydration and health: A review. *Nutrition Bulletin*, *35*(1), 3-25. doi.org/10.1111/j.1467-3010.2009.01795.x

"... water can dilute the delicate balance." Popkin, B. M., D'Anci, K. E., & Rosenberg, I. H. (2010). Water, hydration, and health. *Nutrition Reviews*, *68*(8), 439-458. doi.org/10.1111/j.1753-4887.2010.00304.x

"... What is the right amount of water." Mayo Clinic Staff. (2022, October 12). *Water: How much should you drink every day?* Mayo Clinic. mayoclinic.org/healthy-lifestyle/nutrition-and-healthy-eating/in-depth/water/art-20044256

"... carbonated or flavored water." Pelchat, M. L., Bryant, B., Cuomo, R., Di Salle, F., Fass, R., & Wise, P. (2014). Carbonation. *Nutrition Today*, *49*(6), 308-312. doi.org/10.1097/nt.0000000000000010

"... While scientifically the jury is out." Cuomo, R., Sarnelli, G., Savarese, M., & Buyckx, M. (2009). Carbonated beverages and gastrointestinal system: Between myth and reality. *Nutrition*

Metabolism and Cardiovascular Diseases, 19(10), 683-689. doi.org/10.1016/j.numecd.2009.03.020

"... Eat More Intuitively." Van Dyke, N., & Drinkwater, E. J. (2013). Relationships between intuitive eating and health indicators: Literature review. *Public Health Nutrition, 17*(8), 1757-1766. doi.org/10.1017/s1368980013002139

"... A set daily calorie limit fails." Schaefer, J. T., & Magnuson, A. B. (2014). A review of interventions that promote eating by internal cues. *Journal of the Academy of Nutrition and Dietetics, 114*(5), 734-760. doi.org/10.1016/j.jand.2013.12.024

"... important to develop the skill of listening." Warren, J. M., Smith, N., & Ashwell, M. (2017). A structured literature review on the role of mindfulness, mindful eating, and intuitive eating in changing eating behaviours: Effectiveness and associated potential mechanisms. *Nutrition Research Reviews, 30*(2), 272-283. doi.org/10.1017/s0954422417000154

"... eat slowly and deliberately." Tapper, K. (2022). Mindful eating: What we know so far. *Nutrition Bulletin, 47*(2), 168-185. doi.org/10.1111/nbu.12559

"... Mindful eating helps you eat." Lofgren, I. E. (2015). Mindful eating. *American Journal of Lifestyle Medicine, 9*(3), 212-216. doi.org/10.1177/1559827615569684

"... Practice *Hara Hachi Bu.*" Buettner, D., & Skemp, S. (2016). Blue zones. *American Journal of Lifestyle Medicine, 10*(5), 318-321. doi.org/10.1177/1559827616637066

"... Skimp on the Snacking." Verhoeven, A. A. C., Adriaanse, M. A., Evers, C., & De Ridder, D. T. D. (2012). The power of habits: Unhealthy snacking behaviour is primarily predicted by habit strength. *British Journal of Health Psychology, 17*(4), 758-770. doi.org/10.1111/j.2044-8287.2012.02070.x

"... Snacks of the prepackaged variety." Mielmann, A., & Brunner, T. A. (2019). Consumers' snack choices: Current factors contributing to obesity. *British Food Journal, 121*(2), 347-358. doi.org/10.1108/bfj-05-2018-0309

"... Snacking interferes with meals." Almoraie, N. M., Saqaan, R., Alharthi, R., Alamoudi, A., Badh, L., & Shatwan, I. M. (2021). Snacking patterns throughout the life span: Potential implications on health. *Nutrition Research, 91*, 81-94. doi.org/10.1016/j.nutres.2021.05.001

"... Fasting Sometimes Is Fine." Varady, K. A., Cienfuegos, S., Ezpeleta, M., & Gabel, K. (2021). Cardiometabolic benefits of intermittent fasting. *Annual Review of Nutrition*, *41*(1), 333-361. doi.org/10.1146/annurev-nutr-052020-041327

"... brains and bodies are biologically." Horne, B. D., Muhlestein, J. B., & Anderson, J. L. (2015). Health effects of intermittent fasting: Hormesis or harm? A systematic review. *American Journal of Clinical Nutrition*, *102*(2), 464-470. doi.org/10.3945/ajcn.115.109553

"... variations in blood sugar." Patterson, R. E., & Sears, D. D. (2017). Metabolic effects of intermittent fasting. *Annual Review of Nutrition*, *37*(1), 371-393. doi.org/10.1146/annurev-nutr-071816-064634

"... Skip the Supplements (Probably)." Valavanidis, A. (2016). Dietary supplements: Beneficial to human health or just peace of mind? A critical review on the issue of benefit/risk of dietary supplements. *Pharmakeftiki*, *28*(2), 60-83.

"... The longer answer is: it depends." Wierzejska, R. E. (2021). Dietary supplements: For whom? The current state of knowledge about the health effects of selected supplement use. *International Journal of Environmental Research and Public Health*, *18*(17), 8897. doi.org/10.3390/ijerph18178897

"... inclusions that are not as benign as we might like." Costa, J. G., Vidovic, B., Saraiva, N., Costa, M. D. C., Del Favero, G., Marko, D., Oliveira, N. G., & Fernandes, A. S. (2019). Contaminants: A dark side of food supplements? *Free Radical Research*, *53*(Supplement 1), 1113-1135. doi.org/10.1080/10715762.2019.1636045

"... Several commonly taken supplements." Marik, P. E., & Flemmer, M. (2012). Do dietary supplements have beneficial health effects in industrialized nations. *Journal of Parenteral and Enteral Nutrition*, *36*(2), 159-168. doi.org/10.1177/0148607111416485

"... You don't want to rely." Maughan, R. J., Shirreffs, S. M., & Vernec, A. (2018). Making decisions about supplement use. *International Journal of Sport Nutrition and Exercise Metabolism*, *28*(2), 212-219. doi.org/10.1123/ijsnem.2018-0009

"... Consume Caffeine in Moderation." Barone, J., & Roberts, H. (1996). Caffeine consumption. *Food and Chemical Toxicology*, *34*(1), 119-129. doi.org/10.1016/0278-6915(95)00093-3

"... Slow metabolizers of caffeine." Nehlig, A. (2018). Interindividual differences in caffeine metabolism and factors driving caffeine consumption. *Pharmacological Reviews, 70*(2), 384-411. doi.org/10.1124/pr.117.014407

"... You know you have had the right amount." Smith, A. (2002). Effects of caffeine on human behavior. *Food and Chemical Toxicology, 40*(9), 1243-1255. doi.org/10.1016/s0278-6915(02)00096-0

"... Avoid Alcohol." Ashley, M. J., & Rankin, J. G. (1988). A public health approach to the prevention of alcohol-related health problems. *Annual Review of Public Health, 9*(1), 233-271. doi.org/10.1146/annurev.pu.09.050188.001313

"... Alcohol is especially bad for sleep." Voigt, R. M., Forsyth, C. B., & Keshavarzian, A. (2013). Circadian disruption: Potential implications in inflammatory and metabolic diseases associated with alcohol. *Alcohol Research: Current Reviews, 35*(1), 87.

Chapter 9: Rest

"... using wearable technology." Tanier, M. (2016, October 6). *Next big thing: Sleep science is becoming the NFL's secret weapon*. Bleacher Report. bleacherreport.com/articles/2650188-next-big-thing-sleep-science-is-becoming-the-nfls-secret-weapon

"... player's stress response." Watson, A. M. (2017). Sleep and athletic performance. *Current Sports Medicine Reports, 16*(6), 413-418. doi.org/10.1249/jsr.0000000000000418

"... Like brain research, sleep research." Huffington, A. (2016). *The sleep revolution: Transforming your life, one night at a time*. Harmony.

"... near-magical value for you." Maas, J. B., & Robbins, R. S. (2011). *Sleep for success: Everything you must know about sleep but are too tired to ask*. AuthorHouse.

"... sleep is known to fix or improve." Hernandez, M. (2023). The benefits of sleep. In A. Ratnasekera, M. Neff, K. Yoon-Flannery, & A. Beekley (Eds.), *General surgery residency survival guide* (pp. 165-172). Springer.

"... Overall attractiveness." Axelsson, J., Sundelin, T., Ingre, M., Van Someren, E. J. W., Olsson, A., & Lekander, M. (2010). Beauty sleep: Experimental study on the perceived health and attractiveness of sleep deprived people. *BMJ, 341*, c6614. doi.org/10.1136/bmj.c6614

"... The quality of your nighttime sleep." Porkka-Heiskanen, T., Zitting, K., & Wigren, H. (2013). Sleep, its regulation, and possible mechanisms of sleep disturbances. *Acta Physiologica, 208*(4), 311-328. doi.org/10.1111/apha.12134

"... key practice of the highest performers." Winter, W. C. (2017). *The sleep solution: Why your sleep is broken and how to fix it.* New American Library.

"... Nathaniel Kleitman introduced." Kleitman, N. (1933). Studies on the physiology of sleep. *American Journal of Physiology, 104*(2), 449-456. doi.org/10.1152/ajplegacy.1933.104.2.449

"... different types of waves." Chauhan, P., & Preetam, M. (2016). Brain waves and sleep science. *International Journal of Engineering Science and Advanced Research, 2*(1), 33-36.

"... The timing of the different stages of sleep." Blake, H., & Gerard, R. W. (1937). Brain potentials during sleep. *American Journal of Physiology, 119*(4), 692-703. doi.org/10.1152/ajplegacy.1937.119.4.692

"... stages of sleep that you cycle." Carskadon, M. A., & Dement, W. C. (2005). Normal human sleep: An overview. *Principles and Practice of Sleep Medicine, 4*(1), 13-23. doi.org/10.1016/b0-72-160797-7/50009-4

"... Time for vivid dreaming." Peever, J., & Fuller, P. M. (2016). Neuroscience: A distributed neural network controls REM sleep. *Current Biology, 26*(1), R34-R35. doi.org/10.1016/j.cub.2015.11.011

"... Several factors affect which brain waves." Smagula, S. F., Stone, K. L., Fabio, A., & Cauley, J. A. (2016). Risk factors for sleep disturbances in older adults: Evidence from prospective studies. *Sleep Medicine Reviews, 25*, 21-30. doi.org/10.1016/j.smrv.2015.01.003

"... Ironically, being sleep deprived." Orzel-Gryglewska, J. (2010). Consequences of sleep deprivation. *International Journal of Occupational Medicine and Environmental Health, 23*(1), 95-114.

"... why humans sleep." Freiberg, A. S. (2020). Why we sleep: A hypothesis for an ultimate or evolutionary origin for sleep and other physiological rhythms. *Journal of Circadian Rhythms, 18*(1), 2. doi.org/10.5334/jcr.189

"... A biologist might say." Siegel, J. M. (2022). Sleep function: An evolutionary perspective. *Lancet Neurology, 21*(10), 937-946. doi.org/10.1016/s1474-4422(22)00210-1

"... sleep is so highly productive." Walker, M. (2017). *Why we sleep: Unlocking the power of sleep and dreams.* Scribner.

"... the brain does not rest when you do." Graven, S. (2006). Sleep and brain development. *Clinics in Perinatology, 33*(3), 693-706. doi.org/10.1016/j.clp.2006.06.009

"... Why would the brain be so." Kavanau, J. (1997). Origin and evolution of sleep: Roles of vision and endothermy. *Brain Research Bulletin*, *42*(4), 245-264. doi.org/10.1016/s0361-9230(96)00331-0

"... there really is no trade-off." Suni, E. (2020). *How much sleep do we really need?* National Sleep Foundation. sleepfoundation.org/how-sleep-works/how-much-sleep-do-we-really-need

"... because you almost certainly need it." Dement, W. C. (2005). Sleep extension: Getting as much extra sleep as possible. *Clinics in Sports Medicine*, *24*(2), 251-268. doi.org/10.1016/j.csm.2004.12.014

"... Scientists agree that humans need." Ferrara, M., & De Gennaro, L. (2001). How much sleep do we need? *Sleep Medicine Reviews*, *5*(2), 155-179. doi.org/10.1053/smrv.2000.0138

"... sleep requirements exist on a spectrum." Grandner, M. A. (2022). Sleep, health, and society. *Sleep Medicine Clinics*, *17*(2), 117-139. doi.org/10.1016/j.jsmc.2022.03.001

"... You know you have had enough sleep when." Horne, J. (2010). Sleepiness as a need for sleep: When is enough, enough? *Neuroscience and Biobehavioral Reviews*, *34*(1), 108-118. doi.org/10.1016/j.neubiorev.2009.07.009

"... Because the business day waits for no one." Takahashi, M. (2012). Prioritizing sleep for healthy work schedules. *Journal of Physiological Anthropology*, *31*, 1-9. doi.org/10.1186/1880-6805-31-6

"... Desirable Dreaming." Nir, Y., & Tononi, G. (2010). Dreaming and the brain: From phenomenology to neurophysiology. *Trends in Cognitive Sciences*, *14*(2), 88-100. doi.org/10.1016/j.tics.2009.12.001

"... Some dreams occur." Baird, B., Mota-Rolim, S. A., & Dresler, M. (2019). The cognitive neuroscience of lucid dreaming. *Neuroscience and Biobehavioral Reviews*, *100*, 305-323. doi.org/10.1016/j.neubiorev.2019.03.008

"... Dreaming is a cognitively." Revonsuo, A. (2000). The reinterpretation of dreams: An evolutionary hypothesis of the function of dreaming. *Behavioral and Brain Sciences*, *23*(6), 877-901. doi.org/10.1017/s0140525x00004015

"... REM gives you a chance to process emotions." Scarpelli, S., Bartolacci, C., D'Atri, A., Gorgoni, M., & De Gennaro, L. (2019). The functional role of dreaming in emotional processes. *Frontiers in Psychology*, *10*, 459. doi.org/10.3389/fpsyg.2019.00459

"... If you were being monitored." Dang-Vu, T., Desseilles, M., Albouy, G., Darsaud, A., Gais, S., Rauchs, G., Schabus, M., Sterpenich, V.,

Vandewalle, G., Schwartz, S., Maquet, P., & Thien, T. (2005). Dreaming: A neuroimaging view. *Swiss Archives of Neurology, Psychiatry, and Psychotherapy, 156*(8), 415–425. doi.org/10.4414/sanp.2005.01655

"... dreaming is a marvel." Hobson, J. A., Pace-Schott, E. F., & Stickgold, R. (2000). Dreaming and the brain: Toward a cognitive neuroscience of conscious states. *Behavioral and Brain Sciences, 23*(6), 793–842. doi.org/10.1017/s0140525x00003976

"... Productive Daydreaming." Zedelius, C. M., Protzko, J., Broadway, J. M., & Schooler, J. W. (2021). What types of daydreaming predict creativity? Laboratory and experience sampling evidence. *Psychology of Aesthetics, Creativity, and the Arts, 15*(4), 596–611. doi.org/10.1037/aca0000342

"... You have probably had this experience." Delaney, P. F., Sahakyan, L., Kelley, C. M., & Zimmerman, C. A. (2010). Remembering to forget: The amnesic effect of daydreaming. *Psychological Science, 21*(7), 1036–1042. doi.org/10.1177/0956797610374739

"... can feel so charged or even emotional." Poerio, G. L., & Smallwood, J. (2016). Daydreaming to navigate the social world: What we know, what we don't know, and why it matters. *Social and Personality Psychology Compass, 10*(11), 605–618. doi.org/10.1111/spc3.12288

"... Napping the Day Away." Lovato, N., & Lack, L. (2010). The effects of napping on cognitive functioning. In G. A. Kerkhof & A. P. A. van Dongen (Eds.), *Progress in brain research* (pp. 155–166). Elsevier. doi.org/10.1016/b978-0-444-53702-7.00009-9

"... well-being, performance, and progress." Jones, B. J., & Spencer, R. M. C. (2020). Role of napping for learning across the lifespan. *Current Sleep Medicine Reports, 6*(4), 290–297. doi.org/10.1007/s40675-020-00193-9

"... Napping continues to be studied." Mantua, J., & Spencer, R. M. (2017). Exploring the nap paradox: Are mid-day sleep bouts a friend or foe? *Sleep Medicine, 37*, 88–97. doi.org/10.1016/j.sleep.2017.01.019

"... all the disadvantages of." Rosekind, M. R., Gregory, K. B., Mallis, M. M., Brandt, S. L., Seal, B., & Lerner, D. (2010). The cost of poor sleep: Workplace productivity loss and associated costs. *Journal of Occupational and Environmental Medicine, 52*(1), 91–98. doi.org/10.1097/jom.0b013e3181c78c30

"... a little sleep deprived." National Center for Health Statistics. (2023, February 23). *Sleep health.* US Centers for Disease Control and Prevention. cdc.gov/nchs/fastats/sleep-health.htm

"... Sleep deprivation has been shown." Grandner, M. A. (2022). Sleep, health, and society. *Sleep Medicine Clinics, 17*(2), 117–139. doi.org/10.1016/j.jsmc.2022.03.001

"... as long as you reprioritize." Krause, A. J., Simon, E. B., Mander, B. A., Greer, S. M., Saletin, J. M., Goldstein-Piekarski, A. N., & Walker, M. P. (2017). The sleep-deprived human brain. *Nature Reviews Neuroscience, 18*(7), 404–418. doi.org/10.1038/nrn.2017.55

"... sleep factors very highly." Goel, N., Rao, H., Durmer, J., & Dinges, D. (2009). Neurocognitive consequences of sleep deprivation. *Seminars in Neurology, 29*(4), 320–339. doi.org/10.1055/s-0029-1237117

"... If you get more high-quality sleep." Litwiller, B., Snyder, L. A., Taylor, W. D., & Steele, L. M. (2017). The relationship between sleep and work: A meta-analysis. *Journal of Applied Psychology, 102*(4), 682–699. doi.org/10.1037/apl0000169

"... Be Rigidly Consistent." Chaput, J. P., Dutil, C., Featherstone, R., Ross, R., Giangregorio, L., Saunders, T. J., Janssen, I., Poitras, V. J., Kho, M. E., Ross-White, A., Zankar, S., & Carrier, J. (2020). Sleep timing, sleep consistency, and health in adults: A systematic review. *Applied Physiology, Nutrition, and Metabolism, 45*(10 (Suppl. 2)), S232–S247. doi.org/10.1139/apnm-2020-0032

"... ideal routine." Mayo Clinic Staff. (2022, May 7). *Sleep tips: 6 steps to better sleep.* Mayo Clinic. mayoclinic.org/healthy-lifestyle/adult-health/in-depth/sleep/art-20048379

"... decreases how well your physiological." Wahl, S., Engelhardt, M., Schaupp, P., Lappe, C., & Ivanov, I. V. (2019). The inner clock: Blue light sets the human rhythm. *Journal of Biophotonics, 12*(12). doi.org/10.1002/jbio.201900102

"... Blue light is known to disrupt." Hatori, M., Gronfier, C., Van Gelder, R. N., Bernstein, P. S., Carreras, J., Panda, S., Marks, F., Sliney, D., Hunt, C. E., Hirota, T., Furukawa, T., & Tsubota, K. (2017). Global rise of potential health hazards caused by blue light-induced circadian disruption in modern aging societies. *NPJ Aging and Mechanisms of Disease, 3*(9). doi.org/10.1038/s41514-017-0010-2

"... aren't getting too much disruptive blue light." Lawrenson, J. G., Hull, C. C., & Downie, L. E. (2017). The effect of blue-light blocking spectacle lenses on visual performance, macular health, and the sleep-wake cycle: A systematic review of the literature. *Ophthalmic and Physiological Optics, 37*(6), 644–654. doi.org/10.1111/opo.12406

"... Invest in Getting the Setting." Turner, N. (2010). *The hormone diet.* Random House Canada.

"... Assess Daytime Napping Honestly." Mantua, J., & Spencer, R. M. (2017). Exploring the nap paradox: Are mid-day sleep bouts a friend or foe? *Sleep Medicine, 37*, 88–97. doi.org/10.1016/j.sleep.2017.01.019

"... Napping should be a complement." Ficca, G., Axelsson, J., Mollicone, D. J., Muto, V., & Vitiello, M. V. (2010). Naps, cognition, and performance. *Sleep Medicine Reviews, 14*(4), 249–258. doi.org/10.1016/j.smrv.2009.09.005

"... because of the importance of sleep." Wells, M. E., & Vaughn, B. V. (2012). Poor sleep challenging the health of a nation. *Neurodiagnostic Journal, 52*(3), 233–249. doi.org/10.1080/21646821.2012.11079859

"... Sleep is so important." Pilcher, J. J., & Morris, D. M. (2020). Sleep and organizational behavior: Implications for workplace productivity and safety. *Frontiers in Psychology, 11*, 45. doi.org/10.3389/fpsyg.2020.00045

Chapter 10: Interact

"... Suppose you have the opportunity." Meinel, M., Maier, L., Wagner, T., & Voigt, K. I. (2017). Designing creativity-enhancing workspaces: A critical look at empirical evidence. *Journal of Technology and Innovation Management, 1*(1). papers.ssrn.com/sol3/papers.cfm?abstract_id=3051058

"... You would be faced with a new kind of office." Engelen, L. (2020). Does active design influence activity, sitting, well-being, and productivity in the workplace? A systematic review. *International Journal of Environmental Research and Public Health, 17*(24), 9228. doi.org/10.3390/ijerph17249228

"... You would notice all kinds of furniture." Haynes, B. P. (2008). The impact of office comfort on productivity. *Journal of Facilities Management, 6*(1), 37–51. doi.org/10.1108/14725960810847459

"... best possible performance." Shafaghat, A., Keyvanfar, A., Ferwati, M. S., & Alizadeh, T. (2015). Enhancing staff's satisfaction with comfort toward productivity by sustainable Open Plan Office Design. *Sustainable Cities and Society, 19*, 151–164. doi.org/10.1016/j.scs.2015.08.001

"... The idea is that mixing and mingling." Zhou, J., & Hoever, I. J. (2014). Research on workplace creativity: A review and redirection. *Annual Review of Organizational Psychology and Organizational Behavior*, *1*(1), 333-359. doi.org/10.1146/annurev-orgpsych-031413-091226

"... Workers can feel a sense of." Venkataramani, V., Labianca, G. J., & Grosser, T. (2013). Positive and negative workplace relationships, social satisfaction, and organizational attachment. *Journal of Applied Psychology*, *98*(6), 1028-1039. doi.org/10.1037/a0034090

"... foster interaction, connection, belonging." Rizana, D., Muafi, M., & Helmy, I. (2023). Workplace friendship influences innovative work behavior: The mediating role of psychological empowerment and knowledge sharing. In A. Hamdan, A. Harraf, A. Buallay, P. Arora, & H. Alsabatin (Eds.), *Studies in systems, decision, and control: Vol. 47. From industry 4.0 to industry 5.0: Mapping the transitions* (pp. 101-111). Springer. doi.org/10.1007/978-3-031-28314-7_10

"... Research (including my own) attests that social interaction." Molina-Morales, F. X., & Martínez-Fernández, M. T. (2010). Social networks: Effects of social capital on firm innovation. *Journal of Small Business Management*, *48*(2), 258-279. doi.org/10.1111/j.1540-627x.2010.00294.x

"... satisfied in their job." Winstead, B. A., Derlega, V. J., Montgomery, M. J., & Pilkington, C. (1995). The quality of friendships at work and job satisfaction. *Journal of Social and Personal Relationships*, *12*(2), 199-215. doi.org/10.1177/0265407595122003

"... employees with richer social bonds at work." Bandiera, O., Barankay, I., & Rasul, I. (2010). Social incentives in the workplace. *Review of Economic Studies*, *77*(2), 417-458. doi.org/10.1111/j.1467-937x.2009.00574.x

"... Our brains are highly motivated." Hagerty, B. M., Williams, R. A., Coyne, J. C., & Early, M. R. (1996). Sense of belonging and indicators of social and psychological functioning. *Archives of Psychiatric Nursing*, *10*(4), 235-244. doi.org/10.1016/s0883-9417(96)80029-x

"... our own social standing, support, and opportunities." Repetti, R. L., & Cosmas, K. A. (1991). The quality of the social environment at work and job satisfaction. *Journal of Applied Social Psychology*, *21*(10), 840-854. doi.org/10.1111/j.1559-1816.1991.tb00446.x

"... Google witnessed first-hand the benefit." Poleo, F. A. (2023, October 31). *Innovation strategies: Unpacking Google's 20% time policy.*

DANAconnect. danaconnect.com/the-power-of-dedicated-innovation-time-unpacking-googles-20-time-policy

"... Forging social connections." Hagerty, B. M., Lynch-Sauer, J., Patusky, K. L., Bouwsema, M., & Collier, P. (1992). Sense of belonging: A vital mental health concept. *Archives of Psychiatric Nursing*, *6*(3), 172–177. doi.org/10.1016/0883-9417(92)90028-h

"... motivational gold for individual work." Zhao, X., Yi, C., & Chen, C. (2022). How to stimulate employees' innovative behavior: Internal social capital, workplace friendship, and innovative identity. *Frontiers in Psychology*, *13*, 1000332. doi.org/10.3389/fpsyg.2022.1000332

"... prevalence of social information processing." Rock, D. (2009, August 27). *Managing with the brain in mind*. Strategy + Business. strategy-business.com/article/09306

"... Further, it turns out that most neural networks." Rock, D. (2009). *Your brain at work: Strategies for overcoming distraction, regaining focus, and working smarter all day long*. HarperCollins.

"... Social information, decision-making." Waber, B. N., Olguin, D. O., Kim, T., & Pentland, A. (2010). Productivity through coffee breaks: Changing social networks by changing break structure. *Social Science Research Network*. doi.org/10.2139/ssrn.1586375

"... Because of the importance to our survival." Lieberman, M. D. (2013). *Social: Why our brains are wired to connect*. Crown Publishing Group.

"... why our brains might be so socially oriented." Arioli, M., Crespi, C., & Canessa, N. (2018). Social cognition through the lens of cognitive and clinical neuroscience. *BioMed Research International*, *2018*(1), 4283427. doi.org/10.1155/2018/4283427

"... we get survival-critical resources from other people." Denworth, L. (2020). *Friendship: The evolution, biology, and extraordinary power of life's fundamental bond*. W. W. Norton & Company.

"... social needs can often override." Petersen, M., Roepstorff, A., & Serritzlew, S. (2009). Social capital in the brain? In G. T. Svendsen & G. K. H. Svendsen (Eds.), *Handbook of social capital: The troika of sociology, political science, and economics*. Edward Elgar Publishing.

"... significant impact on your brain." Reyes, S., Giovannoni, G., & Thomson, A. (2018). Social capital: Implications for neurology. *Brain and Behavior*, *9*(1). doi.org/10.1002/brb3.1169

"... than those with weaker social ties." Becht, A. I., Wierenga, L. M., Mills, K. L., Meuwese, R., Van Duijvenvoorde, A., Blakemore, S. J.,

Güroğlu, B., & Crone, E. A. (2020). Beyond the average brain: Individual differences in social brain development are associated with friendship quality. *Social Cognitive and Affective Neuroscience*, *16*(3), 292–301. doi.org/10.1093/scan/nsaa166

"... more and higher-quality social ties." Kwak, S., Joo, W. T., Youm, Y., & Chey, J. (2018). Social brain volume is associated with in-degree social network size among older adults. *Proceedings of Royal Society B: Biological Sciences*, *285*(1871), 20172708. doi.org/10.1098/rspb.2017.2708

"... Another study found." Offord, C. (2020, July 13). *How social isolation affects the brain.* Department of Psychiatry and Behavioral Neuroscience, University of Chicago. psychiatry.uchicago.edu/news/how-social-isolation-affects-brain

"... mental and cognitive performance." Baron, R. A., & Markman, G. D. (2000). Beyond social capital: How social skills can enhance entrepreneurs' success. *Academy of Management Perspectives*, *14*(1), 106–116. doi.org/10.5465/ame.2000.2909843

"... increase in proportion to the number of people." King, M. (2022). *Social chemistry: Decoding the patterns of human connection.* Penguin Random House.

"... Not only is work where we earn our living." Seibert, S. E., Kraimer, M. L., & Liden, R. C. (2001). A social capital theory of career success. *Academy of Management Journal*, *44*(2), 219–237. doi.org/10.5465/3069452

"... how connected to and supported by." Denworth, L. (2020). *Friendship: The evolution, biology, and extraordinary power of life's fundamental bond.* W. W. Norton & Company.

"... Even in a modern context." Lundqvist, D., Fogelberg Eriksson, A., & Ekberg, K. (2018). Managers' social support: Facilitators and hindrances for seeking support at work. *Work*, *59*(3), 351–365. doi.org/10.3233/WOR-182690

"... and ultimately success as a professional." Tymon, W. G., & Stumpf, S. A. (2003). Social capital in the success of knowledge workers. *Career Development International*, *8*(1), 12–20. doi.org/10.1108/13620430310459478

"... Because social processing happens in." Olson, I. R., Plotzker, A., & Ezzyat, Y. (2007). The enigmatic temporal pole: A review of findings on social and emotional processing. *Brain*, *130*(7), 1718–1731. doi.org/10.1093/brain/awm052

"... what our brains process as social rewards." Brann, A. (2022). *Neuroscience for coaches: How coaches and managers can use the latest insights to benefit clients and teams*. Kogan Page.

"... Our emotional states, stability, psychological safety." Jasiński, A. M., & Derbis, R. (2023). Social support at work and job satisfaction among midwives: The mediating role of positive affect and work engagement. *Journal of Advanced Nursing, 79*(1), 149-160. doi.org/10.1111/jan.15462

"... how much we feel we belong." Dalgleish, T. (2004). The emotional brain. *Nature Reviews Neuroscience, 5*(7), 583-589. doi.org/10.1038/nrn1432

"... important to monitor and nurture social." Mori, T., Nagata, T., Odagami, K., Nagata, M., Adi, N. P., & Mori, K. (2023). Workplace social support and work engagement among Japanese workers: A nationwide cross-sectional study. *Journal of Occupational and Environmental Medicine, 65*(7), e514-e519. doi.org/10.1097/JOM.0000000000002876

"... Because you must work with people." Pulles, N. J., & Hartman, P. (2017). Likeability and its effect on outcomes of interpersonal interaction. *Industrial Marketing Management, 66*, 56-63. doi.org/10.1016/j.indmarman.2017.06.008

"... predictive of how happy and successful." Sanders, T. (2006). *The likeability factor: How to boost your L-factor and achieve your life's dreams*. Crown Currency.

"... help you, collaborate, and cooperate with you." Carnegie, D. (1958). *How to win friends and influence people*. Pocket Books.

"... Social standing, status, relationships." Seibert, S. E., Kraimer, M. L., & Liden, R. C. (2001). A social capital theory of career success. *Academy of Management Journal, 44*(2), 219-237. doi.org/10.5465/3069452

"... support can be used to gain financial capital." Thomas, A., & Gupta, V. (2021). Social capital theory, social exchange theory, social cognitive theory, financial literacy, and the role of knowledge sharing as a moderator in enhancing financial well-being: From bibliometric analysis to a conceptual framework model. *Frontiers in Psychology, 12*, 664638. doi.org/10.3389/fpsyg.2021.664638

"... Many studies assert the importance of having friends." Persin, N. (2023, May 30). *The importance of having friends at work*. i Creatives

Staffing. icreatives.com/iblog/the-importance-of-having
-friends-at-work

"... Exit interviews show." Lee, T. W., Burch, T. C., & Mitchell, T. R. (2014). The story of why we stay: A review of job embeddedness. *Annual Review of Organizational Psychology and Organizational Behavior*, *1*(1), 199–216. doi.org/10.1146/annurev-orgpsych-031413-091244

"... When people like and feel connected." Carmeli, A., Brueller, D., & Dutton, J. E. (2008). Learning behaviours in the workplace: The role of high-quality interpersonal relationships and psychological safety. *Systems Research and Behavioral Science*, *26*(1), 81–98. doi.org/10.1002/sres.932

"... it benefits both the individual and the organization." Frazier, M. L., Fainshmidt, S., Klinger, R. L., Pezeshkan, A., & Vracheva, V. (2016). Psychological safety: A meta-analytic review and extension. *Personnel Psychology*, *70*(1), 113–165. doi.org/10.1111/peps.12183

"... The ideal would be that." Bridge, K., & Baxter, L. A. (1992). Blended relationships: Friends as work associates. *Western Journal of Communication*, *56*(3), 200–225. doi.org/10.1080/10570319 209374414

"... it will benefit you in multiple ways." Liao, H., Su, R., Ptashnik, T., & Nielsen, J. (2022). Feeling good, doing good, and getting ahead: A meta-analytic investigation of the outcomes of prosocial motivation at work. *Psychological Bulletin*, *148*(3–4), 158–198. doi.org/10.1037/bul0000362

"... There are many ways to be more prosocial. " Helliwell, J., Aknin, L., Shiplett, H., Huang, H., & Wang, S. (2017). *Social capital and prosocial behaviour as sources of well-being* (Working Paper 23761). National Bureau of Economic Research. doi.org/10.3386/w23761

"... both at and outside of work." Paukcsztat, B., & Grech, M. R. (2022). Building social support: The impact of workgroup characteristics, the COVID-19 pandemic, and informal interactions. *Work*, *72*(4), 1175–1189. doi.org/10.3233/WOR-220020

"... Listen more." Springman, J. (2011, October 27). Marketers, calculate your talk-listen ratio. *Harvard Business Review*. hbr.org/2011/10/marketers-calculate-your-talk

"... the other to be listening to them." Zenger, J. (2017, August 17). Listening and speaking: The leader's paradox. *Forbes*. forbes.com/sites/jackzenger/2017/08/17/listening-and-speaking-the-leaders-paradox

"... Avoid the four unsocial Cs." Carnegie, D. (1958). *How to win friends and influence people*. Pocket Books.

"... Demonstrate the four prosocial Cs." Dunfield, K. A. (2014). A construct divided: Prosocial behavior as helping, sharing, and comforting subtypes. *Frontiers in Psychology, 5*, 958. doi.org/10.3389/fpsyg.2014.00958

"... can improve interpersonal interactions." Bellucci, G., Camilleri, J. A., Eickhoff, S. B., & Krueger, F. (2020). Neural signatures of prosocial behaviors. *Neuroscience and Biobehavioral Reviews, 118*, 186–195. doi.org/10.1016/j.neubiorev.2020.07.006

"... Use open body language." Saraev, N. (2021, December 7). *Open body language: How to look confident, with science*. Medium. nicksaraev.medium.com/evolution-body-language-how-to-get-ahead-in-your-career-with-science-493b32bc9f77

"... Body language is one of the loudest forms of communication." Collett, P. (2017). *How to tell what people are thinking*. HarperCollins.

"... Use the Halo Effect." Lucker, G. W., Beane, W. E., & Helmreich, R. L. (1981). The strength of the halo effect in physical attractiveness research. *Journal of Psychology, 107*(1), 69–75. doi.org/10.1080/00223980.1981.9915206

"... people who are perceived to be good looking." Landy, D., & Sigall, H. (1974). Beauty is talent: Task evaluation as a function of the performer's physical attractiveness. *Journal of Personality and Social Psychology, 29*(3), 299–304. doi.org/10.1037/h0036018

"... Compared with those deemed less attractive." Little, A. C., & Roberts, S. C. (2012). Evolution, appearance, and occupational success. *Evolutionary Psychology, 10*(5), 782–801. doi.org/10.1177/147470491201000503

"... hired, promoted, and paid more." Scholz, J. K., & Sicinski, K. (2015). Facial attractiveness and lifetime earnings: Evidence from a cohort study. *Review of Economics and Statistics, 97*(1), 14–28. doi.org/10.1162/rest_a_00435

"... Take care of your physical self." Spence, C. (2021). The scent of attraction and the smell of success: Crossmodal influences on person perception. *Cognitive Research, 6*(1). doi.org/10.1186/s41235-021-00311-3

"... Be upbeat." Grosz, M. P., Leckelt, M., & Back, M. D. (2020). Personality predictors of social status attainment. *Current Opinion in Psychology, 33*, 52–56. doi.org/10.1016/j.copsyc.2019.07.023

"... A smile is one of." Reysen, S. (2006). A new predictor of likeability: Laughter. *North American Journal of Psychology, 8*(2), 373. link.gale.com/apps/doc/A159922614/AONE?u=anon~38557f0e

"... Project confidence." Giang, V. (2022, September 9). *How to look confident: Body language and posture.* American Express. americanexpress.com/en-us/business/trends-and-insights/articles/4-ways-your-body-language-can-project-confidence

"... Control Social Comparisons." Suls, J., & Wheeler, L. (2012). Social comparison theory. In P. A. M. Van Lange, A. W. Kruglanski, & E. T. Higgins (Eds.), *Handbook of theories of social psychology* (Vol. 1, pp. 460–482). SAGE Publications. doi.org/10.4135/9781446249215.n23

"... you would typically end up feeling." Pillemer, J., & Rothbard, N. P. (2018). Friends without benefits: Understanding the dark sides of workplace friendship. *Academy of Management Review, 43*(4), 635–660. doi.org/10.5465/amr.2016.0309

"... unhealthy competition." Wheeler, L. (2000). Individual differences in social comparison. In J. Suls and L. Wheeler (Eds.), *Handbook of social comparison: Theory and research* (pp. 141–158). Springer. doi.org/10.1007/978-1-4615-4237-7_8

"... Choose Your Companions Wisely." Wells, G. (2007). Who we become depends on the company we keep and on what we do and say together. *International Journal of Educational Research, 46*(1–2), 100–103. doi.org/10.1016/j.ijer.2007.07.010

"... challenges in our social interactions at work." Donohue, W. A., & Cai, D. A. (2014). Interpersonal conflict: An overview. In N. A. Burrell, M. Allen, B. M. Gayle, & R. W. Preiss (Eds.), *Managing interpersonal conflict: Advances through meta-analysis* (pp. 22–41). Routledge. doi.org/10.4324/9780203149041

"... expectations create opportunity for stress." Roloff, M. E., & Chiles, B. W. (2011). Interpersonal conflict: Recent trends. In M. L. Knapp and J. A. Daly (Eds.), *The SAGE handbook of interpersonal communication* (4th ed., pp. 423–443). SAGE Publications.

"... Communicating Boundaries Proactively." Mellner, C., Peters, P., Dragt, M. J., & Toivanen, S. (2021). Predicting work–life conflict: Types and levels of enacted and preferred work-nonwork boundary (in)congruence and perceived boundary control. *Frontiers in Psychology, 12*, 772537. doi.org/10.3389/fpsyg.2021.772537

Chapter 11: Think

"... To succeed at difficult things in life." Duckworth, A. L., Peterson, C., Matthews, M. D., & Kelly, D. R. (2007). Grit: Perseverance and passion for long-term goals. *Journal of Personality and Social Psychology*, 92(6), 1087–1101. doi.org/10.1037/0022-3514.92.6.1087

"... Like muscles, mental abilities get stronger." Fava, G. A., & Guidi, J. (2020). The pursuit of euthymia. *World Psychiatry*, 19(1), 40–50. doi.org/10.1002/wps.20698

"... That something is almost always." Barczak, N., & Eklund, R. C. (2018). The moderating effect of self-compassion on relationships between performance and subsequent coping and motivation. *International Journal of Sport and Exercise Psychology*, 18(2), 256–268. doi.org/10.1080/1612197x.2018.1511620

"... you aren't at the mercy of your own wayward thoughts." Neck, C. P., & Manz, C. C. (1992). Thought self-leadership: The influence of self-talk and mental imagery on performance. *Journal of Organizational Behavior*, 13(7), 681–699. doi.org/10.1002/job.4030130705

"... intentionally working on this is critical." Latham G. P. (2006). *Work motivation: History, theory, research, and practice*. SAGE Publications.

"... Fixed versus Growth Mindsets." Dweck, C. S. (2006). *Mindset: The new psychology of success*. Ballantine Books.

"... A Mindset Beyond Growth." Taleb, N. N. (2012). *Antifragile: Things that gain from disorder*. Random House.

"... to the context of human mindset." Karam, S. (2023, September 23). Thriving in chaos: Unpacking Nassim Taleb's "antifragile." Medium. medium.com/@karamsharkas/thriving-in-chaos-unpacking-nassim-talebs-antifragile-47cdd94afaf9

"... you develop the new neural connections." Fava, G. A., Sonino, N., Lucente, M., & Guidi, J. (2022). Allostatic load in clinical practice. *Clinical Psychological Science*, 11(2), 345–356. doi.org/10.1177/21677026221121601

"... Likely the most powerful, persuasive, and relevant voice." Kim, J., Kwon, J. H., Kim, J., Kim, E. J., Kim, H. E., Kyeong, S., & Kim, J. J. (2021). The effects of positive or negative self-talk on the alteration of brain functional connectivity by performing cognitive tasks. *Scientific Reports*, 11(1). doi.org/10.1038/s41598-021-94328-9

"... Positive self-talk." Rogelberg, S. G., Justice, L., Braddy, P. W., Paustian-Underdahl, S. C., Heggestad, E., Shanock, L., Baran, B. E.,

Beck, T., Long, S., Andrew, A., Altman, D. G., & Fleenor, J. W. (2013). The executive mind: Leader self-talk, effectiveness, and strain. *Journal of Managerial Psychology, 28*(2), 183–201. doi.org/10.1108/02683941311300702

"... how you train and respond to your own internal narratives." Tod, D., Hardy, J., & Oliver, E. (2011). Effects of self-talk: A systematic review. *Journal of Sport & Exercise Psychology, 33*(5), 666–687. doi.org/10.1123/jsep.33.5.666

"... Embrace Change." Vaja, S. (2023, July 11). Open to change: Developing a growth mindset. *Law Society Journal*. lsj.com.au/articles/open-to-change-developing-a-growth-mindset

"... Companies that know this." Elias, J. (2020, November 27). *Google is tackling mental health challenges among employees through "resilience training" videos.* CNBC. cnbc.com/2020/11/27/google-tackling-mental-health-among-staff-with-resilience-training.html

"... Use the Novelty Effect to Your Advantage." Edwards, M. (2018, May 7). Mix it up Monday: Consider the novelty effect. *Matt Edwards*. edwardsvoice.wordpress.com/2018/05/07/mix-it-up-monday-consider-the-novelty-effect

"... generally interesting or exciting." Hidi, S. (2006). Interest: A unique motivational variable. *Educational Research Review, 1*(2), 69–82. doi.org/10.1016/j.edurev.2006.09.001

"... Be curious." Suma, D., & Budi, B. A. S. (2021). The effect of curiosity on employee performance: A case study in Indonesia. *Journal of Asian Finance, Economics, and Business, 8*(3), 1385–1393. doi.org/10.13106/jafeb.2021.vol8.no3.1385

"... A willingness to experiment and be curious." Lievens, F., Harrison, S. H., Mussel, P., & Litman, J. A. (2022). Killing the cat? A review of curiosity at work. *Academy of Management Annals, 16*(1), 179–216. doi.org/10.5465/annals.2020.0203

"... Improvements and professional growth often come." Chang, Y. Y., & Shih, H. Y. (2019). Work curiosity: A new lens for understanding employee creativity. *Human Resource Management Review, 29*(4), 100672. doi.org/10.1016/j.hrmr.2018.10.005

"... *kaizen* is the principle of continuous improvement." Singh, J., & Singh, H. (2009). Kaizen philosophy: A review of literature. *IUP Journal of Operations Management, 8*(2), 51–72.

"... more significant improvements over time." Omoush, M., Moflih, M., & Almetrami, R. (2020). Evaluating the five *kaizen* success measurements through employees work improvement and its effects on overall work and quality of services: Empirical study of insurance companies in Jordan. *International Review of Management and Marketing, 10*(4), 43-52. doi.org/10.32479/irmm.9994

"... Instead, focus deliberately on the more manageable things." Clear, J. (2018). *Atomic habits: An easy and proven way to build good habits and break bad ones.* Avery.

"... small amount of concerted attention." Duckworth, A. L., Kirby, T. A., Tsukayama, E., Berstein, H., & Ericsson, K. A. (2010). Deliberate practice spells success. *Social Psychological & Personality Science, 2*(2), 174-181. doi.org/10.1177/1948550610385872

"... it left little time for the actual work." Geimer, J. L., Leach, D. J., DeSimone, J. A., Rogelberg, S. G., & Warr, P. B. (2015). Meetings at work: Perceived effectiveness and recommended improvements. *Journal of Business Research, 68*(9), 2015-2026. doi.org/10.1016/j.jbusres.2015.02.015

"... Fall in Love with the Process." Logan, T. (n.d.). *Falling in love with the process, not the results.* Conscious Magazine. consciousmagazine.co/falling-in-love-with-the-process-not-the-results

"... Relinquishing some need for control will let you be more." Olson, K. (2022, April 18). *Why letting go of your tight grip actually gives you more control.* Tiny Buddha. tinybuddha.com/blog/why-letting-go-of-your-tight-grip-actually-gives-you-more-control

"... Forget About Perfect." Flett, G. L., Blankstein, K. R., Hewitt, P. L., & Koledin, S. (1992). Components of perfectionism and procrastination in college students. *Social Behavior and Personality: An International Journal, 20*(2), 85-94. doi.org/10.2224/sbp.1992.20.2.85

"... Expecting perfection from yourself or others." Childs, J. H., & Stoeber, J. (2010). Self-oriented, other-oriented, and socially prescribed perfectionism in employees: Relationships with burnout and engagement. *Journal of Workplace Behavioral Health, 25*(4), 269-281. doi.org/10.1080/15555240.2010.518486

"... judging yourself doing it." Stoeber, J., Lalova, A. V., & Lumley, E. J. (2020). Perfectionism, (self-)compassion, and subjective well-being: A mediation model. *Personality and Individual Differences, 154,* 109708. doi.org/10.1016/j.paid.2019.109708

"... which also threatens a sense of hope." Umandap, J. D., & Teh, L. A. (2020). Self-compassion as a mediator between perfectionism and personal growth initiative. *Psychological Studies, 65*(3), 227-238. doi.org/10.1007/s12646-020-00566-8

"... Follow Your Passion." Vallerand, R. J., Salvy, S., Mageau, G. A., Elliot, A. J., Denis, P. L., Grouzet, F. M. E., & Blanchard, C. (2007). On the role of passion in performance. *Journal of Personality, 75*(3), 505-534. doi.org/10.1111/j.1467-6494.2007.00447.x

"... Positive psychology scholars." Seligman, M. E. P. (2011). *Flourish: A visionary new understanding of happiness and well-being.* Atria Books.

"... a good fit for their natural interests, passions, or skills." Ho, V. T., Wong, S. S., & Lee, C. H. (2009). A tale of passion: Linking job passion and cognitive engagement to employee work performance. *Journal of Management Studies, 48*(1), 26-47. doi.org/10.1111/j.1467-6486.2009.00878.x

"... Cultivate Inner-World Awareness." Rock, D. (2010). *Your brain at work: Strategies for overcoming distraction, regaining focus, and working smarter all day long.* HarperCollins.

"... When you speak to yourself in a supportive and encouraging way." Neff, K., & Davidson, O. (2016). Self-compassion: Embracing suffering with kindness. In I. Ivtzan and T. Lomas (Eds.), *Mindfulness in positive psychology* (pp. 37-50). Routledge.

"... believe in your abilities, improve your confidence." Breines, J. G., & Chen, S. (2012). Self-compassion increases self-improvement motivation. *Personality and Social Psychology Bulletin, 38*(9), 1133-1143. doi.org/10.1177/0146167212445599

"... Actively challenge negative thoughts." Frewen, P. A., Evans, E. M., Maraj, N., Dozois, D. J. A., & Partridge, K. (2007). Letting go: Mindfulness and negative automatic thinking. *Cognitive Therapy and Research, 32*(6), 758-774. doi.org/10.1007/s10608-007-9142-1

"... Conjure Compassion for Yourself." Neff, K. (2021). *Fierce self-compassion: How women can harness kindness to speak up, claim their power, and thrive.* HarperCollins.

"... which are beneficial for career advancement." McEwen, B. S. (2020). The untapped power of allostasis promoted by healthy lifestyles. *World Psychiatry, 19*(1), 57-58. doi.org/10.1002/wps.20720

Conclusion: Putting It All Together

"... the BRAC sequence of your brain's." Lloyd, D., & Rossi, E. L. (Eds.). (2008). *Ultradian rhythms from molecules to mind*. Springer. doi.org/10.1007/978-1-4020-8352-5

"... A Workday Schedule Fit for Your Brain's Rhythms." Pink, D. H. (2018). *When: The scientific secrets of perfect timing*. Riverhead Books.

"... Wind down in the evening." Sonnentag, S., Tian, A. W., Cao, J., & Grushina, S. V. (2021). Positive work reflection during the evening and next-day work engagement: Testing mediating mechanisms and cyclical processes. *Journal of Occupational and Organizational Psychology*, 94(4), 836–865. doi.org/10.1111/joop.12362

"... You need extended breaks." Pang, A. S. K. (2016). *Rest: Why you get more done when you work less*. Basic Books.

"... Honor Your Unique Brain, Rhythms, Self, and Process." Roenneberg, T. (2012). *Internal time: Chronotypes, social jet lag, and why you're so tired*. Harvard University Press.

Further Reading

Barrett, L. F. (2021). *Seven and a half lessons about the brain.* Mariner Books.
Brann, A. (2022). *Neuroscience for coaches: How coaches and managers can use the latest insights to benefit clients and teams.* Kogan Page.
Brizendine, L. (2006). *The female brain.* Morgan Road Books.
Brizendine, L. (2010). *The male brain.* Broadway Books.
Carter, R. (2009). *The human brain book.* DK Publishing.
Doidge, N. (2008). *The brain that changes itself.* Penguin Books.
Duckworth, A. (2016). *Grit: The power of passion and perseverance.* Scribner.
Eagleman, D. (2017). *The brain: The story of you.* Vintage Books.
Eagleman, D. (2016). *Incognito: The secret lives of the brain.* Canongate Canons.
Kahneman, D. (2011). *Thinking, fast and slow.* Farrar, Straus and Giroux.
Medina, J. (2011). *Brain rules: 12 principles for surviving and thriving at work, home, and school.* ReadHowYouWant.com.
Palmer, C. M. (2022). *Brain energy: A revolutionary breakthrough in understanding mental health—and improving treatment for anxiety, depression, OCD, PTSD, and more.* BenBella Books.
Perlmutter, D., & Loberg, K. (2015). *Brain maker: The power of gut microbes to heal and protect your brain—for life.* Little, Brown and Company.
Pink, D. H. (2011). *Drive: The surprising truth about what motivates us.* Canongate Books.
Rock, D. (2009). *Your brain at work: Strategies for overcoming distraction, regaining focus, and working smarter all day long.* HarperCollins.
Seligman, M. E. P. (2011). *Flourish: A visionary new understanding of happiness and well-being.* Atria Books.
Siegel, D. J. (2012). *Pocket guide to interpersonal neurobiology: An integrative handbook of the mind.* W. W. Norton & Company.

About the Author

DR. BRYNN L. WINEGARD, HBSc, MBA, PhD, is a multiple-award-winning professor, represented professional speaker, and expert in applied neuroscience and positive psychology for professionals. She has helped clients such as Google, AMEX, Walmart, Pfizer, Johnson & Johnson, and Coca-Cola use the latest brain discoveries to improve human potential and employee performance. She teaches at several universities, engages in research, and is active with the McLean Institute of Coaching. Dr. Brynn is a regularly featured expert in TV, radio, and print. She has had a lifelong obsession with the human brain and its functioning and feels purpose-driven to help professionals use their own brains better, especially at work, so they may live their own best, most successful lives. Dr. Brynn lives with her husband in California. Find out more at DrBrynn.com.

Optimizing Your Working Brain *Even More*

THANK YOU for reading *The Working Brain*!

As a forward-thinking, high-achieving professional, you likely want to ensure that you and your people are as informed and equipped as possible to use your brains to their fullest potential, optimize each workday, and realize the most success out of work and life. Here's how I can help you further:

- **Invite me to speak:** I love disseminating knowledge through speaking, so I primarily develop and deliver customized keynotes, talks, training, courses, workshops, and seminars for conferences, corporate events, meetings, and panels. Have an idea for an event, meeting, or training but not sure of the fit? Reach out for an exploratory chat—I'm always happy to discuss programs, events, and curricula, even if they're in the initial stages of planning or development: info@drbrynn.com.

- **Share *The Working Brain*:** Give a copy of this book to a colleague, direct report, spouse, or friend. When the people you surround yourself with are better equipped, informed, and functioning, so are you and your business. Everyone has a human brain, and just about everyone could improve the use of theirs even just that little bit more.

- **Purchase *The Working Brain* for your team:** The best way to ensure your people do their best work each workday is to give them the missing manual for using their incredible human brain more optimally. Bulk purchases come with a publisher discount. Please contact us (DrBrynn.com/contact) so we can put you in touch.

- **Visit DrBrynn.com:** Here you'll find articles, webisodes, ideas, content, course offerings, testimonials, photos, biography, past clients, and more. While you're there, sign up for our newsletter.

- **Connect & post on social:** Post a key takeaway of yours from *The Working Brain* on your social pages and tag us. Please also like, subscribe, follow, or invite me to connect—I love to be connected with readers! You'll find me on LinkedIn, Instagram, Facebook, X, and YouTube at @DrBrynn.

- **Leave a review:** Leave your insights about *The Working Brain* for new readers on your preferred book-buying platform. Reviews help new readers find the book, read it, and benefit from the learning—another way you can pay it forward.

- **Keep in touch:** Need something custom, specific, and not listed above? If I can help you, I will—DrBrynn.com/contact.

To your very good health and even more functional brain. Thanks again for reading and take good care.

www.ingramcontent.com/pod-product-compliance
Lightning Source LLC
Chambersburg PA
CBHW060549080526
44585CB00013B/500